THE EXPANSION OF AWARENESS

By the same author:
THE FUTURE IS NOW
THE AXIS AND THE RIM
THE MEANING OF PERSONAL EXISTENCE

ARTHUR W. OSBORN

THE EXPANSION OF AWARENESS

One Man's Search for Meaning in Living

With a Foreword by
RAYNOR C. JOHNSON, M.A. (Oxon.), Ph.D., D.Sc. (Lond.)
Master of Queen's College, University of Melbourne

A QUEST BOOK
Published under a grant from The Kern Foundation

THE THEOSOPHICAL PUBLISHING HOUSE
Wheaton, Ill., U.S.A.
Madras, India / London, England

© Copyright 1961 The Theosophical Publishing House, India

*Quest Book edition 1967 published by
The Theosophical Publishing House, Wheaton, Ill.,
a department of
The Theosophical Society in America,
by arrangement with
The Theosophical Publishing House, Adyar, India.*

MANUFACTURED IN THE UNITED STATES OF AMERICA

"This is my prayer, that I may know before I die,
Why the earth called me to her arms."

RABINDRANATH TAGORE.

"We live in succession, in division, in parts, in particles. Meantime, within man is the soul of the whole; the wise silence; the universal beauty to which every part and particle is equally related; the eternal One."

RALPH WALDO EMERSON, *The Over-Soul*.

"Our life, like a river, strikes its banks not to find itself closed in by them, but to realize anew every moment that it has its unending opening towards the sea."

RABINDRANATH TAGORE, *Sadhana: The Realization of Life*.

FOREWORD

I am glad to have the opportunity of commending this important book to the thoughtful reader. The author, Mr. Arthur W. Osborn, is a personal friend—and perhaps I may be permitted to say, is an unusual and remarkable man. He combines in his person the efficiency and capacities of a business executive with the deeper interests of a student of philosophy. As the reader of this book will quickly discern, he brings a first-class mind to a consideration of the ultimate problems of life and existence, but he points us finally beyond the reach of intellect to the mystic's way.

Many thoughtful people to-day are searching for the meaning of life. They do not find any clues in Science, impressive though its achievements are in our time. Philosophers, for the most part, seem to be concerned with academic issues which do not answer the questions the plain man is asking; nor do they generally write in terms which he can understand. Religion, which enshrines many of the profoundest truths, is not presented to-day in a way which appeals to many people. It is, in any case, not easy to separate the mystical insights from the accumulated dogmas and the institutional forms. A book such as this, written by a man of outstanding intellectual honesty, is worthy of study by every sincere seeker after truth. It is an attempt to answer our profoundest questions; is closely reasoned and clearly written. It points the searchlight of an honest and penetrating mind on to those enduring questions which have always been with us, and always will be until we ourselves come to Enlightenment.

I therefore warmly commend this book.

Raynor C. Johnson

INTRODUCTION TO THE INDIAN EDITION

THE distinguished author of this book, Arthur Osborn, has asked me to write an introduction to his very remarkable and thought-provoking thesis on *The Expansion of Awareness*. When I read this book in 1956 I felt a keen desire to meet its author, and the opportunity to meet him came in 1958 when I was in Melbourne (Australia) in connection with my lecture tour. I need not say I felt with Arthur Osborn a deep comradeship of spirit, and the friendship formed at that first meeting has grown in depth with the passage of years. I am therefore very happy to pen a few words of introduction to this book.

I regard *The Expansion of Awareness* as one of the major contributions in the field of thought. It is true that more and more books on subjects of metaphysics and mysticism are being written these days—but most of them are unable to distinguish between super-physical perception and spiritual insight. Arthur Osborn has dealt with the subject of Awareness from the standpoint of the Super-physical as also from the deeper standpoint of the Spiritual or the Mystical. Today when the limitations of physical science are being recognised in an ever-increasing manner, this distinction between the super-physical and the spiritual is of vital importance in coming to right evaluation of things and events. The super-physical perception indicates only an extension of the methods of science into non-physical realms, and, as such, it has more or less the same drawbacks as are to be found in the approach of science.

There are indeed fundamentally two categories of knowledge—Knowledge by Ideation and Knowledge by Being. All scientific knowledge, whether physical or super-physical, belongs to the first category. Such knowledge is based on the duality of the observer and the observed. In spiritual perception, however, there is Knowledge by Being—it arises in that state where the duality of the observer and the observed has vanished. This is the very core of direct or what is otherwise called the Mystical experience. To-day the researches of Para-psychology are initiating man more and more into the realms of Extra-Sensory perception. While these researches are greatly to be welcomed, it is necessary for man not to arrive at false values of life due to this extension in the field of his awareness. Man needs to-day not only an extension of awareness but also an expansion of awareness. The super-physical perception induces an extension of awareness even as spiritual insight indicates an expansion of awareness. Man must rise to a higher dimension of living if he is to come to a satisfactory solution of many a baffling problem of life.

Arthur Osborn has indeed rendered a great service to humanity by writing this book, for he has brought to many a thinking mind, a much needed clarification on the subject of the super-physical and the spiritual. I have no doubt the book will be of great help and inspiration to many both in the East as well as the West in as much as it will enable them to come to a clearer comprehension both of the extension as well as the expansion of awareness.

ROHIT MEHTA

Varanasi, India
3rd August 1961

PREFACE

This book represents my attempt to think a way out of a mood of uncertainty and scepticism regarding the purpose of living. By worldly standards I should have been well satisfied to accept life as I found it. My health has been sound, and as much success as is good for me has come my way. Yet from early years I have experienced a deep sense of dissatisfaction which has forced me to look below the surface of things. It has also so happened that I have been brought into touch with people whose experiences are unusual; some of a " psychic " nature and others with mystical glimpses. Also, for many years I have closely studied the records of psychical research and have made my own investigations and received sufficient evidence to disturb any complacency I might have had that the commonsense world was the only reality. I am constantly meeting people who, while apparently immersed in this world's activities, are not so in reality. They are inwardly groping for some explanation of their existence. They are not what are called " deep thinkers ", nor natural students, yet they are thoughtful, well educated, and are burdened with unanswered questions. Normally such people would accept the doctrines of the conventional religions, but they find themselves unable to do so although they are religious.

This state of chronic scepticism can be painful even to the extent of causing psychic and physical ill-health.

Those who are unattached to any particular religion or organized movement may find in these pages a new approach to their problems. Many are honestly convinced that there is no final truth which resolves all doubts, and in terms of intellectual propositions the history of philosophy would seem to prove them right. Yet this book, which commences with doubt and uncertainty, ends with certainty; but it is a certainty based on an estimation of mystical experiences. In other words, the appeal is to the facts of direct realization. Although reason alone cannot disclose the final secret, the supreme truth when it is revealed is not unreasonable. While it is true that each of us must traverse his own path, yet we are not unaccompanied, and as inevitably my intellectual journey is paralleled by that of many others, these pages could serve as one more link between those many thousands who " speak the same language " but acknowledge no organization.

CONTENTS

		PAGE
	Foreword	6
	Introduction to the Indian Edition	7
	Preface	9
I.	The Problem Stated	13
II.	Appearances and Assumptions	20
III.	Mind and Body	29
IV.	Backgrounds and the Ego	33
V.	The Paranormal	38
VI.	Implications of Telepathy	43
VII.	What Do We Mean by Survival?	50
VIII.	Survival of Personality	57
IX.	The Problem of Non-Physical Bodies	61
X.	Proofs of Survival	69
XI.	The Rhythm of Births and Deaths	74
XII.	Time, Space and the External Universe	104
XIII.	The Future in the Light of Precognition	141
XIV.	The Influence of Mind on Physical Things	178
XV.	Mysticism and Allied States	194
XVI.	The Meaning of Living	219
XVII.	The Attainment of Enlightenment	232
XVIII.	Final Reflections	248
	List of Books and Journals	257
	Index	269

CHAPTER I

THE PROBLEM STATED

"Where do we find ourselves? In a series, of which we do not know the extremes, and believe that it has none. We wake, and find ourselves on a stair: there are stairs below us, which we seem to have ascended; there are stairs above us, many a one, which go upward and out of sight."

RALPH WALDO EMERSON, Essays. *Experience.*

Aimlessness.—The planet sustains its teeming millions of living creatures, born without choice, yet struggling to avoid the inevitable end—death. Man alone, discontented with entirely purposeless living, tries to reason out a meaning.

But many, harassed by the pressure of circumstances, with energies absorbed in " the red mists of doing ", do not lift their eyes to distant horizons but seek justification for living in immediate goals. It is enough to live, to procreate so that others may live to procreate. There are grandiose schemes of social improvement, of stupendous scientific advancement filling the world with switches and levers releasing the energies of the Universe in the service of man's desires.

Yet death takes men in the midst of their dream. These things which shall be are not for us but for those to come, to whom death also will come as they dream of their future.

And so the planet spins in the great void, carrying its struggling burden. Why? Is the Universe a product of design and purpose? Why were we born? And having been born, why do we live?

These questions are not the product of an arid intellectualism. Indeed, in some natures they are often a poignant cry for light, and few there are who can live without asking, " What's the use of it all? " The question becomes urgent when suffering and frustration are experienced, but even life at its best assumes a shallow impermanency unless we can at least glimpse some pattern.

The contemporary mood is one of scepticism, and men who grope over a darkened landscape attach most importance to objects near at hand. Things which should be means, become ends.

That which is palpable and obvious to the senses masquerades as " Reality ". Science, in its rôle of organized commonsense provides the tools of physical conquest. Matter is real; all else is illusory. Men still struggle for " ideals ", but the ideals are of this kingdom.

The Materialistic Mood.—Not even in religion, as practised in the churches, have we a refuge from the prevailing materialism. For the most part belonging to a church means little more than being a member of a social group. There is of course a group adherence to a set of teachings usually founded on various interpretations of Scripture, but the general atmosphere is doctrinal rather than spiritual.

The leaders are concerned to preserve frozen frontiers of thought; therefore they become organizers and not men who through seership and deepened understanding reveal new truths. They are content to pass on the interpretations of other men's seership.

So we witness an army of priests and professional religionists engrossed with organizational routine, ceremonial forms, morality-preaching and social uplift against a background of doctrines which offend the reason because their inner significance has been lost. For the most part they are accepting without much thought what may be called place-of-birth religions: religions which have been inherited, not acquired. Buddhists, Mohammedans, Hindus, Christians are such because of geographical situation.

And psychology, once described as the science of the soul, is now sceptical about the soul in the sense of consciousness having any independence of the brain. In this mood psychology finds popular favour when it " explains " man as a functional product of " conditioned reflexes ", thereby reducing psychology to a branch of physiology. Other schools of psychology are similarly based on the tacit assumption that only the body is real. Even psycho-analysis, in spite of its genuine psychological approach, is basically materialistic. Man becomes primarily a body with mind as a by-product, yet it is this by-product which knows the body and all the theories about the body! And here we find ourselves abruptly confronted with a peculiar paradox.

We are clearly only directly aware of the contents of our own minds, therefore our bodies, strictly speaking, are phenomena within our minds. Yet these minds are capable of extinguishing their own reality by a process of self-hypnosis which causes them to become identified with their own perceptions under the names body and matter. We fall in love with the projections of our own consciousness, and eventually come to believe that our children are our ancestors: that matter, which is a constituent of our own minds, is the origin of our minds. We have much knowledge of the mechanisms of life and yet have no vision of life's meaning. We are living a span of existence between two unknowns. We know we were born and we know we shall die, but within the framework of commonsense experience both ends of the span are lost in a mysterious abyss.

The mystery is not lessened by what we know of heredity and the immortality of the germ-plasm, nor should our sense of wonder be dimmed by words such as evolution, for when analysed these terms prove to be more descriptive than explanatory. In spite of all we know about the mechanism of evolution, it is still mysterious that you and I should exist on this planet as conscious individuals capable of thinking about our origin and destiny, and even constructing such theories as evolution.

We appear to be thrust helplessly into existence—

" What, without asking, hither hurried *Whence*?
And, without asking, *whither* hurried hence."

Religion and Mental Peace.—When the prevailing mental climate was more religious in tone, men had at least a vague conception of God as Creator of the Universe, and felt however dimly, that their lives had meaning in a divine plan.

No " Back to God " movement can restore this state of innocence. We have advanced too far along the path of critical intellectualism. But if we pursue the path of intellectualism with minds poised and dedicated to truth, ruthlessly disregarding emotional preferences, there is evidence to show we can regain the mental peace of the age of " faith ", on a level which includes profound insight and intellectual maturity. But the aim must not be to seek peace, but truth.

The mental state of large numbers to-day is aimless. The conventional religions are committed to doctrines which seem little better than myths to the modern intellectual. The creeds are frankly not believable for increasing numbers of educated people. Yet those who have not simple faith and find the creeds incredible are often fundamentally religious people who realize that life means more than bread and economic security; that in fact the physical world is strangely incomplete, unsatisfying and obviously ephemeral, for death broods over all forms.

Those who have lost their religion may be haunted by a latent fear that the Universe is not even friendly to its creatures, for evil, injustice and pain lurk like spectres in the shadows, clouding joy with a sense of transiency and making goodness itself seem liable to extinction in the desperate struggle against evil.

Naturally, it is the more keenly intellectual and sensitive minds which suffer a sense of frustration at what seems to be the meaninglessness of the Universe. Some psychologists consider that the failure of religion to satisfy the spiritual needs of the more intellectual and earnest is a major cause of neurosis in the modern world. So we find Jung saying, " During the past thirty years people from all the civilized countries of the earth have consulted me. . . . Among my patients in the second half of life—that is to say, after thirty-five—there has not been one whose problem in the last resort was not that of finding a religious outlook on life. It is safe to say that every one of them fell ill because he had lost that which the living religions of every age have given to their followers, and none of them has been really healed who did not regain his religious outlook. This, of course, has nothing whatever to do with a particular creed or membership of a church."

But it is easier to diagnose than to effect a cure. Considerable money is invested in the many religious organizations which maintain thousands of officials, clergy, ministers and expensive establishments, the primary purpose of which is to preserve religion in some form or other. Yet their creeds have ceased to be vital factors in the lives of perhaps the majority in Western countries.

Framing the Question.—Is it possible to answer the question, " What is the meaning of life? " It has been asked often enough, and believed by many to be unanswerable. Let us therefore at least be clear as to the type of answer we are seeking.

Life in the abstract may have no meaning, for meaning can only have relevance for individual consciousness, in other words, for you and me. What type of experience is ordinarily described as having meaning? I think it will be found on examination that an event or experience seems to us to have meaning to the extent that it has reference to some future aim or goal we are pursuing. Or an event has meaning when it is perceived as an essential part of a pattern. To twiddle one's thumbs might be considered a meaningless act, but should it be part of an exercise to increase manual dexterity, the act assumes meaning. It is being part of a pattern which gives it meaning. Similarly, to the extent that we see our personal lives as part of some wider pattern they have meaning.

So it is that purely bodily behaviour is considered to be understood and to have meaning when seen in the frame of biological need: hunger, self-preservation, and so on.

Actually, therefore, we feel we have explained and understood a particular piece of human behaviour when we have succeeded in assigning it a place in some general pattern. For instance, the behaviour and peculiarly complex customs of some primitive peoples are just puzzling oddities unless studied as part of a cultural and physical background.

When, therefore, we ask, " What is the meaning of Life? " the search for an answer drives us relentlessly to a study of background, and that means we must make up our minds about the kind of universe into which we are born.

Thinking Philosophically.—Our individual lives can only assume meaning to the extent that we achieve an aim based on a steady conceptual background, or as it is usually called, acquire a philosophy. However, many will, I am afraid, derive little help from the academic philosophers. Sometimes the history of philosophy seems largely a record of one philosopher cleverly refuting his predecessors as fashions in thought come and go.

Yet in spite of the absence of a generally accepted body of philosophical doctrine similar to that of science, men will never cease to philosophize, for reason needs to know why—we cannot exist content with merely knowing *how*.

Science is an organized system of " know-how ", but when we think philosophically we enter a more abstract realm, for we are seeking basic principles; we are indeed striving to give ultimate meaning to the findings of science itself.

Our quest, therefore, for meaning forces us to use our minds to their highest capacity, and in thinking philosophically we participate in a rich intellectual heritage which does something more important than provide us with a set of final conclusions. Rather do we come to a clearer appreciation of fundamental questions, and acquire a training in scepticism and synthesis. Like Thrasymachus under the gentle pressure of Socratic questioning, we gradually drop many of our naïve notions, and learn to appreciate the implications of the questions we ask.

But some may come to an even more significant conclusion. As we grapple with our problems we may come to a realization that logical thinking can only lead us part of the way. Eventually our minds are forced into a mood of humility before the final mystery, and we become prepared for a deeper level of experience to rise within us and illumine the gropings of our pedestrian thinking. Of this I shall have something to say later. But at this stage the problem of our existence presents itself in intellectual terms.

The Significance of our Question.—We ask, " Why are we here? " Let us pause a moment at the question itself. Is it not rather peculiar and significant that we ask the question at all? The asking of such a question implies a dissatisfaction with an apparently arbitrary existence, even when conditions are pleasant, and particularly so when they are not.

This dissatisfaction is a curious psychological attitude, and is indirect evidence that some deeper level of consciousness is stirring within us. It is almost like a latent memory of a more ideal state of being which dimly infiltrates our outer awareness, preventing us from becoming wholly immersed in outer existence.

If existence as we outwardly know it were complete, it is hard to understand why we should challenge it, and demand to know why we are here. It is the kind of question a man might ask if he were hypnotized and reawakened in unfamiliar surroundings.

Why am I here? Where am I? are instinctive questions when there has been a break in the continuity of consciousness, and memory has not regained its clarity.

CHAPTER II

APPEARANCES AND ASSUMPTIONS

"Recognizing that the physical world is entirely abstract and without 'actuality' apart from its linkage to consciousness, we restore consciousness to the fundamental position instead of representing it as an inessential complication occasionally found in the midst of inorganic nature at a late stage of evolutionary history."

A. S. EDDINGTON, *The Nature of the Physical World.*

"But there are beliefs—such, for example, as the belief that physical objects exactly resemble our sense-data—which are entertained until we begin to reflect, but are found to melt away when subjected to a close inquiry."

BERTRAND RUSSELL, *The Problems of Philosophy.*

Answers on Different Levels.—I shall later consider some evidence which will support the view that the answer to the meaning of life lies in the recognition that man lives on various levels of consciousness and that what is a satisfactory answer on one level is meaningless on another. Consequently there can be many answers to any question, each satisfactory according to the level of comprehension, and in the case of such a question as, "Why are we here?" the answers may grade off until the mind reaches a certainty beyond reason.

Actually the form in which a question is put often discloses a whole world of thought and accepted premises, and before attempting to answer the question it is necessary to examine the premises on which it is based, and frequently such a critical analysis demonstrates that the question requires no answer because in the form in which it is put it is unanswerable.

What are the presumptions involved in the question, "Why are we here?" Firstly, let us consider the adverb, "Why". We would not ask "Why" unless we had some notion of cause and effect. There is a tacit assumption of a universe governed by law behind such a question, and a series of answers each usually beginning with "because" are necessary to satisfy the questioner according to his degree of profundity.

Some will find adequate the reply that we are here because of the circumstances of our parentage; the laws of heredity and environment. Those who remain satisfied with replies on this level of physical sequence would usually be called materialists, who are content to know the machinery of our existence and show no curiosity as to why there should be any machinery. So from their point of view the question "Why are we here?" is adequately answered by science.

Assumptions.—But for others the question, "Why are we here?" remains still unanswered, and they probe more deeply for an answer. In doing this they reveal a background of thought involving certain assumptions, and it is these assumptions which create the problem.

Obviously the person who accepts man as wholly a material creature will feel no need to ask why we are here when he is familiar with the physical facts of procreation and birth. But the man who craves for further light on our existence has quite a different set of assumptions.

For a variety of reasons he believes man to be fundamentally non-material, or as he may put it, he believes "man has a soul". Also, he usually accepts the existence of God, who is somehow responsible for man's existence. If in addition he has certain fixed ideas as to the nature of God, such as His goodness and omnipotence, then indeed for such a man we cannot even attempt to answer the question "Why are we here?" without uncovering the assumptions involved in the question itself. For we find the question is asked against a background-system of theological concepts, including the ancient problem of the existence of evil in a universe created by a good and omnipotent God.

The questioner is really asking, "How can we reconcile this turmoil of existence shot through with evil if God is all-embracing, omnipotent, good, and complete in perfection?"

It is clear therefore that although the same words "Why are we here?" are used, the question is asked against a variety of backgrounds, and it is these conceptual backgrounds which must be examined. In doing so we may find the question has disappeared.

Existence in the Light of Commonsense.—Our uncritical commonsense impressions of our existence take the following form.

Firstly, we have an unshakable conviction that we exist, which we describe as self-consciousness. This awareness of Self seems the core of our being. Each one of us says " I ", and the multifarious experiences of life are related to and cluster round ourselves as seemingly separate " I's ". Our language reflects this in such words as " I think ", " I feel ", " I will ".

But equally fundamental in our primary experience is an awareness of things and persons other than ourselves. Gradually this realm of experience which is so outside ourselves assumes concrete dimensions, and seems " out there ", an external environment which is an objective fact and remains external no matter how hard we close our eyes and imagine otherwise.

These then are the two poles of our separate existence: the inner world of our selfhood with its conscious states, and an external world of things and events. From this experience we derive the general conceptions of mind and matter, which seem to be an irreducible duality intertwining the multifarious phenomena of the universe.

If we could take this duality as self-evident, as it appears in our experience, it would simplify our task of explaining the universe. The great external universe symbolized by the abstraction we call " matter " would be regarded as the field into which living creatures are born, evolve and die; the vast cold environment of matter remaining " out there ", the permanent stage for millions of successive creatures to live their little life-spans through endless time.

This is the unreflective view of practical men who are unconcerned about origins and consider the testimony of their senses as final truth: the world is as it appears to be. What is seen, touched, smelt, and heard is accepted as real—out there, or as it is called, " objective ".

But we soon grow out of the naïve acceptance of the testimony of the senses at its face value.

The mind is forced constantly to correct our judgment based on mere appearance. The sun does not move across the sky; a stick seen through water is not really bent; and the landscape is not actually rushing past our train window.

So with our other senses we have learned to distrust the immediate impressions received, and believe we obtain a truer report of what is objective by means of scientific instruments and experiments which in many cases positively contradict our unaided percepts. Even the solidity of matter, which every dictate of commonsense assures us is a fact, vanishes into the mathematical formulae and electronic energies of the physicists.

We cannot escape the problem of the distinction between appearance and reality, which has exercised the philosophers for centuries, and has crowded library shelves with treatises of subtle reasoning, which often are clever rather than enlightening.

But on this problem we crave for enlightenment, for our search for the meaning of life drives us relentlessly to penetrate beyond the screen of appearance.

It may not seem on first acquaintance that it need be unduly difficult to discover reality behind appearance. The plain man will readily agree that appearances deceive. He will realize that all sorts of scientific tests and experiments must be conducted in order to discover the real nature of things. The moon may look like green cheese but he is satisfied on scientific grounds that it is not.

On this level of thinking scientific observation will dispel the illusions of sensory impressions. All that is necessary is more intensive research; more sensitive instruments, and increasingly keen observation. The basic concept being that nature is " out there ", a something which is arbitrarily presented to our senses and which although deceptive on the surface can be made to disclose its real nature by the methods of science aided by instruments and laboratory tests.

The Retreat from Commonsense Appearance.—It is only with reluctance that this rather naïve, although attractive, conception is rejected. We are not prepared to desert the commonsense view without a fight.

Yet regretfully we must.

It is the rôle of philosophic thinking to examine the validity of many views which often seem axiomatic, and one of these commonsense views is the notion that there is " out there " an objective world having characteristics not fundamentally different from the report of our senses. That is to say, a world of physical objects, trees, mountains, tables, houses and so on.

Now to get a clearer view of the difficulties in holding this opinion, let us ask ourselves a few questions. Firstly, " How do we know the external world?" We naturally answer, " By means of our five senses." But surely not by means of the senses alone? The senses merely respond to external stimuli, and these stimuli need interpretation, and that is done by the mind.

Here lies the crux of the matter. How much does the mind contribute, and how much is external, independent of mind? It is clear in the first place that whatever may exist externally can only be known by what takes place internally—that is, within our own minds.

When, for instance, we say we see a red apple, what actually occurs is that our optic nerve has been stimulated in a certain way so as to produce the impression " red ". A complicated series of events has occurred. Light waves stimulate nerve cells, starting a chain of chemical reactions which end in the sensation " red ".

How it comes about that this mechanical sequence of light waves and chemical changes arrives at the terminal to produce the conscious message " red " is a mystery beyond the capacity of any mechanistic theory to explain.

" Red ", therefore is not a quality of the apple independently of a mind to perceive it. All that we know directly is a mental apprehension called " red " which arises as the result of an astonishing capacity of the mind to translate the significance of a complicated mechanical sequence of waves and chemical changes into the sensation " red ".

A similar analysis can be made for each of our other sensory impressions. A complete description of the apple resolves itself into a catalogue of sensations. In other words, a description of changes occurring in our minds.

So the seemingly objective apple, standing out so independently from other objects, is at the most merely the source of a set of stimuli, but the " apple itself " remains an unknown X.

Solidity and Form.—Let us amplify this with another example —consider solidity and form. Surely these are existents entirely independent of our minds. Physical objects, we say, are material, and even if we are forced to admit that taste, colour and smell have a large measure of mental content, we stubbornly insist that hardness and shape belong to physical objects and cannot be argued away, and probably feel inclined to bump our opponent's head against the table to prove our point.

But sadly for this commonsense view a reasoned examination of what occurs when we perceive solidity shows that this quality also is a creation of our senses. The more we learn about matter the less solid we find it to be. Nothing that we know of the nature of the atom conforms to our notions based on appearances. The language of commonsense is useless for accurate description of the physicist's discoveries. Our senses have deceived us. Where we perceive deadness and immobility the physicist finds energy and vibration. Things which we handle and describe as solid are now known to be mostly space, and the impression of solidity which things make upon us is imposed on our minds because of the limitations of our senses.

If our senses were different, the appearance of the world would change correspondingly. What a radically different world we should experience if, for instance, our eyes were able to respond to X-rays! A considerable proportion of objects would not then be visually perceptible as solid.

Similarly if our sense of touch were altered our tactile experiences of objects would differ. We know, for instance, that certain diseases cause the nerves to report softness instead of the normal hardness.

Our impression of solidity therefore is relative to our sensory constitution, so the surface of a pond is solid to a mosquito, liquid to us, and a sort of atmosphere to a fish.

Nor can we accept shapes at their face value. A table, for instance, has various shapes depending upon the angle from which it is viewed. When seen from, say, a balcony, its shape may be a narrow oblong supported by two short legs: but from a corner of the room its sides would seem to converge with three legs only visible. In short, it would have as many appearances as there were places from which to view it.

Add to these the variations of shades and colours which would occur as we change our position, and it becomes clear that we are hard put to it to say which of these appearances we should declare to be the " real " table, and our judgment becomes still more confused if we examine the table by means of instruments such as reveal variations of texture of grain, and so on.

Logically, how can we promote any one of these appearances to the status of " real " table? There is no arbitrary standard which, for instance, compels us to claim that the table as seen from the balcony is the " real " table. The other appearances are equally valid.

The word " table " therefore is a descriptive term for a complex of sense impressions. In other words, it is a concept or idea based on a variety of percepts.

We sum up these sense data and say that an object, which we call " table ", is before us. Our direct sensory experience is not of a " table " but of colours, shapes, hardness, and so on. These impressions are within our perceptual consciousness, and on them images of an external world of objects are based. Objects therefore are projections of our own consciousness.

The Shared World.—But here the reader's commonsense will revolt if he supposes that the above statement implies that nothing exists independently of our personal consciousness. This is not what is meant.

Yet it should be mentioned in passing that there are those who maintain that the external world is a sort of dream, having no independence apart from the dreamer.

Nor is it easy to disprove such a view, for is not a vivid and connected dream accepted as reality by the dreamer while the dream lasts? In the dream state we move in a world as apparently external as our waking world. We perceive houses; travel in trains; roam over landscapes; converse with people, and so on. Only on awakening do we say that all these experiences were purely subjective. Could our so-called " waking experience " also be another dream?

However, to return to our statement, " objects are projections of our consciousness ", this does not imply the non-existence of an external world.

As individuals we obviously possess a world in common. When a number of people simultaneously perceive what we call a " table ", clearly something independent of their individual consciousness is affecting them. The question is, what?

Matter.—The naïve will immediately reply that the external world is composed of "matter ", and although we may perceive it from an infinite variety of viewpoints, it remains a material, external reality which we can touch, see, smell, taste and hear.

But each of these sensations takes place within our minds, and when we say that a material something causes them, we have made a statement which it is impossible to prove.

The word " matter " represents an idea in our mind. For no one has ever contacted this mysterious " matter ". We know directly only our own sensations, and then proceed to speculate on the origin of these sensations.

It so happens that the generation to which we belong invented the term " matter ", and unreflectively we have become accustomed to accept this word as though it described a real objective substance, whereas it is purely a mental construct.

If the reader doubts this, he should be asked to state clearly what he means by " matter ", and nothing he can say will exceed the range of his own sensations, which are modifications of his own consciousness.

He will find himself saying, " Matter is that which can be touched, seen, etc., etc.", which of course is begging the question, for our desire is to know what existence this elusive substance has apart from those states of mind we call " sensations ".

Persistent introspection of how we perceive the so-called external world will reveal that matter, in the usual sense of the word, is a pure fiction, having no existence apart from our mind. When therefore materialists of the older school dogmatically assert that " matter " is a dead substance, they are only indulging in speculation as to the origin of their sensations. The problem of the relationship of such incompatibles as mind and matter no longer exists. We have largely been tantalizing ourselves with a verbal problem.

CHAPTER III

MIND AND BODY

" To-day there is a wide measure of agreement, which on the physical side of science approaches almost to unanimity, that the stream of knowledge is heading towards a non-technical reality; the universe begins to look more like a great thought than like a great machine."
SIR JAMES JEANS, *The Mysterious Universe.*

" Then if we explain material things in terms of mind, we explain things little known in terms of things better known; whereas if we explain mental things in terms of matter, we are elucidating things inadequately known by means of things less known."
EDWARD CARPENTER, *The Art of Creation.*

The Body as the Cause of Mental Changes.—It will no doubt occur to the reader that although we have been at pains to point out that the external world is a mental construct based on sense-impressions, we have ignored the fact that our senses themselves are physical in origin, and as our senses are under the control of our brains we come round full circle to another type of materialism in which man is no more than a product of brain-functioning, therefore brain and mind are one.

The materialist case for the dependence of mind on body rests very largely on the common experience that alterations in bodily functioning are accompanied by changes in consciousness. So far as it goes this is obvious enough. But here we must be on our guard. Everyone knows that his mental condition is intimately associated with the state of his body. To say this is merely to describe our daily experience. The materialist, however, says more than this. He says that bodily changes *cause* the mental changes, in fact that mind is actually a product of the body.

Now this statement is pure theory, but its plausibility, especially when expressed in more subtle ways, deceives many into thinking that it is an inevitable deduction from the facts.

Of course it is not. Logic does not require such a conclusion. The materialist is as entitled to theorize as anyone else, but theories are not proof.

As a preliminary to clear thinking, therefore, let us state what does logically follow from the facts. All that we can legitimately say is that changes in bodily functioning correspond with changes in mental functioning. The evidence only warrants a conclusion regarding a relationship between body and mind. That relationship is not necessarily one of cause and effect.

Theories.—We do not know what the nature of the relationship is, without pondering on the significance of the facts. Some say that body is the cause of mind, and others that mind causes body. Others insist that there is no relationship of cause and effect, but merely that the two sets of phenomena are parallel series. Then there are the various monistic schools of thought who see no fundamental duality of mind and matter, their views ranging from innumerable types of Idealism to extreme materialistic Monism. Also there are the Neutral Monists, who see mind and matter as but two aspects of a fundamental unity or Absolute. All these philosophers speculate on the same body of facts; facts which assume significance only in proportion to the profundity or intuition of the philosopher.

The only theory which necessarily precludes even the possibility of mind existing apart from body is that which postulates that consciousness is merely a by-product of matter, a theory which is sometimes called " Epiphenomenalism ". It belongs to classical Materialism and had its greatest vogue in the nineteenth century, but in less crude forms it is still with us; an expression of it, for instance, is seen in Watson's *Behaviourism.*

For the sake of simplicity I shall use the common term " Materialism " to cover those theories which virtually by their fundamental principles reduce consciousness to a function of matter. I perhaps should add that the word " Materialism " should carry no derogatory significance. The materialist interprets life according to his experience, and it is to his credit that he resolutely takes his stand on the most solid basis of evidence he can find. We all know that many who profess so-called " spiritual " views have neither evidence, reason, nor personal experience to support them.

The Paradox of Regarding Body as Prior to Mind.—Now it is rather curious that we should feel compelled to postulate body as primary to mind because each one of us is immediately aware of himself as a conscious being and it is by means of our mind that we become aware of our body. Body, therefore, is a concept in our minds. As we have already observed, our immediate awareness is of certain sensations, such as heat, cold, light, sound, smell, etc., which evoke conscious responses and are unified by the idea or concept, " body ". This idea we call " body ", then, is the mind's interpretation of innumerable perceptions.

Does it not seem strange that we, whose only certain and immediate knowledge is of ourselves as conscious individuals, should conceive ourselves as being a product of our own concept? It would seem more in accordance with experience to say that all is mind rather than that all is matter. For we only have experience of matter being apprehended by mind.

What then are our bodies? They are the means whereby mind is focused for the purpose of functioning in certain limited conditions. Mind in itself is not located anywhere, for it cannot be contained by space or limited by time. Yet manifestation implies limitation, and it is within the bounds of organized forms that mind achieves definition and expression.

But bodies are not alien so-called material substances; they are orders of life which serve as vehicles for other forms of life each in its degree a manifestation of mind. On this view the whole universe is an expression of mind in myriad forms.

This view is the entire reverse of the conception of mind being in some mysterious way an evolutionary by-product of matter.

Materialism Refutes Itself.—Any theory which denies mind as the primary fact of our experience can be reduced to an absurdity. For, if consciousness is only a phase of material mechanism, the theory of materialism itself collapses, because as a theory it is a mental concept, and it is the aim of materialism to reduce mind to chemical and other changes in physical bodies.

If the materialist succeeded in doing this, then mental events would only be the reflection of a series of material changes and the theory of materialism itself would have the same status as any other chemical change, such as the formation of chlorophyll in plants or oxidization in metals.

In other words, mental events would be merely the reverse side of physical events, and as such would not have any philosophic significance as true or false. The materialist, having triumphantly reduced himself to a machine, has lost his mind, which holds his precious theory, and therefore paradoxically is denied the means of proving its truth!

We may doubt the existence of the external, but never can we doubt the reality of ourselves without making ludicrous any theory we may build up about the supposedly real external. For the very ability to construct any theory presupposes the existence of the self who thinks it.

To such an extent can the learned become narrowly concentrated on a particular theory that they can with ponderous and humourless erudition ask us to accept that matter—the object perceived—is the cause of the self perceiving it.

We shall later return to the problem of the status of the external world. We cannot easily dismiss the brute empirical facts of our existence.

CHAPTER IV

BACKGROUNDS AND THE EGO

"However one may define self, it is always something other than the ego, and inasmuch as a higher understanding of the ego leads on to self the latter is a thing of wider scope, embracing the knowledge of the ego and therefore surpassing it."

Dr. C. G. Jung.   Foreword to D. T. Suzuki, *Introduction to Zen Buddhism*.

Viewpoints.—We have already observed that the question, "Why are we here?" is asked by people holding the most diverse views regarding the nature of the universe, and often the best way to answer is to challenge the background against which the question is asked.

In the pre-Galileo period, when the world was accepted as flat, and the firmament was peopled by gods, the explanation of man's existence would be in terms of the arbitrary wills of the gods.

Similarly to-day those who hold anthropomorphic conceptions of God have to face the perennially disturbing problem of evil in a universe which they conceive as being the special creation of a good and omnipotent Deity. So against this background we have theories of man's free will, which are designed to relieve God of all responsibility for evil.

Obviously an explanation must always be addressed to some system of accepted premises, and granted the premises, the explanation is usually perfectly logical.

If a clap of thunder is the voice of God then it is logical and sensible not to neglect the religious ceremonies appropriate to the occasion.

We can well imagine an elaborate system of ceremonies with rival theologians advancing subtle arguments for and against the relative efficacy of ceremonial procedures. Yet the whole elaborate structure of theological disputation collapses immediately it is accepted that God is not shouting at us through a thunder-cloud.

So with our present enquiry into the meaning of our existence it is essential to postulate the background against which we ask our question.

The reader no doubt will already detect the type of cosmic scenery against which we pose the question of our existence. We have at least seen that the universe is not as it appears to be, and it will probably be agreed that if we are to choose between a universe of " dead " matter out of which life emerges, or a universe of life with matter as a form of conception, then we shall choose the living universe, for by making such a choice we have a more satisfactory basis for explaining the facts of our experience, and one more in conformity with our deepest intuitions.

Yet although this choice is of fundamental importance and is fraught with far-reaching consequences in our interpretation of the facts of our existence, it raises its own particular problems.

Separate Egos.—We may have by-passed some of the stubborn problems of the materialist, and at least we are not called upon to explain the emergence of life out of a dead universe. Yet we must still try to understand what we poor lonely individual units of life are doing on this planet. For we are lonely in our separate, personal lives.

We may try to overcome this sense of lonely separateness by gregarious community-living, but each one of us lives within a carapace of separate selfhood where we are strangers even to our intimates.

When we discussed the problem of appearance and reality in connection with our perception of an outside world we came to the conclusion that our senses deceived us. Can it be possible that we are subjected to a similar illusion in connection with our psychological sense of separateness?

It is worth while examining this question, because it brings us to closer grips with the central theme of our life's purpose.

We certainly do feel ourselves to be separate egos, and, apart from rare heroic moments and strivings, seem largely governed by the law of self-preservation and self-interest, and some psychologists would say we are wholly creatures of self-interest.

Even our moments of apparent self-sacrifices would be explained by impulses below the threshold of normal consciousness, which lead us into self-effacing actions not because of impersonal conscious idealism, but rather on account of suppressed infantile attitudes which have formed complexes.

Thus our egoism is extended even into the nether regions of our personalities. Needless to say, there is much experimental evidence for this, and a great deal of useful psychiatric work has been achieved in terms of these theories.

It is indeed a notable advance in the understanding of our natures to have extended the frontiers of our personalities into the deeper levels of the subconscious. The therapeutic value of the modern psychological approach is daily being demonstrated in innumerable ways, and even those of us who cannot be said to require the technical services of a psychiatrist have at least had our smugness disturbed, and have learned to detect our rationalized motives.

Egos Perhaps Not Separate.—But all this being granted, and due tribute being paid to the greatly extended area of the personality which has been uncovered, there are grounds for believing we are still only on the surface of our consciousness.

We shall later have to consider the experiences of many people who have been privileged to attain an unusual degree of insight and in consequence see life at a more fundamental level. The testimony of these seers and mystics forces upon our attention a view of human nature in many respects contradictory to our ordinary experience and the natural tendency would be to ignore it, except for the fact that a study of the records makes it obvious that some profound common experience is being described. We can detect this unity of experience although the seers belong to every race, creed, religion, or even when no religion is professed.

But first let us see if, even on the grounds of ordinary experience, we can accept the surface evidence which causes us to think that our egos are separate psychological cores impenetrable and isolated from all other egos.

The first observation we must make is that it is only our own ego that we know. We quite naturally infer that other people also function from what we call an egoic centre, but this is an inference from our own experience.

In its essence this ego with which we seem to be so familiar is our sense of I-ness. It is a sort of centre to bind our experiences into a unity; or it could be described as a thread on which are strung the phases of our changing personal patterns. Yet introspection can never detect the " I " as a separate entity. We discover instead only the changing phases of our consciousness, pleasure, pain, sensations and so on. The " I " as a changeless centre escapes our introspection. If therefore we relied on reason alone we could argue that there is no self, but only an ever-changing flow of conscious states without any self to connect them. But we are intimately aware of our self, and most of us are prepared to trust our feeling of selfhood and suspect our reasoning. In other words we are confronted with what philosophers call an antinomy; in this case a direct contradiction between a conclusion based on reasoning and an immediate awareness requiring no proof.

If, however, we postulate the " I " as the unifying centre of our personality, it could be considered as having only a functional nature, and therefore would be without qualities, and consequently the same in everyone.

We could from this draw two conclusions—firstly, we might consider the " I " to be a psychological illusion, or we might adopt the view that there is only one " I " or self, and that it is the separate self which is illusory.

On this second view there is a basic unity of selfhood behind the changes which manifest themselves in the time and space of personal experience.

For the moment we will not try to decide which of these views might most reasonably be accepted. We can, however, now state that there is certainly something which needs considerable amendment about the ordinary views of the human personality.

It really is a nuisance that our commonsense notions continue to be an inadequate guide. If they were acceptable at their face value we should not have the bother of so much discussion and probing.

Unusual Facts.—There are facts lying all around us like bricks of unusual shapes which although apparently useless, for the type of houses we are building, yet obviously must have their proper place if only we could plan the right structure.

It is some of these odd facts which disturb our complacency about our usual notions of mind and personality. For instance, the conception that our minds are isolated in our brains and have no means of communication with other minds except through the senses has almost the status of a dogma.

The materialist must defend this dogma without compromise. Quite shocking damage could happen to the foundations of his materialistic structure if he were forced to admit that mind could contact mind without the aid of any physical sense!

Even a materialist is not exempt from the instinct to suppress a heresy. He has built his house with bricks of a conventional shape, and it rests on foundations of his own choosing, and now we have the effrontery to show him gaps in his foundations to which he must attend, and worse still, attend by somehow fitting in these queer-shaped bricks! But to do this he has to rebuild on the basis of a new ground-plan.

CHAPTER V

THE PARANORMAL

"It is certain, I suppose, that there still are more things in heaven and earth than are at present mastered by science. And Bergson has reminded us that millions of men have lived for thousands of years in a world vibrating with electricity, without ever suspecting that there was such a thing. Are we not probably now in the presence and under the influence of unknown forces or beauties or loyalties, which are beyond the range of our exact knowledge, and power of definition, but by no means beyond the reach of an undefined but strong and even passionate feeling. . . ."
  Dr. Gilbert Murray, O.M., *S. P. R. Proceedings*, vol. xlix., p. 169.

"The evidence seems to stand, and if we dogmatically reject it we shall be open to the reproach of laying down what *ought* to be the order of nature, instead of observing what *is*."
  Lord Rayleigh, Sc.D., LL.D., F.R.S., *S. P. R. Proceedings*, vol. xlv., p. 17.

The Growing Recognition of the Paranormal.—A consideration of psychical phenomena is only incidental to my main theme, yet their revolutionary implications demand our attention.

I do not think it is an exaggeration to say that as the occurrence of these phenomena gains recognition, present views of the nature of the universe will face a major crisis.

Those who are alert to the evidence which is now assuming impressive proportions feel they are witnessing the crumbling of one era of thought and the early stage of radically new conceptions. No doubt it will remain for future generations to realize the full significance of the facts which psychical research workers are quietly and patiently trying to establish.

Of course there is nothing new in paranormal phenomena. They are recorded in the folk-lore and beliefs of every people, and continue to be reported to-day. Culture, education and scepticism do not cause these accounts to cease. In fact, spontaneous phantasmal appearances often occur with startling suddenness to people who normally have neither interest nor belief in such experiences.

Often they are disturbing in their unexpectedness, yet cannot be ignored because, as in some cases of telepathic visions, they convey veridical knowledge of events beyond the percipient's normal capacity to know.

Gradually there has come into existence a vocabulary which in a crude rule-of-thumb manner seeks to name the various types of supernormal phenomena.

Although such terms as " clairvoyance ", " clairaudience ", " psychometry " and " telepathy " are unsatisfactory and even misleading, they have served as convenient labels for widespread types of psychical experience.

Added to these mental types of phenomena we have equally widespread records of physical and semi-physical paranormal manifestations, such as " hauntings ", " poltergeists ", and movement of objects by unknown means.

In view of the long history of these phenomena it may be asked why I consider them so significant to-day. The reason is that pioneer thinkers are now accepting the challenge to investigate these facts, and the experiments and records published by the Societies for Psychical Research—particularly the English and American Societies—over the last half century contain intellectual dynamite for current conceptions about the human personality and the universe.

This field still awaits its Newton and its Darwin, or even its Freud, to synthesize and interpret these tantalizing facts. But facts they are, and sooner or later they will have to be consolidated with the general body of knowledge. We can however see in what direction they point, and their relevance for our search for meaning in living.

Inhibitions.—One of the reasons for the past neglect of systematic study of the paranormal is the inhibitory influence of certain prevailing assumptions. We have already examined some of these. But intellectual recognition that common-sense experience is deceptive is alone not enough to dispel the overwhelming effect sense-impressions make upon us.

Close observation of physical phenomena and inductive reasoning have been the means of establishing a well-knit system of laws and physical sequences which have given us command over our environment.

Science now is almost a popular religion. This is a wholesome change from superstition and fear-engendering religions, provided we preserve the open-mind attitude which does not resist new truth.

The scientific tradition requires us to take cognizance of all facts, no matter how novel they may be.

But in practice a curious selective process comes into operation. Each one of us has built around himself a body of beliefs and accepted attitudes. This forms a mental mesh and acts as a screen through which new facts have to filter. Facts are accepted or rejected according to the nature of our mental screens. The scientist will readily admit this when he witnesses this psychological process in connection with narrow religious attitudes.

He realizes that it is almost useless to marshal the facts of evolution in the hope of convincing a Fundamentalist. The ideas cannot penetrate such minds, or if they do, fail to be appreciated as significant.

The narrow sectarian has acquired a particular type of mental constitution which automatically rejects alien facts, as a sick stomach refuses food.

This makes the scientist feel superior, yet he suffers from the same limitation in another form. We all do, more or less, but naturally much less so when we lose our arrogance and become aware of our mental bias.

The Possible and Impossible.—The Fundamentalist " knows " that evolution cannot be true, because it conflicts with God's scriptural revelation. There we have a closed system of thought, with its own laws of what is possible or impossible.

A similar dogmatism prevails with some scientists. They " know " that paranormal phenomena cannot occur because they conflict with their accepted view that the universe is basically a product of mechanical forces.

Some years ago a correspondent, in reply to a letter I wrote to a University journal said: " . . . telepathy is to be rejected because it implies a theory of mind which is false." This particular correspondent was, I think, a psychologist, but the incident is typical of the easy dismissal of inconvenient facts. Obviously, anyone who possesses the " true " theory of mind is well buttressed against facts which conflict with it.

New facts slip into the mind without resistance when they conform to the conventional pattern, but those which have no home in this pattern are rejected like illegitimate children from a respectable family.

These children, however, have a habit of growing up and becoming a nuisance when they threaten the family complacency.

Paranormal facts are also a nuisance because they disturb our faith in some assumptions which conventional thinking, based on commonsense, has rather smugly taken for granted.

Personal Frailty.—We should also note in passing that recognition of paranormal phenomena does not, especially in academic circles, tend to enhance one's reputation. Parapsychology is now a serious study, but until recently it was not academically respectable. A friend of mine, a professor in one of the leading Universities, who had made a close study of the evidence, was nicknamed " Professor of Spooks ".

Of course, strong personalities are not affected by this kind of banter, and many, indeed, rather enjoy opposition in a worth-while cause. But the fact remains that more timid natures are very afraid of the opinion of their confrères, particularly so when their economic interests could be affected by adverse criticism.

It is hard to say to what extent personal frailty has been a retarding influence in preventing the recognition of the paranormal, but it is not unusual to find people who in private conversation acknowledge the paranormal, yet professionally prefer their real attitude to remain unknown.

The subject does trail in its wake a good deal of superstition and downright fraud, and men as a rule prefer to be regarded as hard-headed and tough rather than credulous.

I am perhaps thinking more of the past than the present. My own acquaintance with the paranormal goes back over many years, and in earlier days it was certainly not a prestige-enhancing subject. Now, however, a great change of intellectual climate is taking place, so we can expect the paranormal to become an important branch of our normal studies.

CHAPTER VI

IMPLICATIONS OF TELEPATHY

" Man has a general sensitivity, more subconscious than conscious. It reacts to other men, to human objects, even to nature. One might say that the sensory sensitivity of consciousness is only one particular case of its general sensitivity."

RENÉ WARCOLLIER, *Experiments in Telepathy.*

Assumption that Telepathy Occurs.—The impressive array of facts accumulated by various Psychical Research societies is no longer being neglected. The English Society of Psychical Research in particular, with its high standard of evidence and its scholarly investigators, is now at the stage where its Proceedings and Journal present a challenge to the intellectual world which it would be discreditable to ignore. Those who have not studied these records and followed with care the latest findings and critical discussions have denied themselves acquaintance with data of crucial significance for any understanding of human personality. It would be a very foolish procedure to-day to try to construct a theory of mind without taking into account the facts of Psychical Research.

Consider, for instance, the implication of telepathy. The evidence for its occurrence is overwhelming. So much so that Dr. Thouless feels able to say in his presidential address to the S.P.R. (Vol. XLVII, July 1942, p. 13), " If we meet sceptics as to the reality of the phenomena we are studying, let us refer them to the researches of Rhine, of Soal and of Tyrrell, and not succumb to the temptation of trying to satisfy them ourselves."

This is advice which it suits our present purpose to take. Nothing would be easier than to crowd these pages with accounts of experiments; but to the sceptic they would lack the convincing power of the original records. So I must leave those who are undecided about telepathy to study the technical publications of the English and American Societies for Psychical

Research. For my own part I shall proceed on the assumption that telepathy has been demonstrated to occur, and the contrary opinion of those whose education has not made them familiar with the evidence can be ignored.

Menace to Materialistic Concepts.—In order to appreciate to what extent the facts of telepathy menace some popular materialistic concepts of mind let us remind ourselves what we are accustomed to accept about our mental functioning.

Firstly, I suppose most of us would feel fairly confident that our minds were private affairs. We have a comfortable assurance that our thoughts are secret unless we choose to reveal them, or unless perhaps they are detected by others through some facial movement or unconscious gesture which inadvertently allows people to read our minds when we would rather keep our thoughts to ourselves.

Nevertheless we do believe we can keep our thoughts to ourselves, and if there are strong reasons for secrecy we are not opposed to a bit of acting so as to make doubly sure our thoughts remain private. This conviction of privacy seems to be reasonably supported by the experiences of our daily intercourse with people.

Admittedly now and again we are a bit startled when someone suddenly speaks our thoughts, or perhaps we may ourselves perceive in a sort of flash a person's real attitude. Sometimes two people suddenly speak the same name. However, for the most part such incidents do not bother us much and can easily be explained by coincidence or as being due to a common stimulus. We ordinarily have undisturbed faith that our minds are closed chambers, and that we can guard the entry and exit doors if we want to.

If we happen to feel some need for theory, then naturally we find our commonsense daily experience supported by theories which conceive the mind as a product of brain. Here we really do feel securely isolated in our ivory citadels.

Within these skulls we can study the neurones, and note that messages can come and go along the wires of efferent and afferent nerves. Everything is neat and tidy and beautifully mechanical—or would be except for our conscious minds which happen to be the observers of all this skull machinery! However, within the limits of materialistic theory we can at least be certain that no nonsense like telepathy can occur!

But telepathy does occur!

What does this mean? It means that mind is more than brain; which of course many of us, in spite of the materialists, have suspected all along. So we have to discard the brain-box theory of thought, and look to other theories which are better able to accommodate the new facts.

Brain as an Instrument of Limitation.—Bergson's theory that the brain is an instrument to limit thought rather than a factory in which thought is produced does no violence to the facts. The brain on this view is like a wireless set which excludes more than it lets through. Mind, it would seem, overlaps the brain.

Mind indeed can be conceived as universal, and brains are instruments whereby our attention is focused and our consciousness achieves definition of life in terms of the discrete experiences we call physical existence.

If we can accept this theory of mind we at least have a better basis for explaining telepathy, for consider what happens in cases of telepathic communication.

An idea in one mind becomes known by another when all normal means of communication have been ruled out as impossible.

Not only are all the physical channels closed, but most careful experiments have been devised to eliminate chance coincidence, this being done by calculating the odds against chance in controlled experiments with Zener cards, and so arriving at a figure plus or minus which would constitute significance. But I must adhere to my decision to refer the sceptical to the original experiments. Those who like their evidence in statistical form could for a start read *S.P.R. Proceedings*, Vol. XLVI, June, 1940.

Is Telepathy Due to Brain Waves?—So then in telepathy we are witnessing phenomena which cannot be explained by any materialistic theory of mind.

Of course, efforts have not been lacking to discover brain waves, and indeed we know that electrical impulses are detectable in the brain. But it would have to be a very peculiar type of brain-vibration to explain telepathy.

All known physical vibrations vary in strength inversely to the square of the distance involved. What sort of vibration would it be that displays complete disregard for this law?

The clarity and strength of telepathic communications are entirely unaffected by the distance between the minds concerned. It does not matter whether the persons in telepathic contact are in the same room or hundreds of miles apart.

Now if some type of physical vibration were at work we could plot its variations through space; note that obstacles, such as walls or mountains, impeded it, and so on. But no such vibration has been discovered, nor can we conceive any organ in the brain capable of producing it.

Also we have another baffling phenomenon. In some experiments with Zener cards and pictures the target card or picture is not guessed correctly; but correct hits are scored on the next one or two cards about to be exposed. In other words, there is a displacement in time to the extent that a card or event is cognized before it actually occurs in what we call the present moment.

Naturally there are considerable discussions and differences of opinion regarding the interpretation of a phenomenon which was detected quite unexpectedly during the experiments. We shall refer to pre-cognition later; but we can at least say now that mechanical theories of brain-vibration have little relevance.

Bold Hypotheses Needed.—Those who have closely studied the evidence are convinced that the time has come for bold hypotheses and new concepts in handling these facts which lie so tantalizingly outside the bounds of classical theories. To keep harking back to mechanical notions is like trying to fit the modern mathematical concepts of space-time into the forms of flat-earth Geometry.

As we have already mentioned, the phenomena for which the popular term " telepathy " has been coined are but a phase of a whole group of extraordinary facts which are called loosely and often misleadingly, " clairvoyance ", " prevision ", " telekinesis ", and so on. The need for a neutral term has long

IMPLICATIONS OF TELEPATHY 47

been felt and the Greek letter " Psi " is now coming into general use as a non-committal term to describe all paranormal phenomena.

Our concern here, however, is not the technical one of the laboratory worker in Psychical Research, who must discover a hypothesis which will synthesize the facts and also serve as a tool for gaining new knowledge.

It is indeed certain that until we can fit these paranormal phenomena into some general concept of law they will not command the attention they deserve.

We assent to certain propositions almost unconsciously, because they dovetail with our pre-suppositions. We are brought up to accept the laws of gravitation. Evolution and the whole climate of scientific thought are bred into our mental structure. New facts are automatically explained by invoking laws which we uncritically accept as being absolute universal sequences.

For practical purposes this is a great gain, and it comes as a shock when fundamental concepts which form the background of our thought are challenged, as, for instance, Hume's destructive criticism of the so-called " Law of Causality " itself. All explanation must be in terms of some system of pre-suppositions. Certain things are accepted as axiomatic. We cannot proceed with Euclid's Propositions unless his Axioms are accepted as not requiring proof.

The explanations which some primitive and uneducated people accept as valid are just as logical if we grant the mental climate of pre-supposition against which the " explanations " are made. There is nothing illogical in explaining certain natural phenomena as being caused by spirits or magical powers of Witch Doctors, when the group-thought accepts without a shadow of doubt that Nature is animistic. Nor would there be a lack of experimental evidence that some Witch Doctors are not to be trifled with.

We repeat, therefore, that all " explanations " are relative to the system of thought accepted by the group into which we are born. The movements of the planets are adequately " explained " by Newton's " Laws of Gravitation "; but what of the future, when Einstein's mathematical concepts become the popular background?

Already we have discarded the Newtonian concept of " Force ". The planets, it was supposed, would move in straight lines with uniform velocity if it were not for the influence of a force which exercised a pull and caused eliptical movements. " Force ", of course, was merely an hypothesis rendered necessary by certain pre-suppositions. Change the pre-suppositions and you change the explanations, so that to-day explanations of the planetary movements would be in terms of modifications of space-time.

We require a similar radical change of outlook if we are to " explain " the phenomena of Psychical Research. But we can at least see the most fruitful direction to take. It will be away from materialistic mechanism.

Levels of the Personality.—My purpose in drawing special attention to the facts of paranormal phenomena is because they provide evidence that mind and consciousness transcend physical limits. This point is crucial for any understanding of the meaning of life—of our lives. As one browses over the records and links the formal documented accounts with those of our own experience it becomes increasingly clear that our familiar waking consciousness, or, as we might call it, " our phenomenal self", is only a partial expression of an inexpressibly more profound reality.

Quite apart from study of paranormal phenomena it is nowadays widely accepted that there are vast tracts of the human personality below the threshold of the waking consciousness. Freudian terms are almost the patter of knowledgeable youngsters, who chatter with slick familiarity about the subconscious complexes, fixation and so on.

Memorizing a glossary deceives some people into the belief that they have acquired real knowledge. Behind the psychological terms lie the experiences of human beings, and we must proceed beyond the words to the facts themselves. This applies even to such words as " sleep " and " trance ". Their very familiarity creates a false sense of knowledge, whereas there is much that is mysterious about these states of consciousness.

In some trances the understanding is deepened to the point of enlightenment, and knowledge is derived beyond normal limits. We will consider some of the implications of trance-experiences later. We can, however, say now that the human personality functions on various levels, and it is our conclusion that some of these levels extend the boundaries of the mind beyond the limits of brain-functioning, though of course if the experiences on a " higher " level are to be communicated to the consciousness of our normal waking level the brain must function as a channel.

CHAPTER VII

WHAT DO WE MEAN BY SURVIVAL?

"If there are other worlds than this . . . who knows whether with some stratum of our personalities we are not living in them now, as well as in this present one which conscious sense-perception discloses?"
PROFESSOR H. H. PRICE,
S.P.R. Proceedings, vol. 50., p. 25. "Survival and the Idea of Another World."

Believers and Sceptics.—So far my aim has been to etch the general background against which we can pursue our quest for a meaning in life. In my book, *The Superphysical*, I reviewed in more detail some of the evidence which supported the view that consciousness transcends physical limits.

There is one question which now demands specific consideration, for it bears directly on the meaning of living. Do we survive bodily death? Those who answer "Yes" are of three types. Firstly, the religious people, who accept on the basis of scriptural and doctrinal authority; secondly, those whose general philosophic conceptions make survival an almost inevitable corollary; and thirdly, we have those who have been convinced by specific evidence derived from experience in psychical research. Those who answer "No" are naturally the materialists, who are convinced that life cannot exist apart from physical forms. Then, of course, there are the many agnostics, who honestly cannot make up their minds.

It need hardly be stressed that on a matter which is so personally important we should spare no effort to resolve our doubts. Yet it must be admitted that these doubts exist most acutely in those who reject all intimations from life except those in logical form. Can there be any significance in the fact that the majority of people show hardly any concern about the matter? They live for the moment. Is this an unconscious testimony to the fact that they need not be concerned, because they are immortal? Sometimes truth is better expressed by unreasoned attitudes than it is by intellectual formulations.

Be this as it may, clarity of thought is indispensable, and particularly is it so on the question of Survival.

The Word "Survival" Misleading.—Now it should be noted at once that there is a question-begging implication about the word "Survival" itself. To survive is to outlive, or continue in existence, and this as applied to our consciousness conveys the impression that our personal mind, or, for short, let us say Soul, is a product of our physical organism, and manages to acquire sufficient energy and integration to continue some sort of existence after the death of the body which originally supported it.

If this view were correct, arguments for survival would rest on a very dubious foundation. In fact it would be highly improbable that survival of a complete personality could occur. The best we might expect would be that some loosely-integrated memory-elements might persist like the after-glow of a suddenly snuffed-out light, or an echo in the hills. Not much more, in fact, than the hypothetical " psychic factor " of Dr. Broad.

But if our mind and personality is not rooted in the body but stems forth out of the universal life and consciousness, the word " Survival " is not appropriate. We do not ask whether electricity survives the loss of an electric light globe. Once again we realize that all problems must be considered against a background of accepted premises, and it is clear that if we conceive the universe as fundamentally an expression of life and consciousness, then our personal lives, and the lives of all creatures, are embraced in a universality which is timeless. Expressed in religious terminology, our immortality is assured because God exists.

Although this conception of the universe, by assuring us of immortality, makes the problem of survival, strictly speaking, irrelevant, yet minds nurtured in inductive thinking will not be happy with deductive conclusions alone.

The Difficulty of Conceiving Survival.—Actually there is much to confuse us in the usual conception of survival. Even though we may be convinced on general principles that we do continue to exist in some form after the death of the body, we hardly know how to conceive what form our survival takes.

In the first place, what is it that is usually meant by Survival? The assumption is that we continue after the death of the body in full possession of our sense of personal identity; that we retain a memory of earth events, and continue more or less the historical sequence experienced on earth; also that we retain some form which renders us recognizable. Here we have some very concrete requirements.

Is it thinkable that in the light of what we know about the human personality it could survive bodily disintegration?

Now the first obvious fact about ourselves is that we live a double life. One part is visible and the other invisible. Our bodies are tangible and visible, but our minds are apprehended in an entirely different way. I think it will be usually conceded that the most important elements of our personality are the invisible ones. For here we have memory, sense of selfhood, and all those qualities of character which distinguish one person from another. We must not be trapped into accepting the argument based on appearance, that these psychical characteristics are due to physical conditions. This is an unproved assertion. Logically there is no reason to suppose that our invisible part ceases to exist when our visible part perishes. But it may be argued, surely a very profound change in the personality must occur when it is severed from its physical constituent!

The Body and Survival.—Whatever views we may hold regarding the relationship of mind and body, our practical experience is one of intimate identification with our bodies, and a large part of our lives is devoted to the satisfaction of our physical needs. Much of our personality-pattern, indeed, forms itself around the social norms connected with eating, exercising, dress, adornments, and awareness of our physical appearance. The mere possession of a beautiful body may be the dominant influence in forming character and personality, and still more so is this the case when the body is ugly and deformed.

As the body is such an important ingredient of the complex we call personality, how are we to regard personal existence without the body? Then again, as we recognize other people largely by their physical appearance, how may we know them in a bodiless state?

Now these are the sort of questions which inevitably arise through looking at the human personality from below upwards, as it were. Almost unconsciously we are again accepting the body as the orginating cause of our conscious states. So let us again note that it is *we* who are thinking about our bodies. Our bodies are not thinking about us! Nevertheless our bodies are part of our personalities, and death has the appearance of severing the personality so drastically as to create a doubt whether the *post mortem* state could be recognizably continuous with the incarnate state.

Organic Wholes.—I suggest that much of our difficulty in conceiving *post mortem* existence arises from the tyranny which sense-experience imposes on our thinking. In our practical affairs we take the identity of things for granted. Chairs, trees, pens, and objects of all sorts are assumed to be substances with qualities. A pen we say is made of such and such a material, and is numerically identical throughout a period of time. But actually, as we have seen, we have no direct experience of objects, but only of qualities, or as they are called sense-data.

Although the world does appear to be filled with separate objects existing in space and enduring unchanged through time, we have no warrant for believing this to be anything more than appearance. Indeed, any so-called separate object has no meaning in isolation. A complete definition of any object requires us to describe its relationship with other objects. In other words, the linkage between objects is just as important as the objects themselves, and indeed the relationship may be said to be part of the object.

This is particularly apparent when we again consider wholes such as our bodies. They are composed of millions of parts, such as cells, blood corpuscles, liver, kidneys, bones and so on. None of these individually identifiable things has any meaning apart from the organic whole within which it exists. In fact the character of the whole determines its nature.

How Does the Body Maintain Its Unity?—Here indeed we are confronted with a mystery. How does this whole maintain itself? A tiny embryo, the human zygote, a single cell about 125th of an inch in diameter, grows into a complex organism, a marvel of adaptive functioning. Specialized organs are developed, and millions of living cell-units are organized, disciplined, and held to their special tasks, their growth being limited or increased always according to the needs of the body as a whole. New cells constantly replace old ones, and as our bodies pass through the phases from infancy to old age the materials of our bodies are renewed over and over again.

Cells and organs may under certain conditions exist independently of the body of which they are normally a part, but within the body they behave as members of a well-disciplined community. In the normal body arms and legs do not grow to inordinate and irregular lengths and shapes; the heart does not become a gigantic muscle beyond the body's needs.

All the other organs, each composed of millions of cells, obey some directive which holds them in check and restrains any tendency to anarchic behaviour likely to endanger the community-life of the whole.

How is this unity maintained? Of course, we all know something about glandular secretions. It is a commonplace of popular talks on physiology to explain monstrosities and abnormal growths as being due to the deficiency or superfluity of this or that hormone or glandular secretion. So also are we familiar with the process of Mitosis—cell-division—and accept that our bodily structure is determined by the genes within the chromosomes.

But what is all this? Surely it is hardly more than an interesting piece of description. It is like knowing everything about the machinery of a car except that it was made by man. We only explain a car when we discover that it is a product of intelligent planning.

I am not here considering the strongly-contested theories of Vitalism and Mechanism. Let the Mechanist proceed as far

WHAT DO WE MEAN BY SURVIVAL? 55

as he can with his investigation of the chemical-and-cell-structure of organisms—a useful and fascinating study—but he will never, while confined to this specialist plane of thought, approach those conceptions which we call " explanations ".

In terms of mechanism it remains a mystery how organisms hold their diverse parts in place, and impose upon a multiplicity of simple cells the disciplined behaviour-patterns or organic functional unities we call living organisms.

The whole is so much more than the parts that no analysis of the separate parts could ever enable us to predict the qualities of the whole. Carbon, oxygen, hydrogen, nitrogen, sulphur and phosphorous are ingredients of our bodies, but as parts of the whole they become living flesh.

The mystery of our bodies is that, although they are ever-changing and comprise millions of separate units, yet they themselves also exist as a unity. To our senses our bodies seem identical objects throughout. Changes, we know, are taking place, but so gradually that we observe a recognizable identity throughout our lives.

Psychological Wholes.—Now a similar phenomenon occurs with our psychological states. These also are in constant flux. Moods, thoughts, sensations, memories, change unceasingly, and not only is this restless activity taking place in our surface consciousness but we know that below the threshold of our waking state lie active fields of psychological influence, forming complexes and revealing their presence through dreams and irrational impulses. Sometimes, indeed, certain elements of this psychic ferment split off to form a new personality, or dual and multiple personalities may reveal themselves.

How then are we to regard Survival if the human personality is a sort of kaleidoscope of changing psychological states based on the shifting foundation of equally changing bodily states? There seems nothing permanent to survive.

In any case, what sort of survival might we expect? Does a child continue for ever as a child, or, if we conceive it as growing in the other world, does it grow into the form its body would have assumed if it had lived? Does an idiot continue as an idiot? And in cases of split personality do both Dr. Jekyll and Mr. Hyde continue to exist?

Partial Views.—These are the kinds of questions which inevitably arise when partial views masquerade as whole views. It is quite true that our personalities can be viewed as changing sequences of mental and bodily states. We can similarly regard a house as bricks, timber, glass, steel and so on. But the significant fact is that it is a house, and the significant fact about all these mental and bodily states is that they are aspects of a personality.

We are aware of ourselves as personalities, but there is no harm in splitting ourselves up into bits for the purpose of special study, provided we do not lose the personality by becoming entangled with the bits!

The personality is a whole, and therefore is more than its parts. But the term *whole* does not mean that the personality is a " thing ". We usually think of things as objects made of substance, which have duration in space and are supposed to have certain qualities. We have already shown that we have no direct experience of physical objects.

But commonsense still dominates our thinking, and we almost irresistibly conceive permanence in terms of unchanging objects. That is why, even though we may subscribe theoretically to some belief of man having a soul, we find ourselves imagining the soul as a substantial something. We would not do this if we regarded man as *being* a soul, instead of having one.

What, however, we must keep in mind is that almost every line of enquiry into the nature of reality ends with a rejection of some aspect of our commonsense notions. The physicist starts with solid particle-like conceptions, and ends with energies, electrical potentials and mathematical abstractions. The philosophers, no matter how they differ in their philosophies, find themselves driven to abstractions which are almost unintelligible in commonsense terms. Clearly therefore if we are to cling to our notion based on sense-impressions we shall increase our difficulty in thinking about survival.

CHAPTER VIII

SURVIVAL OF PERSONALITY

"All we can cause or can observe is variety of *motion*—never creation or annihilation. And even the motion is *transferred* from one body to another, and transformed in the process; it is not generated from nothing, nor can it be destroyed. Special groupings and appearances are transitory; it is their intrinsic and constructive essence which is permanent. . . . We shall argue that personality or individuality itself dominates and transcends all temporal modes of expression, and so is essentially eternal wherever it exists."

SIR OLIVER LODGE, *Man and the Universe.*

"The Soul is a spiritual being, with its home in heaven—the heaven that is within us, even while it is in the body. But it has brought down this heaven with it into the time-process in which it energises."

WILLIAM RALPH INGE, *The Philosophy of Plotinus.*

Rejection of Unchanging Substances.—We have already seen that our personalities are changing wholes. Let us forget about things and substances. What we immediately know is ourselves. No doubt it can be argued that introspection actually does not reveal a self, but only some sensation or particular perception, but we should not expect to get evidence for that which is self-evident, and no one can be persuaded that he is not aware of himself.

Having got rid of notions of concrete things as a basis for permanence, we need only think in terms of states of consciousness, and realize that bodily forms are apprehended by consciousness and have no reality apart from consciousness.

But consciousness has its forms of expression and these forms appear as bodies. The personality may, when analysed, seem a phantasmagoria of change, but the changes are only aspects within a whole. It is the whole which is crucial for any consideration of existence outside the physical form.

Forms of Survival.—Let us look again at the questions we asked about the forms of survival. How are we to regard the death of a child? We asked: Does it continue in the after-life as a child? The answer must surely be " No ", for what we call a " child " is an immature body, and the body does not continue to exist.

It would indeed be rather a dreary prospect to imagine an indefinite continuance of each personality without change at the precise point where death occurred. But no doctrine of survival requires us to visualize in this materialistic manner.

Actually the problem of child-survival or idiot-survival is a false one. All bodies, whether immature, perfect or deficient, represent a particular order of life on one level of expression. They are examples of the principle that forms of life in addition to existence on their own level can also provide vehicles for, or render it possible for, other forms and types of life to manifest. The stream of changing life we call the body is embraced within the totality of the human personality.

But even if we regard the personality as another example of the law of wholes and parts, the question still persists as to what happens to a whole when it loses some of its parts. Again we observe the natural tug of the mind towards thinking in concrete symbols. The very words " whole " and " part " build up pictures of things which can be cut up into sections and dealt with in terms of arithmetic and geometry. But the human personality is a very different kind of whole. It is a living, conscious whole, and the laws of its being are those of the mind.

Remembering this, we ask again: How is the psychological whole affected when it loses one of its parts—the body? On general principles we might suppose it need not be greatly affected. This statement may cause some surprise, for loss of the body seems such a vital cleavage.

Actually, the loss of the body is only apparent. Admittedly it disappears as far as our sensory life is concerned, but inasmuch as the body has formed part of a conscious whole, the experiences derived through it would be registered by and absorbed into the conscious personality, which is transcendent of the body.

Indeed if the personality continues after death we should expect it to pre-exist the body. Once we have conceded that the mind can function independently of the body, even during the body's life—and evidence from psychical research supports this view—then the personality should hold within its conscious awareness the memory and essence of its experiences derived from its temporary association with and manifestations through a physical organism.

If therefore this organism happened to cease at the childhood stage, then the child-form image would be retained in consciousness. This would also apply to any other phase of body experience. Even cases of so-called Split Personalities, inasmuch as they provided well-formed vehicles of conscious experience, must be presumed to be synthesized within the psychological whole we call a human personality. The same principle would apply to idiots, but to make this clear we would need to define what we mean by idiocy.

In many cases a deficiency in the brain merely causes a frustration of consciousness, and shows itself as a general backwardness. Here the mind is denied expression, and the *post mortem* state would be deficient to this extent. What therefore appears from the view we are expounding is that *we are not at home in the body*. Our true home is on another plane of existence, with a different order of time and space.

Identification with the Form.—We have a natural narcissistic tendency towards identification with the outer rind of our being. It is a familiar phenomenon of hypnosis for people under the influence of suggestion to become incarnate, as it were, in a set of fictitious scenes and suggested character-rôles. If these people were not awakened we might imagine them continuing their illusory lives completely identified with their assumed characters.

It is interesting to speculate what would happen if a hypnotic subject were kept constantly under the influence of a particular character-suggestion, and then died. It would seem likely on our hypothesis that this character, which had its existence in the subconsciousness, would continue in the after-death state at least until such time as the normal personality asserted itself.

Whatever holds our awareness in the realm of consciousness persists, and that it does persist beyond the death of the body we need not doubt. Indeed, we would not doubt it except for this hypnotic-like tendency to become immersed in our bodily sensations. Evidence is available that this is not the case with all people. There are many who have experienced almost complete detachment from their bodies. See for example the experiences of Dr. Wiltze, S.P.R., VIII, and of Sylvan Muldoon, related in his book, *The Projection of the Astral Body*; also William Gerhardi's book, *Resurrection*. In fact, pages could be filled with examples of bi-location of consciousness. Those who have had this experience simply could not be persuaded that they were only physical bodies.

CHAPTER IX

THE PROBLEM OF NON-PHYSICAL BODIES

"By Body I understand the mode which expresses in a certain determined manner the essence of God insofar as He is considered as an extended thing."
The Ethics of Spinoza.

"I have always taught you that all phenomena and their developments are simply manifestations of mind. All causes and effects, from great universes to the fine dust only seen in the sunlight come into apparent existence only by means of the discriminating mind."
The Lord Buddha,
The Surangama Sutra

Bodies as Living Vehicles.—The query still arises as to whether we can conceive consciousness without a body. All consciousness as we know it is associated with a body, and a bodiless consciousness is difficult to imagine.

Actually we need not do so. There is no logical reason why bodies should be restricted to the physical level. As long as consciousness is functioning on a finite level, there must be the limiting factor we call body. And here we stress that we are not dealing with a dichotomy of life and matter. We conceive Reality as all-inclusive consciousness, and within this absolute consciousness all things have their being. We will later discuss the problem of finite existences. It is sufficient to note now that finite existence implies definition, and this takes the form of consciousness limited by body. But as we have stated previously, the bodies themselves are living " wholes ", not combinations of an imaginary " dead matter ".

Our physical organism is a stream of living cell life obeying laws belonging to its own order of existence, yet providing a vehicle for the manifestation of our self-consciousness. The body may be thought of as a habit-pattern governed largely by hereditary automatisms which are only partially influenceable by the self-consciousness.

Yet it should be noted that under certain psychological conditions the personal consciousness does profoundly affect the functioning of the body, in some cases even dramatically, as when so-called miraculous cures occur. Dr. Alexis Carrel reports in his book, *Man the Unknown*, that under the influence of prayer such diseases as " Peritoneal Tuberculosis, Cold Abscesses, Osteitis, Suppuration Wounds, Lupus, Cancer, etc." have been almost instantaneously cured. And, of course, our daily experience testifies to the effect of emotions on our glandular secretions. We are indeed profoundly ignorant of the latent powers which reside within us, and our difficulty in understanding is increased by the modern method of specialized research. Man is a unity, and no matter how necessary it is to take him apart for special study we inevitably drift into error if specialist-descriptions of the behaviour of a part are mistaken for more than they are.

The Focusing of Consciousness.—We return once again to the fundamental datum of our experience, our self-existence. We exist. This needs no proof. It is our piecemeal examinations which cause confusion. Much of the difficulty of understanding man arises from treating a mental construct or abstraction as though it were an actuality, whereas it is no more than a useful mental tool to facilitate a particular study. So, when we split up man into two irreconcilable parts which we label matter and mind, and then proceed on the assumption that these are actual isolated realities, we merely bedevil our capacity to understand.

The body is only an aspect of our total being. While our awareness is focused on the physical level it is confined to a limited range of responses, and is as sharply focused as light through a camera lens. We can suppose that this concentration of attention to a particular field of experience is due to an inherent need for creative clarity which enriches the personality in its deeper aspects. It is these upper reaches of the personality which are most important, and give meaning to our periphery-experiences.

Inevitably this concentration of consciousness through a narrow focus crowds out a whole universe of other possible experiences. A man during prolonged observation through a microscope can have his attention absorbed by the phenomena seen through the powerful lens to the exclusion of what is going on in the room. But it is his life as a man which gives meaning to his life as concentrated on the microscopical phenomena.

Bodies After Death.—When our attention is withdrawn from physical life, as in death, why should we suppose we have not organized forms appropriate to other aspects of our personal consciousness?

The difficulty for most people would be their inability to conceive the substance or material out of which a non-physical body could be made.

So once again we find our minds held captive by the commonsense notion that qualities and functions must belong to substances and things. In our analysis of matter we failed to find physical objects, but discovered only sense-data. If, therefore, non-physical bodies exist, we similarly would expect to know them as a mode of perception. This does not mean they would be imaginary or subjective. They would possess for our consciousness as lively an objectivity as do our physical bodies. It is all a matter of relativity.

The non-physical bodies must be conceived of as " solid ", relative to the changed shift in our awareness. Our physical bodies seem substantial to us in spite of our knowledge that they are spheres of active life, and even in spite of the fact that they are virtually empty space in terms of atoms and electrons. If it seems mysterious to us that we should continue after physical death associated with other bodily vehicles of consciousness, let us remind ourselves that our association with our physical bodies is equally mysterious.

The Nature of Non-Physical Bodies.—It may be asked how are these non-physical bodies created? We are so familiar with the processes of physical progeniture that we have ceased to wonder at the marvellous adaptive functioning we witness in the organic forms of what we call Nature. Nature, we say, has produced these forms in infinite variety. We patiently observe and classify with meticulous care, and eventually find the order and law we call evolution.

But all these intellectual formulations of the sequences and behaviour of the forms of life still fall short of understanding. We are observing phenomena on the surface of a living ocean. Why should life press for expression in these myriad forms? Evolution may tell us how they survive, but not why they originate, and there is mystery even in the familiar processes of histolysis and histogenesis in insects, where the internal organs are disintegrated to the point of complete destruction, and then by some mysterious power of inner organization the creature is re-formed into an entirely new being—a butterfly.

All through nature we witness these strange manifestations of creative principles within the heart of life. We see only the effects. The causes are invisible. The form-building powers of life operate in the darkness of the womb and in the kernel of the seed buried in the soil. Invisible, silent, and cryptic, life works beyond the range of our perception until the forms appear which disclose the secret work. The process is from within outwards.

We cannot imagine any manifestation of life except in terms of this duality of inner and outer, or at the conscious level of self and not-self, and this implies consciousness and body. As the personality is transcendent, the dissolution of the physical organism merely means a shifting of awareness.

We will still be ourselves with forms which will seem external and material. But as with our physical bodies, they will not be material, but other organizations of life. Or, as we have expressed it above, they will be living wholes no more and no less mysterious than the living whole we call our physical body.

We naturally may feel the need to visualize these bodies as being composed of some type of matter, but it is better to try to break clear of imagery of this kind, particularly so as the physical body itself is, in spite of its seeming solidity, mostly a void, the atoms which comprise it being relatively vast spaces, within which the electrons occupy about as much relative space as do the planets in our solar system. Sir A.S. Eddington in his book, *The Nature of the Physical World*, says,

THE PROBLEM OF NON-PHYSICAL BODIES

" If we eliminated all the unfilled space in a man's body and collected his protons and electrons into one mass, the man would be reduced to a speck just visible with a magnifying glass."

Yet this tenuous sphere of electronic energy is apprehended in normal perception as the substantial body of bones, flesh and blood! The body as discovered by the physicist is utterly unlike the body of appearance. For practical purposes we accept the appearance as real, but it resembles the body of electrons as little as does music the perforations on a piano-player roll. In other words, the body of appearance is a product of mental interpretation.

Now a precisely similar registration in consciousness is what we would expect to occur in connection with non-physical bodies. From the point of view of our consciousness our immediate awareness would be that we were appropriately embodied. Only secondarily might we concern ourselves with what the bodies were " made of ". Actually they would be made of just as little as are our electronic physical bodies. In fact they could be conceived as other modes of energy organized in vibratory spheres to enable consciousness to function in definite and limited ways necessary for the changed phase of existence.

As our consciousness expands and alters focus, corresponding changes in body would occur. For it follows on our view that any doctrine of personal survival requires us to postulate existence in terms of forms. These forms must be apprehended as " solid " and objectively definite for the experiencing consciousness. Also they would be part of a general environment of other apparently real external phenomenal existences.

Spiritualistic literature purports to give descriptions of the conditions of life in the other world. Most of these accounts may seem naïve and materialistic, for the " spirits " are described as living very much in a world of things and people. Many people, indeed, were rather shocked by the materialistic descriptions in Sir Oliver Lodge's *Raymond*.

Yet this is only what we should expect if survival is a fact. If our consciousness survives, it must do so as part of a phenomenal realm as seemingly real as our physical world. No doubt we can imagine " progress " of some sort, and a progressive sloughing away of the grosser material imagery as the consciousness awakens to new aspects of reality, but until the final enlightenment the illusion of separate existence in an external environment will persist.

Have We Non-physical Bodies Now?—Are we to suppose that these non-physical bodies come into existence only after death, or have we them now? They are part of the total personality. Although our consciousness is at this stage pin-pointed on the physical level, it is simultaneously functioning on other levels, as is evidenced by clairvoyance, telepathy and some trance experiences. I would surmise that these and other psychical phenomena, such as hauntings and poltergeists, etc., imply some definite mechanisms which we could call bodies.

Here I should perhaps refer to the widely-held belief in the existence of bodies which to some extent are counterparts of the physical body. The Egyptians believed in the Ka, and *The Tibetan Book of the Dead* gives techniques for the release of the counterpart body when a person is about to die.

The reader will also no doubt be familiar with the extensive Theosophical literature which records detailed descriptions of the astral and other bodies. According to Theosophical teaching man has seven bodies, but this number seems rather arbitrary. The bodies are described as being composed of varying degrees of subtle matter. The finest or subtlest matter is referred to as the " highest ", and the densest matter as the " lowest ".

Actually the planes on which these bodies exist are supposed to interpenetrate one another. There is none really higher or lower than another. The densest planes may be regarded as those in which the matter is most concentrated, and therefore occupies less space than the more rarefied.

The expression " passing from plane to plane " is often used, but this is misleading. To " pass " from one plane to another, it is not necessary to alter one's position, but merely to extend the consciousness so that it becomes aware of increasingly finer grades of matter. An Adept, for instance, sitting in contemplation, might become conscious of any plane upon which he concentrated his attention.

It is claimed that these bodies are visible to the trained clairvoyant. In fact, detailed descriptions have been published with illustrations of the human aura and expositions of the meaning of the colours and degrees of radiance clairvoyantly seen.

Caution against Accepting Clairvoyant Descriptions Literally.—Providing we are on our guard against a too-literal acceptance of these descriptions, the general concept of non-physical bodies gives a structural form to our thinking about survival. I feel sure the clairvoyant is seeing something. There is significant corroborative testimony from widely different sources to support this conclusion. But it is not my purpose here to review this evidence. The point I now make is that we can no more accept the interpretations of the clairvoyants at their face value than we can the commonsense interpretations of the physical world.

The clairvoyant no doubt is sensitive to an increased range of stimuli, but the descriptions will naturally be coloured by the clairvoyant's thought-pattern. Yet in fairness to the Theosophical scheme we should recognize that there is plenty of " room " within the physical body in its known electronic structure for an almost infinite range of energy modes, which can be conveniently called bodies inasmuch as they give form and definition to conscious functioning. In fact it is impossible to imagine consciousness without association with organized form.

I might, in passing, refer to an objection which, while it does not affect the validity or otherwise of non-physical bodies, does, it is claimed, render their existence unattractive. It has been argued that if the cells and atoms of the physical body are interwoven with a sort of astral counterpart, we might expect cancer cells, for instance, to have their astral replicas. We could agree with this. But even so, the idea need not be repulsive. Cancer cells are only ordinary cells out of control, and the problem of disease is the breakdown of organizational wholeness. This may take place in the physical body and need not necessarily affect any supposed non-physical counterpart, for the counterpart elements could be regrouped into the wholesome pattern when freed from the physical conditions which caused the disorganization we call " Disease ".

Non-physical Bodies make Survival More Thinkable.—The conception of non-physical bodies at least may be an aid to making survival more thinkable. Those who consider " body " to be the primary datum might be appeased somewhat if they could accept the non-physical body concept. In fact it would be legitimate to be quite materialistic and yet accept survival. On the physical level personality is considered a composite product of psychical and physical elements or, as it is called a " psycho-somatic " effect. Obviously this does represent the facts of our present conscious experience. We are body-mind creatures. This is so even if we consider body to be only a percept of mind. The mind does perceive a body, and to this extent our minds are modified by our own percepts. If therefore we accept this body-mind complex as continuing on successive non-physical levels of expression we do not break away so violently from our accustomed thinking about the personality.

CHAPTER X

PROOFS OF SURVIVAL

"A great deal of confused philosophical thought has its origin in obliviousness to the fact that the relevance of evidence is dictated by theory. For you cannot prove a theory by evidence which that theory dismisses as irrelevant."

A. N. WHITEHEAD, *Adventures of Ideas*.

The Nature of Proof.—Is proof of survival possible? Clearly this depends on what we mean by proof. In Law a set of rules for evidence is accepted, and within the limits of these rules proofs can be advanced which are generally regarded as valid.

Proof must always start from some point which needs no proof. When a number of witnesses with good eyesight corroborate without collusion that they have observed a certain event, it is implicitly assumed that normal eyesight is capable of reporting the occurrence of an event, and after proper precautions have been taken to establish the truthfulness and independence of the witnesses, we can proceed with proof according to rules which the court will accept.

If, however, a case of alleged survival were up for judgment, all the ordinary assumptions would be changed. The witness may testify that he had seen a deceased parent and that information was received which it was reasonably believed could only have been given by the deceased person. The witness may also claim to have heard and recognized his parent's voice with all its intimate inflexions and personal characteristics. This experience may have been repeated frequently, and in the presence of others who knew the parent. All the witnesses might be known as truthful men and women of sound judgment. Would their evidence be accepted even as a basis for establishing proof? It would not be, because a new set of assumptions would be involved, and a number of alternative hypotheses are available from which to choose. Our witnesses for survival have not only to establish that they have seen, heard, recognized a departed friend and intimately discussed matters known only by the deceased and themselves; they have also to prove that their experience was not due to telepathy, clairvoyance, cosmic memory, existence of a psychic factor, or perhaps a manifestation of the medium's capacity for dramatization based on knowledge obtained by cryptaesthesia.

There are cases where it is admitted that the information could have been known only by the dead man as, for instance, in the case of James L. Chaffin, who died without revealing that he had made a new Will, the Will only being discovered through one of Chaffin's sons having vivid dreams in which the father appeared and showed where the new Will was hidden. The case is well documented, as a law suit followed the finding of the new Will.

But even here it is possible to invoke theories other than survival. We could, for instance, say that Mr. Chaffin before his death may telepathically have conveyed the information about his Will to his son, and that this telepathically-conveyed information had remained latent, only to emerge some years later in the form of dreams.

Provided one is prepared to credit the living mind with almost unlimited powers of telepathy, clairvoyance, or, to use the modern term, Psi faculty, then obviously proof of discarnate minds is almost impossible. All that we can hope to do is to establish various grades of probabilities.

Actually, this is also the case with physical science. We have for the most part to be content with the highly probable. It is highly probable that the sun to-morrow will rise in the East; but it is not absolutely certain that it will do so. Most of the so-called laws of science are empirical sequences, and, strictly speaking, are not laws at all. They are observed regularities, and we have a reasonable expectancy that they will continue. In a sense they represent a system of assumptions which we accept because they are part of the intellectual climate of the generation to which we belong.

Through sheer familiarity we are apt to consider these assumptions as though they were inherently necessary; but they have not the self-evidence of certain general mathematical propositions, or *a priori* knowledge. The facts which are discovered by experience have only relative validity, and need to be re-interpreted over and over again as our minds grasp new and wider abstract principles.

The Preference for Hypotheses other than Survival.—Why is it that so many people find almost *any* theory preferable to that of survival? It is because, unconsciously, they have accepted a set of presumptions which virtually have imposed limits to what they regard as possible and impossible. They have accepted the testimony of sense-experience at its face value, and see the material sequence as final and absolute laws beyond which there can be nothing else. When, therefore, they are confronted with a theory of survival, their minds are abashed by the notion, for it appears nonsense against the set of assumptions which automatically come into play as a controlling influence determining their acceptances and rejections.

Is it so improbable that man should survive the death of his body? Yes, improbable to the point of impossibility of belief if one has accepted this world of sense-experience as the only reality. Such a man is in the position of Plato's cave-dwellers, who mistook the shadows for the reality.

Survival, therefore, is probable or improbable according to our philosophic assumptions. Mere evidence alone cannot convince. Evidence has to be assessed, and this will necessarily be done against the background of our accepted system of thinking.

Looking back over our intellectual past we can smile at the pontifical statements which have been made as to what can and cannot happen in the universe. Fortunately, there have always been those who grasped the deeper significances of facts, and refused to have their minds imprisoned by dogmatism.

Added Difficulties in Proving Survival.—In some ways psychical research has made it more complicated to offer direct evidence of survival. There was a time when the phenomena of trance-mediumship and manifestations of *soi-disant* deceased persons would have established a *prima facie* case for survival. But we now know more about the extra-sensory powers of the human mind, and consider we must explore these supernormal faculties to their utmost limit before adopting the survival hypothesis.

Yet it is often not sufficiently realized that these supernormal powers themselves presuppose a degree of psychic independence of the physical organism which almost makes survival an inevitable corollary.

If the human mind, while *embodied*, is able to transcend the normal limits of time and space as it does when exhibiting Psi phenomena—particularly prevision—why should being disembodied affect a faculty which is inherently non-spatial? The physical body cannot be the originating source of faculties which so clearly out-range the known limits of sense-response.

The function of the brain and nervous system in this connection seems to be that of a passive channel of communication for the mind's enlarged awareness.

The more psychical research demonstrates the supernormal powers of consciousness, the clearer become the implications of the mind's transcendence, and this is the crux of the survival problem. Yet those engaged in the practical work of psychical research are forced to seek for fruitful hypotheses which can be tested. One of the aims, therefore, of research is to investigate whether or not there is in the human personality anything which can be conceived to survive.

This is the conventional scientific approach, and is perhaps the only one which is propitious for devising useful techniques for investigation and practical working hypotheses. Obviously, if research does isolate, as it were, certain elements in the human personality which can be shown to be capable of separate functioning, apart from the sensori-motor system, then positive evidence would be provided in a form to satisfy our scientific temperaments.

A Paradoxical Definition?—But while warmly supporting the patient research along these lines, there is something paradoxical in the way the problem is stated. We start from the observation that we are body-mind creatures. But the mind is clearly immaterial, and by the time we have finished defining its nature in contrast with matter we have made for ourselves an unbridgable gulf between the incompatible opposites of matter and mind. If, therefore, our definitions were sound, we would have no need to ask whether mind survives, because our definition of its immateriality implies its independence of its material opposite.

This analysis into an arbitrary duality of incompatible elements is not philosophically fashionable to-day. Yet even to the extent that body and mind are conceived as a single functional whole we find that when our definitions of consciousness proceed to their logical limit we have by our very definitions credited mind with all the elements which imply its survival, and then proceed to ask whether in fact it can survive!

The sense of personal awareness is the core of all our other experiences, including the so-called body-mind relationship. If, however, we invent theories and attitudes which confuse our primary, self-evident intuitions, then we must proceed full circle through the labyrinth of research in order to verify our self-existence, which could not have been doubted in any case. It is our materialistic assumptions which cause our difficulties.

CHAPTER XI

THE RHYTHM OF BIRTHS AND DEATHS

" The essences of our souls can never cease to be because they never began to be, and nothing can live eternally but that which hath lived from eternity. The essences of our souls were a breath in God before they became living souls; they lived in God before they lived in the created souls, and therefore the soul is a partaker in the created souls, and therefore the soul is a partaker of the eternity of God."

WILLIAM LAW.

" And as to you, Life, I reckon you are the leavings of many deaths.
(No doubt I have died myself ten thousand times before.)"

WALT WHITMAN, Song of Myself.

" Were an Asiatic to ask me for a definition of Europe, I should be forced to answer him: It is that part of the world which is haunted by the incredible illusion that man was created out of nothing, and that his present birth is his first entrance into life."

SCHOPENHAUER, Parerga and Paralipomena.

The Individual and Circumstances.—Our research for meaning in living brings us back constantly to the primary awareness of our self-existence.

The other pole of our awareness is the non-self, the world of things, bodies and events which seem outside our self and constitute a field which conditions our existence.

Our sense of selfhood is unchanging and is a constant background to all our other experiences.

We may in moods of philosophic detachment realize the transcendence of our consciousness and feel inwardly free. But even though the external world is realized as largely a mental construct, the practical problems of our living remain. We seem to emerge out of a blank sea of unconsciousness and through the womb of a woman come into contact with a strange, external, ever-changing scene.

The speck within the mother grows and takes form in the darkness and emerges into the light with a cry. The helpless infant follows the pattern of the race. The form increases in stature, becomes adult and gradually declines and disintegrates into the primeval elements. But, as the countless individuals emerge and vanish from the outer scene, we sense the all-pervading potency of hidden currents as though we existed on a heaving sea of universal life. Nothing is complete on the surface.

Individuals appear and disappear, but the womb of life is eternally pregnant.

We cannot regard the universal life as being impersonal for have not persons emerged from the recesses of its bosom?

Here we come to the crux of our practical problem.

We who are persons have entered through the portals of normal birth into what appears to be an alien external world. Although we have forms, we are not the product of our forms. We have minds which can leap the boundaries of time and space and yearn for universal truth.

The forms we call our bodies have no such conscious yearning.

It is you and I who suffer, struggle and enjoy. It is we who experience the anguish of incompleteness and suffer the pangs of frustration and purposeless living even to the point of throwing away the body by suicide, reckless adventure or heroic sacrifice.

The laws of the body are those of self-survival and mechanistic repetition.

Yet into this realm we call physical appears the sequence of individuals with minds revealing an ancestry of another order; individuals who find their deepest satisfaction in love and the contemplation of the universal values of Truth, Beauty and Goodness.

We may assent on general principles that the individual is more than his bodily form, but why, we may ask, am I associated with this particular form?

Our conception of a universal consciousness carries with it certain implications.

The term itself " universal consciousness " indicates timelessness. Therefore, when viewed from our present standpoint in time, we must say that consciousness pre-exists our corporeal form. But we have already noted that whatever in addition this universal consciousness may be, it at least must include individuals. This means that we, as individuals, pre-existed our present physical appearance.

Law or Chance?—In this chapter we are mainly concerned with those aspects of our lives on the outer plane of daily living.

Even if our true nature is hidden from our phenomenal selves, and though we may inhere in a wider consciousness, yet the pressure of external experience lies heavily upon us.

Our minds are sucked down, as it were, into the stream of sense-experience. Reality may be a unity of bliss, but through the bodies we are creatures of change. We seem to be born into a helpless captivity. And how diverse are the conditions into which individuals are born! Granted that individuals are fundamental in the manifestation of life, what law governs their appearance in physical forms?

In other words, why were you and I born when and where we were? To suppose that we emerge into the time-sequence by chance conflicts with our knowledge of an orderly universe. The body is a product of heredity: should we not also expect our psychical nature to have a causal ancestry? We are not only spiritual beings in some abstract sense, we are also spiritual beings undergoing a process of manifestation, and to this extent we must come under the influence of law.

Even those who deny the universal validity of the law of causality agree that patterns of sequences exist. Events do not just happen arbitrarily and in isolation. Every occurrence has a history, and the present is seen to be a product of its past.

Yet we seem to be thrust into the corporeal stream of existence without discoverable cause! Perhaps you and I are sufficiently comfortably endowed not to feel this arbitrariness unduly. Yet if our minds are sensitive and grope for understanding we must experience moods of dismay at the dismal conditions into which so many are born. On this planet alone during a period estimated in millions of years countless generations of human beings have passed through the portals of birth and death. Their lives have been lived under the most diverse conditions.

The contemporary scene continues to exhibit striking contrasts. Aborigines still exist untouched by the complicated influence of civilization. There are the immature whose mental outlook is that of primitive people. Whatever we may mean by progress it is certainly subject to great ebb and flow. Each civilization seems to carry within it the seed of its own decay.

Our present civilization is the product of relatively few minds, and if these were destroyed our society would collapse for lack of the technical skill and knowledge of basic principles.

The race is sustained not only by the superior minds of its scientists, but also by the great spiritual teachers and saints.

So we find great evolutionary gulfs in the development of individuals. If this is the first experience of manifested life how can there be an evolutionary gulf? There must be some explanation for the difference between a moron and a genius. The problem is not answered by saying that the moron has certain glandular and physical deficiencies. Admittedly this may be the case. On the other hand all normal healthy brains do not reveal genius. Genius may need a peculiar physical organism in order to manifest, but the physical organism does not of itself produce genius, any more than possessing a Stradivarius would enable the untutored to play.

Something is taking place at a level much deeper than that of the physical.

Multi-Existences.—Individuals appear on the periphery we call corporeal existence. They seem to arise from the mysterious abyss of the unmanifested. But if individuals are not made by the body they must have pre-existed the body.

This being conceded, would it not reasonably follow that we as individuals have experienced corporeal existence many times? This conception enables us to answer many problems which confront us in daily living. No longer need the incongruous panorama which is presented by human existence outrage our sense of justice. We are not special creations making a brief contact with the outer world. If this were so we might well feel the helplessness of our plight, for some power other than ourselves must have thrust us into the maelstrom of existence without our choosing, and for no reason that we can grasp.

Faith in God and a vague belief that good will somehow triumph in the end may serve as an escapist philosophy to assuage some of our pains, but reason asks for more than a mood of hopefulness.

We feel an inherent repulsion to totalitarianism on a cosmic scale. Even suffering assumes less poignancy when it is realized to be curative, and part of a process for the unfoldment of latent powers and the achievement of creative mastery over conditions. Then we could say with Edward Carpenter, " Every pain that I suffered in one body became a power that I wielded in the next ".

This conception gives us a glimpse of depths within our individuality from which arise the causes of our present existence. The processes of life are from within outwards. A tree exists in many forms. There is a tree in the seed, and all that follows makes apparent the invisible potencies of the seed. The branches form and spread, becoming clothed with foliage. The leaves fall and are renewed with the cycles of the seasons, but the inward pattern of the tree continues throughout the periodicity of its external aspects.

Our personalities are similarly aspects of a deeper self. If leaves could become aware of themselves as leaves, they might bewail their brief fluttering existence, but if their awareness were extended to embrace the wholeness of the tree's life, the meaning of their life as leaves would be clear to them.

Everywhere we witness the mystery of permanence in the midst of change. Outwardly our lives in forms seem subject to transiency and arbitrary influences. Yet inwardly we feel free and capable of creativeness.

It is this inward sense of a wider self which we must trust, for it is in this direction that we can discover a meaning for our surface lives.

Outwardly we see an incongruous panorama—human beings born into conditions of bewildering diversity, some mature, serene and creative, others diseased, frustrated and doomed to suffering.

It is intolerable to suppose these beings appear causelessly. But if our present embodiment is only one of a cyclic series of expressions of our deeper self, then we may perceive the working of an evolutionary law by means of which we realize ourselves as conscious spiritual beings.

The Logic of Multi-Existence.—It is part of the teachings of all religions that our life on earth is a discipline to prepare us for an eternal and higher life in the hereafter. If this doctrine is accepted it is hard to understand how one brief life on earth can be sufficient for such a grand purpose.

Often it is only in one's later years that some measure of understanding and wisdom is achieved, and at this point we die. But millions die in infancy, and others vanish from the scene with tasks apparently incompleted and characters unformed. Yet current doctrines of immortality in the West attribute the greatest importance to our life on earth as a prelude to immortality. Is it logical to make our eternal life dependent on one experience of embodied existence?

Surely any doctrine of individual immortality implies pre-existence? The idea that we are special creations for a particular body makes it almost impossible to conceive an endless existence after death. And even a limited continuance after death seems less probable if we only come into being with our present bodily form.

Those who are committed to a belief in individual immortality would greatly strengthen the logical foundations of their belief if they accepted reincarnation. The soul then would be conceived as existing in a different time-order from the physical, but as being engaged in an evolutionary process which requires many embodiments. It is difficult to understand why those who have already overcome the difficulty of conceiving a non-physical soul in association with one embodiment should boggle at the idea of the same process occurring many times.

From the deepest mystical point of view, which involves new concepts of time, no doubt reincarnation is only a formalized statement of conscious experiences in a particular time-sequence. But the people who reject the doctrine usually do not do so on such high philosophic grounds. Consequently if we assent to a doctrine of individual immortality, then the doctrine of reincarnation should meet with little intellectual resistance. In fact, we may endorse Hume's statement that " it is the only theory of immortality that the philosopher can look at ".

For those who have neither personal experience nor intuitive intimations which cause a belief in reincarnation, the theory must remain an hypothesis. If it is considered with an open mind, then its acceptance or rejection will depend on its philosophic merits.

The arguments for reincarnation are logical, but as with all arguments, certain premises must be conceded.. It would be silly to discuss reincarnation if one denied the possibility of conscious experiences apart from physical existence.

We need not decide at this stage whether the soul is an entity having a separate existence in the sense that physical objects are supposed to have. Clearly we are functioning now as separate conscious entities, although this may be only a relative description based on sensory limitations of perception.

Most people in western countries who have accepted the doctrine of reincarnation have usually done so because they feel that, rightly interpreted, it provides a solution to the apparent injustice of our differing experiences. When so much in the universe has been found to be an expression of law, we can hardly be content to accept that the manifestations of our souls are arbitrary. If we are prepared to concede the existence of souls, then we are driven by logical necessity to seek for the laws governing their expression. There is an intellectual need to be rid of the notion that we are born by accident. Consequently, the basic concept of the doctrine of multi-existences, that the soul manifests in accordance with law, strongly appeals to our reason. We feel it *ought* to be true.

It relieves the soreness of adversity, and explains apparently unmerited good fortune if the conditions into which we are born are determined by our own activities in previous existences.

We are where we are and what we are because we require just these conditions for our unfoldment, and we are also under the necessity of working out the consequences of past activities.

The soul is thus conceived as a centre of energies which require appropriate fields of expression. These fields of expression we call incarnations.

Reincarnation implies both freedom and determinism. We cannot escape the consequences of the matrix of energies and compulsions which results from a long chain of embodiments. On the other hand we are free to use the law to gain liberation.

Freedom and Law.—Deep within our psychological make-up there is conceived to be an impulse towards manifestation which becomes an irresistible will to live in the realm of form. The realization of this " will to live " brings automatically into play the law of consequence, called in the East " Karma ". Manifestation thus implies Karma, the law which binds, yet becomes the means of freedom.

For eventually a cycle of manifestation is completed and the desire for life in form subsides. The soul draws within itself the quintessence of its experiences, and realizes a fullness of life to which its embodied experiences have given definition.

In its essence the Soul is not separate from the Infinite. Its separateness can be regarded as only apparent, and on this view its finite expression would be a functional aspect of the Absolute.

The process of becoming in time and space actualizes some of the infinite possibilities of the Whole we call God, and excludes others.

We shall return to this theme in a later chapter. We need now only note that if our individual lives are embraced within the cosmic whole, then the powers, qualities, and potentialities of the universal life are reflected in each of us; as microcosms we reveal cosmic processes. The rhythmic sequence of manifestation unfolds some of the infinite potentialities. Thus we may postulate a controlling factor other than Karma determining the path of the soul's experiences. We might symbolically conceive the soul as being briefed to actualize a portion of a cosmic plan. This plan, though fundamentally timeless, would as it unfolds in the time-sequence exercise its influence as a future goal. The soul in its manifested state need not consciously realize this; nevertheless the goal would act as an invisible magnet. We are part of a cosmic drama, having considerable freedom in the way we interpret our part, yet destined to fulfil our allotted task.

The law of Karma corrects our deviation from the cosmic harmony. Our freedom partakes of the absolute freedom of the whole, yet is conditioned by the need to function in limitation.

Karma is the law which registers disturbance of equilibrium. Freedom allows us to disturb the equilibrium, but the consequence is suffering.

Our present life therefore is not the chance occurrence it appears on the surface to be.

The matrix of energies which we have woven as it were into the structure of our inner bodies determines the time of our birth and environment.

The Mechanism of Karma.—Although fundamentally the whole process is a journey in consciousness, it has a mechanistic aspect.

Here we can invoke the concept of non-physical bodies which we discussed in Chapter 9.

These bodies could be vibratory spheres which provide the vehicles for Karma, drawing us into sympathetic relationship with certain groups of people and conditions, and excluding us from others through a complete absence of vibratory response.

It is a familiar concept among occultists that thoughts have forms and may be seen clairvoyantly. There is some evidence for this in certain types of phenomena such as hauntings, and the peculiar " atmospheres " to which sensitives are susceptible in some localities. If therefore we are seeking a mechanism to account for the carrying-over from life to life of Karmic energies, then thought-atmospheres or non-physical vehicles of consciousness provide a useful and thinkable hypothesis. These bodies would be the seed-pods from which stem forth the successive incarnations.

But any hypothesis in mechanistic terms is only a concession to our ordinary mode of thinking.

It is our view that in the ultimate analysis all forms, bodies, and mechanisms are modes of consciousness. Admittedly, uncompromising monism is not easy to maintain when the hard facts of phenomenal existence and practical living force multiplicity so closely upon our attention. We will return to this problem in a later chapter. Obviously, a deeper understanding of this ancient teaching involves a consideration of the nature of Time.

There are always many levels of meaning to any doctrine of significance. However, the central concept of reincarnation is simple enough.

It is in essence a statement of a law of periodicity, and represents one more example of the cyclic manifestation we witness throughout nature. There is a rhythm in the life-histories of creatures and natural phenomena. The concept of reincarnation conceives the soul to participate in this universal process. It would indeed be surprising if it did not.

Some Current Beliefs and Attitudes.—In Christian communities the general assumption is that we have only one incarnation, followed by an eternity in some after-death state.

There is no reason why this doctrine should be entitled to intellectual priority higher than that of an opinion. Admittedly, ecclesiastical and scriptural dogmatism in the West more or less supports the single incarnation hypothesis, but if we give undue heed to the dogmatisms of the world's ecclesiastical systems we shall find there is hardly a fantastic notion which has not somewhere been supported by Scripture or priestly authority. Our approach to the doctrine of reincarnation should be to consider its merits as a hypothesis compared with rival hypotheses.

We have already noted that perhaps its strongest appeal is that, granted certain premises, it offers a solution to the painful problem of apparently lawless inequality.

One could imagine some salutary applications of the doctrine to social attitudes. We might not be so racially intolerant if we believed that persecution and exploitation would bind us to those we hate, and force upon us some form of expiatory service.

Also the modern doctrine of progress might gain new meaning in the light of reincarnation. We are constantly urged to work for posterity. It is the fashion to pay lip-service to this idea, even if we cannot define what we mean by progress on a universal scale. However we would be very smug if we could accept with complacency the toil and sacrifice of untold millions of past generations as being necessary to enable us to enjoy our present civilization, such as it is.

And now it is we in our turn who are to sacrifice for the benefit of future unborn generations. There is an understandable motive for making sacrifices for our immediate offspring. This is a form of vicarious immortality. We live again in our children. But to endure hardship for a more distant future puts a strain on our frail humanity. Our interest in the welfare of the inhabitants of the planet who will live a thousand years hence is for most of us rather academic.

Yet we are engaged in projects which cannot mature until long after we have gone, and we feel in some vague way that we should build for the future. This concern for the future has a new significance in the light of reincarnation. The present is growing into a future which we ourselves will inherit. If there is to be a future Utopia it would be one inhabited by the present generation in new forms and not by a race of alien beings with no roots in the past.

Not only would we be reborn into a particular period but also into appropriate groups with which we have a common affinity. Our fate is not entirely that of a single line of individual destiny. We also participate in the fate or Karma of our group or country. The causal energies of our individual lives are criss-crossed with those of the group to which we belong.

THE RHYTHM OF BIRTHS AND DEATHS 85

Consequently large numbers of people share disasters and benefits in common if the energies of the individual require this group experience.

To accept the concept that nothing which happens to us is accidental, and that we are now generating those energies which determine our future manifestation, would stiffen our will to new effort.

If reincarnation is a fact then the emphasis is on right living, rather than on seeking salvation by believing certain doctrines. If we must have beliefs they should be regarded as of tentative value to evoke right effort.

Our minds grope in an infinite cosmos, and any belief-formulations are as the essays of children about the world they have only vaguely experienced.

Theological speculation, creeds, doctrinal tradition, and ceremonial, which comprise the obligatory beliefs of most of the world's organized religions, satisfy a psychological need.

Each formulation at the time it was made probably represented the clearest statement in words possible within the mental capacity of those to whom it was addressed. Providing these statements are recognized as the halting record of human effort to express what is fundamentally inexpressible, they serve to guide our thinking.

But the history of religious conflict demonstrates the tragic imprisonment of the mind which results from allowing these human approximations to be imposed upon us as the final word of God!

There are certain widely-accepted doctrines which have to be modified or even discarded if reincarnation is true. This is particularly the case with the doctrine of Saviours. Students of Mythology will know how ancient this notion is. In its crudest form the deity is supposed to be willing to accept a sacrifice, and those who believe in the virtue of this sacrifice will be saved. The doctrine of course is modified among the more cultured, but it retains its essential character even in the Christian theology.

On the assumption of reincarnation the vicarious sacrifice of another cannot achieve our salvation. We reap as we sow, and in accordance with the law of cosmic cycles our individual expression completes its part of the Divine mosaic we call manifestation.

The key patterns of each age are exemplified in the lives of our great teachers, saints and seers. These sages illumine the path, but we must tread it ourselves. Still less can we achieve enlightenment by mere belief. We have to become awakened to new levels of consciousness which make us sensitive to the ever-present inspiration of the great ones who are the racial exemplars of the complete life.

We cannot escape the law which determines our existence, and the rhythmic sequence of many lives gives each of us the opportunity to fulfil our destiny.

This idea of law which brings to each man his desert is not entirely congenial. Our childhood attitudes are by no means transcended, and almost instinctively we tend to pray for benefits. Many of the forms of prayer and hymns in current use are petitions to God for special benefits.

The more enlightened churchmen deplore petitionary prayer, but it will persist as long as God is conceived as an omnipotent Father. Also it is very human to seek to bring God over to our side. But it was rather startling recently to read in the press that a well-known boxer in a ringside speech thanked God for his help in knocking his opponent senseless.

Prayer, for the reincarnationist, would be based on an entirely different attitude. If he had enough knowledge his prayer could be very potent. He might even use petitionary forms but he would not be deceived by these for they would only represent a technique for orienting the mind so that certain energies and influences from higher levels could manifest.

The universe is living and the mind has the capacity to evoke strange powers. This requires concentration and some knowledge. But all responses are in accordance with law and it is what we are rather than what we ask for that determines our success.

Single-track Salvation.—As opposed to this view we have what may be called one-track salvation theologies. In the

West we are exhorted to believe in Jesus as our *only* means to God. Great stress is laid on an historical sequence of events, and we are told that an essential preliminary to our salvation is to profess our faith in the efficacy of the death of Jesus. When this exclusive path-to-God theory is accepted with naïve literalness, it must of necessity lead to almost fanatical proselytism.

Obviously not a moment can be spared if the eternal life of millions is dependent on their being given the opportunity of professing the Christian faith.

Mohammedans in their turn exalt belief in another historical figure as a sole pathway to God.

The Hindus however are not by temperament proselytizers. A single incarnation does not assume the exaggerated importance for them that it does for the Christian. Their view is more catholic. They see the majestic pageant of manifestation within the All-embracing life of Brahma, and their seers proclaim in the words of the *Bhagavad Gita*, " However men approach Me, even so do I welcome them, for the path men take from every side is Mine."

But the gulf between practice and precept is often immense, and even in India, the home of the profound Vedanta, the vision of the mountain has become cloudy and distorted to the inhabitants of the valleys, and standing guard over the paths of ascent are the priests of exclusive doctrinal portals who seek to fence off all rival exits.

Actually it is largely the verbal forms in which we are asked to believe which divide us. When we practise the ethics of religion, divergencies due to geography and cultural inheritance become relatively unimportant.

The Problem of Lack of Memory.—While it may be conceded that the general theoretical case for reincarnation is strong, the plain man naturally objects that the absence of memory robs the doctrine of any practical or ethical significance.

Of course for those who have a conviction that they do remember, reincarnation ceases to be theory, because for them it has become knowledge. But the majority of people, we must assume, have no conscious memory of previous existences.

Consequently, whatever allegedly happened to them in some other incarnation happened to another person who has no obvious connection with their present existence.

In other words, there seems to be no causal connection between the various incarnations.

The usual reply to this objection is that *personalities* do not reincarnate, but only the deeper, underlying self of which the personalities are the successive partial expressions. The normal reaction to this statement is to brush it aside as meaningless. Our conscious personalities with their physical accompaniments seem very real to us. In fact, for those immersed in practical affairs, they are the only reality, and this so-called deeper self seems a myth, or even a verbal subterfuge.

The hale and hearty extrovert in particular would take this attitude instinctively, but those of us who are accustomed to introspection and have some aptitude for meditation, experience a more intense inner life which has greater significance than external events.

The fact is, we require to apply definite techniques to enable us to explore our inner consciousness, and those unpractised in these techniques will usually remain unconscious of the psychological contents existing below the threshold of their normal awareness.

It is clear that the linkage between the various personalities of the different incarnations must be sought in the subconscious.

The Subconscious.—The term subconscious is used as a general description for those aspects of consciousness which exist below the threshold of the surface-awareness of the normal waking self, yet are powerful enough to influence and control behaviour and attitudes.

The concept of the subconscious is nowadays a familiar one, and for modern psychology it plays a major rôle, especially in psychiatric practice.

It is indeed largely through treatment of the mentally sick that we have derived our knowledge of these cryptic levels of the human psyche.

Therefore many of the terms used to describe subconscious activation are rather associated with abnormal psychology.

But the various schools of psychology are by no means agreed in their doctrines regarding the subconscious.

There is a wide cleavage of views on fundamental issues, for instance, between Freud, Jung and Adler.

Freud, as is well known, considered the general basic energy, or libido, as being sexual, while Jung regards this concept as too narrow to explain the facts. He considers the libido to be a more generalized psychic energy, sex being only one of its manifestations. Adler on the other hand sees the will to power as the underlying driving force.

This illustrates how research into the subconscious is coloured by the general outlook of the researcher. Jung in particular is fundamentally religious in outlook, whereas Adler was greatly influenced by Schopenhauer and Nietzsche.

It need not surprise us therefore that other investigators, who view the human psyche less narrowly than those whose main interest is psychotherapy, discover other levels of subconscious activity.

Consequently the term subconscious is too vague and general to describe all phenomena, particularly those of *psi* phenomena and trance communications, which not inappropriately could be attributed to a super-consciousness rather than to a subconsciousness which is associated principally with energies on the instinctual level.

The various terms used in psychological study are only descriptive labels to facilitate quick recognitions of particular aspects of consciousness which emerge as the result of applying certain techniques.

Modern psychological theory is very fluid, and our notions of what our subconscious " contains " are of necessity coloured by the type of technique used, and the bias of the investigator, but still more by the peculiarities of the persons who are the subjects of the investigations.

Subconscious and Ordinary Memory Compared.—Of particular relevance to our present discussion is the subconscious memory. Events completely forgotten seem to be indelibly retained by the subconscious. An hypnotic subject can often be directed to recall minute details of early years and even passages from books, and words spoken, of which the normal memory retains not a trace.

A study of modern psychotherapy shows how little reliance we can place on ordinary memory when it comes to explaining certain types of behaviour. The psychiatrist in his efforts to cure neurosis and emotional maladjustment demonstrates to the patient the influence of infantile experiences and repressions beyond recall except by expert aid.

Our ordinary memory is a very patchy record of our life-history. Any of us can prove this by endeavouring to remember in detail the events of even one day. The broad outline can, of course, be recollected of, say, yesterday's experiences, but if we try to re-live yesterday's events meticulously in detail, we find it by no means easy to recall every event with accuracy.

It is indeed an interesting exercise to retrace a day's events, starting with the last, and proceeding backwards to the time we awakened in the morning. It requires considerable concentration, and our first attempts leave us with a feeling of humiliation at our inability to recall in detail our precise experience at each minute of the day.

This is the case even if we confine our attention to the mere recalling of external events, such as meeting this or that person, or visiting particular places and so on. If, in addition, we attempt to re-experience our moods, and mental attitudes and recall our thoughts we find that only the highlights are readily remembered.

Should we continue this exercise to include a week's events, the record in normal memory becomes increasingly ragged. There are blanks which remain unfilled in spite of all our efforts to remember. Taking longer periods, say a year, then the details in their entirety are beyond normal recall.

The memory of our total life-span is hardly more than a recollection of the main highlights. It may be likened to a cinematograph film which has been badly cut. Scenes flash brightly on to the screen only to be followed by flickering blurs and patches of blankness, and the blanks are more numerous than the clear pictures.

THE RHYTHM OF BIRTHS AND DEATHS 91

This, however, is only the film of our normal memory. The subconscious memory does not present these gaps. Under suitable conditions, as in the hypnotic trance, our life-history is retained with exact fidelity and clearness. There are records of people who at the point of death re-experienced the events of their life with vivid clarity, and in detail.

The continuity of the subconscious memory, compared with the broken record of the waking memory, provides a model for the linkage between life and life.

It is now generally recognized that the gaps in our normal memory are often of greater significance than the events we remember.

Our general behaviour-pattern and attitude to life are largely determined by forgotten experiences. Even the normal processes whereby we acquired our education are not remembered. Few of us can remember our first efforts to form the letters of the alphabet, yet our present skill is evidence of what once required our conscious attention.

Instinctual fears, attachments, loves, hates and frustrations are likewise forgotten, and would as far as normal memory is concerned be deemed not to have occurred if it were not for the techniques of modern psychology which uncover the causes of delinquency, maladjustment, fixations and a whole range of phobias as being due to infantile experiences and repressions—forgotten, yet potent to mar or ruin a person's life.

The account which a man might give of his life, relying entirely on his normal memory, would be a very inadequate record, and even deceptive, except to the psychiatrist who is trained to detect rationalizations which cover the real causes of behaviour.

Ordinarily, we live our lives unaware of the subconscious elements in our nature, and by living solely on the surface we could argue quite logically that it is nonsense to suppose important events could happen to us and yet leave no trace in our ordinary memory.

If, also, one has a bias towards moral judgments, there could be a rankling sense of injustice that we can suffer such serious consequences as the result of early repressed experiences beyond the control of the rational, moral self.

Yet such are the facts, and they are within the limits of what is to-day ordinary psychotherapy.

Objections Based on Lack of Memory not Strong.—It is clear therefore that any objections to reincarnation based on the absence of memory are largely robbed of their force when we realize that we may live through experiences and yet retain no trace of them in ordinary memory.

The connection between lives in a similar manner exists in the deeper levels of consciousness—deeper of course than in those of the subconscious of current analytical theory.

The exploration of man's underlying states of consciousness is comparatively new in western countries, but the eastern psychologist has for centuries been accustomed to the application of introspective techniques which, under skilled guidance, have enabled the aspirant to probe his inner self.

The aphorisms of Patanjali represent the crystallized form of a technique practised by countless generations of men who have devoted themselves to the task of achieving psychological liberation, and enabling the consciousness to transcend the limits of normal awareness.

In order to understand, therefore, the theory of reincarnation, we have to keep clearly in mind that the personality as we know it is an emergent of a deeper self, and the successive personalities are, as it were, buckets lowered into the sea of experience to be withdrawn into the reservoir of the enduring transcendent self.

Lack of memory on the periphery of consciousness seems to be a general law, and even a functional necessity. We have already noted how the psychological causes of much normal behaviour are hidden in the subconscious. Similarly the causes of our total life-pattern, such as place and time of birth and so on, are hidden in our deeper structure.

But just as our complexes reveal their existence by obtrusions of emotional tone and compulsions of various types, so may experiences in past lives be conceived to register their effects in the form of inherent faculty and innate skills and dominant tendencies.

It is not necessary to our spiritual evolution to be reborn with a detailed memory of our past. This, in fact, would be as great a hindrance and embarrassment as remembering five-finger-exercises long after a technique has become automatic which leaves the mind free to interpret the music.

There are more types of memory than that of recollection of particular events. Even our bodies are functional memories representing the racial trial and error of ages of evolution.

If reincarnation be a fact we should not expect each life to be burdened by an intolerable memory of detailed experiences. Rather should we expect past experiences to be expressed in the outer consciousness by means of the general environment and fundamental character-pattern.

Yet at certain stages and for particular purposes past-life scenes could flash into the outer consciousness, or even more likely they might manifest by some upsurge of emotion or sudden recognition of another person of vital significance for the current incarnation.

In other words, memories of past lives could disclose their influence similarly to the way in which infantile experiences and repressions protrude into adult behaviour.

We might even surmise that no matter on what level consciousness is functioning, it would always do so in terms of an outer waking self, and a subconscious.

The necessity for focussing on a particular set of experiences inevitably imposes limitations. Definition implies exclusion. Consequently what is not in the forefront of consciousness becomes part of the general background, comprising various levels and degrees of availability for being recalled.

I am rather disposed to think that after death our present life will become subconscious, relative to our after-death waking consciousness.

This may account for the difficulty of communication between one level of consciousness and another.

If it requires the skilled application of certain techniques to become aware of our present subconscious, we can well imagine that similar special efforts and particular training would be required to retrace with clarity the events of the physical life, which, while it is " there " within the conscious whole, yet is not needed in the form of a detailed record.

Some Who Remember.—Although specific memories of past lives would seem to be contrary to the general law which governs our manifestation, yet it is well known that large numbers of people have had the peculiar experience which they describe as " remembering their past lives ".

Numbers of cases could be cited, but they would have little value as proof. Some of the cases are fairly obviously due to illusions of grandeur, when they relate to important historic personages.

However, after discounting cases of this type, there remain others which cannot be lightly dismissed as being due to imagination.

Sometimes the " memory " flashes into consciousness unexpectedly, and with the vividness of a scene in the present. Several people with whom I have been closely associated have had such experiences.

One lady, whose mind is cultured, balanced and critical, has had three such experiences. They have left an indelible impression upon her, and she can give no other explanation of them except to say they were indistinguishable from memories.

One of the scenes which she seemed to be living over again was so poignant that it affects her even now after many years. Also the memories have helped her to understand certain relationships in her present life.

In my book, *The Superphysical*, I gave several cases of " memories ". Some of the memories were unflattering and painful, so could hardly be attributed to a desire for self-aggrandizement.

The significant point to note about these experiences is not just the fact that certain people have had " psychic visions ". These are common enough. It is the overpowering conviction that they have been actually *remembering* a portion of their own history which stamps these experiences with the peculiar intimacy which is the characteristic of our normal memory.

We all of us imagine things at times, but we know beyond doubt when we are remembering, and when we are imagining. Memory is a unique experience. Yet many of our personal memories are unprovable to others, and of course normally we do not need to prove them.

Those who believe they remember some incidents in a previous existence can only testify to their conviction, and others must draw their own conclusions.

So for example Professor Lutoslawski, the eminent Polish savant, states: " For me the subjective certainty of pre-existence is parallel to the certainty of immortality, and it is not a conclusion from any line of argument. I know that I have existed before this life, either on earth as man, or elsewhere in similar conditions. This knowledge is for me not less evident than any mathematical axiom, and needs no proof." (*The World of Souls*, p. 200.)

Such a statement has little value as proof for others. But this is the case with most deep personal experiences.

Words are symbols and their effectiveness as a means of communication depends entirely on our sharing with others a common experience.

Sometimes veridical data are available, as, for instance, when very young children can give details of circumstances relating to a previous incarnation of recent date, and investigators are able to verify the incidents related by the child. In India several cases of this type are on record, some of which I cite in *The Superphysical*.

It would no doubt be an interesting piece of research to collect and edit some hundreds of cases of " memories ", and I wish a comprehensive work of this type were available, similar to that of Gurney, Myers and Podmore's *Phantasms of the Living*.

However, even thousands of such cases would not, I think, constitute proof of reincarnation, but they might provide strong presumptions in its favour, and perhaps even an intuitive conviction that it was true. This of course would be more likely to occur if one were satisfied on general principles that reincarnation is a reasonable theory.*

Prevision and Reincarnation.—Some of the facts of prevision tend to support a theory of multi-existences.

We shall need to consider prevision in connection with a discussion of the nature of time, but the aspect we note here is the possibility of foreseeing events in a person's future.

Many examples of this can be found in the Proceedings of the English Society for Psychical Research, and in numerous books, such as Dr. Osty's *Supernormal Faculties in Man*, Dunne's *An Experiment with Time*, and Dame Edith Lyttleton's *Some Cases of Prediction*. †

Obviously such facts have wide significance in many fields of thought, but I am only concerned at the moment to ask what are the implications of the fact that events in a person's future may be foreseen? It is true that normal inference will enable many events in our lives to be predicted with a fair degree of accuracy. If we know intimately enough a man's character, education, social position, and many of the people with whom he mixes, it would not require supernormal faculties to foresee his career, and we might even guess accurately the girl he would marry, and so on.

But suppose a complete stranger told us we would travel to a particular country when we were planning to leave for an entirely different part of the world, and also gave a description of a person we would meet there who would be of great significance for us; and suppose all this came about, and, still more remarkable, that we discovered that the person we met had years previously been impressed by a strong

---

* I should here draw attention to the work of Dr. Ian Stevenson, Chairman of the Department of Neurology and Psychiatry, School of Medicine, University of Virginia, U.S.A. His research into ostensible memories of past lives, particularly those of children, deserves close study. I have been greatly impressed in my correspondence with him by his open-mindedness, patience and grasp of the nature of the problem. His work is not yet completed but the first results of his investigations may be read in his "Winning Essay of the Contest in Honor of William James," published under the title of *The Evidence for Survival from Claimed Memories of Former Incarnations*. It is along these lines that eventually the reincarnation theory may gain the degree of probability amounting to "proof".

† Also about 50 cases are published in my book, *The Future is Now*. University Books, Inc. New York. 1961.

psychic impulse to wait for someone who would have a decisive influence in her life; might we not suspect that some sort of predestination was at work?

Actually, this chain of events occurred to me, and what is more, when I met the person in question there was an almost visual flash of recognition which established a relationship with a certainty which seemed born of a prior knowledge.

This is only one of several instances where events in my life have been foreseen by clairvoyants. They are not, like that recounted above, of a striking character, and naturally have little evidential value except for myself.

Sometimes the events foreseen in a person's life are of a dramatic nature. As, for instance, when it is predicted that a man will die at a certain time, and details of the type of death are given. The prediction concerning Dr. Tillyard which I related in *The Superphysical* is a good example. On July 7th, 1928, a psychic predicted among other things —actually out of 53 impressions 40 proved correct—that Dr. Tillyard would "die through a railroad or automobile accident", and added, "He has not a long life to live." Dr. Tillyard was only forty-three years of age at the time the prediction was made. There was an exact fulfilment, for he was killed in a motor car accident near Canberra, Australia, on January 13th, 1937.

It is not my purpose here to review the evidence for prevision. Those who are interested will naturally consult the original records. They are abundant, and well authenticated.

There is at present no theory which is adequate to explain all the facts of prevision. Obviously, prevision challenges our ordinary ideas about time. However, the point I wish to make now is about one particular type of prevision, viz., that the precognizing by supernormal or non-inferential means of future events in a personal life would be less difficult to understand if reincarnation were true.

If our present life is a continuation of a long history, then many of the main events of our present life must to some extent be determined. Certainly our place of birth was, and in some cases, perhaps, the mode of our death is.

We cannot generalize. Exceptional people will have exceptional life-histories and often eventful careers. In some cases a certain future may be unavoidable, but in others present actions may modify or cancel what otherwise might have occurred.

People have often received warnings which they have heeded and so escaped a predicted danger; others have also been warned, but the event foreseen nevertheless occurred. We cannot say to what extent our lives are determined, but if reincarnation is true we can say the determination is by some deeper level of one's self.

Decisions made in the past may bind us in the present, but the time-sequence continues until we realize the perfect freedom which lifts us out of the realm of time.

I do not wish unduly to press the facts of prevision into the service of a theory of reincarnation. They have a much wider significance than that. Yet it is at least interesting to note that on the assumption of reincarnation we should not be surprised if sometimes our future can be predicted.

In this chapter we are not concerned with the nature of the time-process as such, but with the question why it is that we as individuals should experience one set of circumstances rather than another, and especially do we ask how is it possible that it can be foreseen that certain events will occur in a person's life.

Should we agree that something in the nature of a skeleton map of a person's total life exists on some causal plane of consciousness, then under suitable conditions we might obtain glimpses of it.

Actually those contacting " the plan " would not be seeing the future, but a present reality which needs time for it to be expressed, even as an architect's drawing exists in the present but manifests sequentially.

Reincarnation would explain the existence of the plan. This might be supposed to represent the core of our causal energies generated during the long history of many embodiments. Our life-pattern would unfold from this causal region even as our bodies emerge from the germ-plasm. It is unfortunate that we are compelled to use analogies which involve spatial imagery. Actually the whole process is an adventure in consciousness.

Alternative Hypotheses to Reincarnation.—If one is prepared to grant that conscious existence transcends the physical organism, then reincarnation as a theory has no serious rival. Naturally, few theological systems can ignore this problem of inequality, and many have tended to expound after-death compensatory systems. Usually the conceptions are vague, but in essence they are promises of better conditions in heaven.

We have already noted that such after-death compensatory schemes do not face up to the real problem of why we were born at all, and that in fact they aggravate the injustice by making eternal existence depend on behaviour in the limited time-sequence.

Other variants of the compensatory type are those which postulate a kind of community sharing of experiences after death, so that the sorrows of one individual are balanced, as it were, by the joys of another.

Conceptions of this type lay stress on some form of group-mind rather than in individual expressions. Consequently there is less need to suppose that each and every individual has to carve out his own sphere of expression. Rather is it more important to realize that the individual is contributing to a wider whole, and within this more comprehensive consciousness the vagaries and injustices which apparently occur to individuals are resolved by a sort of alchemy of blending in a shared state of consciousness.

Such a conception is not necessarily opposed to reincarnation. Many expositions of reincarnation are crude and naïve, and accept the separate individual as the only reality. But even ordinary experience contradicts this notion. Community and individuality are complementary conceptions. Neither can exist without the other.

We are here confronted with basic concepts which colour almost every aspect of our thinking, both philosophically and practically. It is represented in the politics of Socialism versus Individualism, and becomes acute when we try to reconcile the experience of mysticism with the phenomenal facts of multiplicity.

We shall return to this problem, but here we need only observe that reincarnation in terms of individualities is not contradicted by deeper views of Reality.

If we conclude eventually that phenomenal existence is in some sense an illusion, then obviously all separateness and concrete manifestations, including reincarnation as usually understood, must be part of the illusion. We could then say that reincarnation is as true or false as other phenomenal appearances in time and space.

Reincarnation, judged from this ultimate standpoint, becomes part of the general problems of multiplicity and unity.

If reincarnation is rejected on these high principles the rejection will carry with it the whole universe of phenomenal appearances. Truly a philosophical example of throwing away the baby with the bathwater!

I hope as we proceed we shall find it possible to find some purpose in the phenomenal universe, in which case the conception of reincarnation may indeed express a truth at least within the relative terms of time and space.

If in the end we have to reject the individual as ultimate, the curious paradox will arise that it is we, the individuals, who must commit this act of psychological suicide. No matter how complicated or abstract our thinking becomes, it is we ourselves who are doing the thinking. The reality of the thinker cannot be denied without destroying the validity of the product of his thinking.

Reincarnation not Necessarily a Religious Doctrine.—Reincarnation has as much or as little relevance for religion as is the fact that we are born once. All that the doctrine postulates is that the soul manifests in accordance with a law of cycles.

We might make the same statement about the foliage of trees, and other cycles in nature.

Religion in its deepest sense represents our efforts to realize God or the Absolute. While, therefore, the doctrine of reincarnation may satisfy our intellectual need to understand certain aspects of phenomenal existence, it could also prove a hindrance to spiritual effort, if it accentuated a backward-looking tendency. The entry to the Eternal lies in the present.

The spiritual life requires us to make a vertical approach, and away from the horizontal plane of the time-sequence.

All religions which unduly stress an historical series of events as a basis for belief become stultified.

Religion must be a vital experience in the present.

The path to enlightenment does not consist of a scholarly knowledge of sacred records and doctrines formulated by other men. These doctrines therefore, including that of reincarnation, when merely held as beliefs, have not necessarily any value for the achievement of enlightenment.

It is quite different if a person remembers that he has lived before. For him at least reincarnation is a fact, not a belief. But even so unless his previous experiences have brought him to the point where a new orientation of his life is possible and he makes the deliberate effort to gain what is called in the East " liberation ", then remembering his past lives has as much or as little value as our normal memory of incidents in our present life.

As the Indian teacher, Krishnamurti, states: " For me reincarnation happens to be a fact, because I remember certain things." Yet although for him reincarnation is a fact he does not encourage mere belief in it. He adds, " put it out of your mind; and remember only that as you are the product of the past, so you can control the future. You are master of yourself, and in your hand lies eternity." (*Star Bulletin*, March, 1931, p. 8.),

It should however be mentioned that Krishnamurti's indictment of belief, applies to all beliefs. He has a burning zeal to awaken in his hearers a realization of immediate awareness of immortal life and he conceives beliefs as hindrances to this supreme goal.

Reincarnation is, we repeat, not a religious teaching any more than is the theory of evolution.

It has indeed value as a concept or hypothesis, and enjoys no higher status than that of any other statement about natural processes.

The Word Reincarnation Misleading.—The exposition we have given of the doctrine of reincarnation is over-simplified and makes considerable concessions to our ordinary modes of thinking. The result will be to cause an imagery of souls as concrete entities dipping in and out of material forms. We disclaim any such ideas.

The very word " reincarnation " is as misleading as the word " survival ". Reincarnation implies embodiment. But the self is never embodied. The word " reincarnation " should be used merely as a symbolical expression of a series of psychological experiences. The body is included within the sense of selfhood, but can be distinguished from the self. The self in manifestation is always aware of a not-self. The self is constant and unchanging, but its identifications with the not-self vary continually.

There is a form of meditation which consists of a series of disentanglements of the self from the not-self. The object is to realize our self in its essence without the qualities imposed by identification with the body and changing psychological elements, or what William James called the " me " as distinct from the " I ".

A metaphysical statement of the doctrine of reincarnation could be in terms of the Self defining itself through a movement in consciousness which appears as identification with a not-self, and withdrawal. Later chapters will make this conception clearer.

I should perhaps here comment briefly on the Buddhistic conception of the doctrine of rebirth. It is generally supposed that Buddhism denies both God and the Self. Actually however the Buddha refused to speculate about metaphysical problems. His aim was to demonstrate the cause of suffering and its removal. Only by the enlightened can the Supreme be understood, therefore Buddhism concentrated on the practices and way of life which lead to enlightenment.

The Buddhist conception of transmigration does not imply a reincarnating entity or soul. Rather is it a statement of a law of causality whereby acts and their consequences are a continuous stream of change. Yet the chief purpose of the Buddhist way of life is to escape from the wheel of births and deaths. It may therefore be asked who or what is escaping, if there is no enduring entity or soul.

According to Ananda Coomaraswamy, " When the question is pressed, Is there a Self, the Buddha refuses to answer ' Yes or No '; to say ' Yes ' would involve the ' eternalist ' error, to say ' No ' the ' annihilationist ' error." *Gotama the Buddha,* p. 21.

The truth being that while there is no enduring self, there is the eternal immutable Self. This statement, which seems enigmatical, will be discussed more fully in Chapters 15, 16, 17 and 18.

We have already noted that our conception of " things " and " soul entities " is imposed upon us by our sensory limitations.

In the phenomenal world all is change and composite. Each aggregation of elements requires no supporting " entity " to sustain it. That is to say its " soul " is the name we use to describe its functional aspects. Only in the Self is there permanence, and It confers reality on all aggregations.

CHAPTER XII

TIME, SPACE AND THE EXTERNAL UNIVERSE

" We must know that it is only the revelation of the Infinite which is endlessly new and eternally beautiful in us and gives the only meaning to our self."
RABINDRANATH TAGORE, Sadhana.

" In comparing the certainty of things spiritual and things temporal, let us not forget this—Mind is the first and the most direct thing in our experience; all else is remote inference. That environment of space and time and matter, of light and colour and concrete things, which seems so vividly real to us is probed deeply by every device of physical science and at the bottom we reach symbols . . ."
ARTHUR STANLEY EDDINGTON, Science and the Unseen World.
(Swarthmore Lecture, 1929.)

" The human mind is profoundly dissatisfied with any form of absolute dualism, with a religion or a metaphysic for which ultimate Reality is not one and undivided."
ALAN W. WATTS, Behold the Spirit, p. 132.

The External World.—To our ordinary practical consciousness it appears obvious that outside ourselves there exists a world of moving things occupying space; that in fact the universe is filled with independent phenomena which are not the product of our imagination but are brute facts which are discovered by us.

Yet, as we have noted in Chapter 2, we cannot determine what precisely does exist independently of our own consciousness.

Philosophers have argued about this question for centuries, and in the process have adopted two main attitudes represented by the Idealist and Realist schools of Thought. The Idealists assert with various shades of emphasis that we have no direct knowledge of an external world, but know only our own mental states. So we have at one extreme the subjective Idealists whose views lead logically to Solipsism, which is the doctrine that as we can only know our mental states we have no warrant for asserting that anything else exists.

Admittedly something else may exist but all that we know directly are the images and sensations within our own minds. The solipsist therefore can logically maintain an attitude of complete agnosticism as to the existence of an external world, for even if an external world exists, it can only reveal itself to us through the medium of our own mental states.

However, although Solipsism is difficult to refute on purely logical grounds, there are good reasons for believing that a world does exist which is independent of our own mental states, but the problem still remains of determining what is the nature of this independent outside world.

The philosopher Locke (1632-1704) addressed himself specifically to the task of discovering which qualities belonged to the external world and which were contributed by our own minds, and he concluded that only a few qualities, such as extension in space; number, motion and solidity belong to the external world. These he called primary qualities. All the other sensations, such as colour, taste, smell and so on he called secondary qualities, and regarded them as the result of our own mental processes. Behind and supporting the primary qualities Locke also postulated the notion of an external " substance ".

However, Berkeley (1685-1753) took the analysis further and had little difficulty in showing that Locke had no logical justification for postulating that the primary qualities and substance existed independently in the external world. Berkeley indeed expounded a more extreme philosophy, and pressed Locke's attitude to its logical conclusion, namely that nothing existed externally, independently of its being perceived.

This view is usually summarized by the statement that the existence or being of a thing consists in its being perceived.

But surely, it may be asked, it is not contended that the apparently external world is entirely a projected image of our personal consciousness; that there is in fact no world which we share in common with others, or indeed that there may not even be other persons? A lunatic could no doubt live entirely within a self-created world of his own imagining, but would not any reasonable philosopher suspect the processes of his own reasoning if they led to such a conclusion?

Actually, no philosopher would, as far as I am aware, deny that there is a world which exists independently of his own consciousness. Berkeley, as an exponent of objective Idealism, never denied the existence of a shared independent world. But he did deny, in common with most Idealists, that this world comprised physical objects standing out in space and having the characteristics they appear to have, independently of our perceiving them. Although he argued that they do not exist apart from their being perceived, he did not believe they existed only because *we* perceived them.

How then, on Berkeley's theory, does the external world have independence, if its existence is dependent on being perceived? Berkeley's answer is that the things we call external are also ideas in the mind of God. We share these ideas with God. Things do not go out of existence when we cease to perceive them. They still remain as perceptions in the mind of God.

In this way Berkeley escapes the dilemma of Solipsism, which otherwise would be the logical conclusion of his views.

If, however, we are not prepared to grant the existence of a universal mind or God, then subjective Idealism can find no escape from the circle of our own impressions.

Hume (1711-1776) did not hesitate to press Berkeley's views to their logical conclusion. He argued that if all our knowledge is derived from sense experience, then, unless we perceive God through the senses, His existence has no logical justification in terms of Berkeley's philosophy.

It would seem therefore that Hume's theory, rigidly pressed, logically brings us back once again to Solipsism. However, except as an experiment in academic reasoning, few people could accept the world as being a product of our personal minds. Nor is it necessary to accept Solipsism even though we contend that the universe is basically mental in character.

Everything can be a product of mind but not necessarily a product of our minds.

Idealists, inasmuch as they have maintained that everything is mental, have for the most part postulated the existence of a universal Mind, or Absolute, of which our personal minds are part. This type of Idealism is usually called objective Idealism because the world is objective to, and independent of, our individual minds, yet is mental in origin because it exists within an Infinite mind. Hegel of course is the most thorough-going philosopher of this type.

The Realists naturally approach the problem of the external world quite differently. Their basic assumption is that an independent world does exist, but when it comes to defining precisely what does exist, and what is the nature of existence apart from our minds, there is the greatest divergence of opinion, ranging from a naïve acceptance of a commonsense world more or less as it appears, until at the other extreme we have the philosophical physicists such as Jeans and Eddington who have whittled away the external world until we have nothing left except point-events and mathematical symbols. In other words, on either the Idealist or Realist views, the external world has ceased to exist as it appears to commonsense.

In popular parlance we might almost say it's anybody's guess what exists " out there ". We can indeed say with far more certainty what is not " out there ".

We have now arrived at a position where the external features of the world are so nebulous and incomprehensible in terms of sense-experience that our ordinary language has become positively misleading when used to describe the external world as discovered by the physicist.

While therefore it is agreed that there is an external world of some sort, it is one which escapes detection by the senses, but is inferred from certain effects.

The atom, for instance, is never observed directly; we know only certain radiation-phenomena which enable us to build up mental constructs which cause us to postulate what we call the Atom. And similarly with physical objects. These also are not known directly. Instead, we have in direct experience only patches of colours, scents, sounds, tactile sensations and so on, or as they are usually called, sense-data.

Now we do not feel easy in our minds about an external world of this type. It is a patchy sort of affair. Admittedly we may be forced to concede that we only apprehend directly a variety of sounds, shapes, tastes, smells and so on; also it seems we must accept the physicist's world of radiations and mathematical formulae. But the effect upon our minds of this kind of description of the external world is what might be called atomic. We have a picture of isolated elements without any unifying background, like a jigsaw puzzle of bits and pieces, but out in space without any frame to support them.

Our reason craves for some background support for these sense-data and we would be happier if we could accept our sensations as being derived from physical objects. We feel frustrated when psychological analysis shows that we have no direct knowledge in sensory experience of physical objects. Or we might turn in desperation to a belief in some sort of external substance or matter as a medium which supports our multitudinous sensations. But the external substance proves as illusive as do physical objects. It cannot be seen, touched, tasted or smelt. As far as sense-data are concerned, it just does not exist.

Yet our reason continues to seek for some background other than our personal experiences. We do not believe that the universe is a conglomeration of bits of sensation or radiation-potentials without some unity of background, a kind of patchwork quilt without a quilt.

If we are not content to believe that the external world has no existence apart from our perceiving it, what kind of background shall we adopt as a support for its independent origin?

It would seem we can choose either a Universal mind or an all-pervading Substance. Admittedly, sense-experience gives us no knowledge of either alternative. But sense-experience is not our only source of knowledge. The mind has other means of apprehension. This is revealed in certain what are called " a priori " judgments, or even in intuitive certainties which supplement ordinary reasoning.

From what has been said in previous chapters it is clear that we have already made our choice, and that we conceive the Universe as being embraced within the Whole of a universal Mind.

There are serious intellectual difficulties in conceiving that a universal matter or substance should be the sole origin and support of the Universe.

Assuming we are committed to postulate some universal support for the world, why choose something so alien and unknowable as matter? At least we do know our own minds, and these minds surely could only arise in a universe which is mental in nature!

This view implies that Reality is a unity. Consciousness embraces all things. The Universe is not the product of mind and matter, but of mind only. I do not minimize the intellectual difficulties in maintaining monism in the face of our constant experience of differentiation and the opposition of elements which seem other than mental.

Dualism or Monism.—If the Universe were accepted as arising from two or more sources we would have less difficulty in understanding the diversity of experience.

The world of appearance challenges monism. There are recalcitrant facts all round us which stubbornly resist inclusion in a purely mental Universe. Mind is always opposed by something other than itself. In the hey-day of 19th century materialism it was hardly doubted that mind and matter were the warp and weft out of which the fabric of existence was woven. But even the materialists were not content with dualism, for their constant effort has been to reduce mind to a manifestation of the movements of matter. In other words they strove for monism, but of course it was materialistic monism for which they yearned.

And the result of this effort to dethrone mind and make it a by-product of matter has produced one of the most amusing paradoxes in our intellectual history.

The scientist of necessity took the external world for granted, and it presented a picture of bewildering diversity. The environment appeared to be composed of an infinite number of substances, species and creatures. Minerals, plants and living things of every conceivable type seemed phenomena having separate existence, and often without sufficient common characteristics to enable them to be classified. The scientists with insatiable curiosity prodded and pried into every nook and cranny of this apparently outside world which seemed so full of strange new things to be discovered.

But gradually a change came over the scene. The original diversity was too uncongenial for the enquiring mind. Phenomena needed to be grouped and labelled. Law was found to exist where the first impressions were of chaos. Chemical substances eventually became grouped into 92 elements.

Slowly a new world-picture began to emerge. It was found possible to account for all the phenomenal diversity as being due to combinations of fewer and fewer things, until to-day every living thing or substance is conceived as having as its basis one kind of thing—which is not a thing—namely the atom.

Yet the atom itself has never been observed by any of our senses, and its reality can only be grasped in terms of abstruse mathematical formulae. In other words, the so-called physical world with all its diverse phenomena, has been reduced to something singularly like a mental concept. This is indeed a paradoxical situation! The scientist sets out to investigate a world of independent physical things, and ends by passing beyond sense-experience into a realm of intellectual abstractions!

The urge to seek for unity in the midst of diversity is very deep-seated. But although the physicist seems to have gone almost to the limit as far as his methods allow, there still remains that hard core of otherness.

The physicist, we must assume, is in contact with an environmental fact which, no matter how hard it is to describe in commonsense terms, does represent something discovered and not created by the physicist's mind.

In the light of what we have written elsewhere there is no need to suppose that the physicist is not observing phenomena which have reality independently of his consciousness, but this does not mean he is in contact with a non-mental reality.

The problem however which any monistic conception has to face, is how to account for diversity in that which is fundamentally a unity.

The monistic hypothesis does not permit us to invoke any outside principle to account for diversity. The unity is infinite, and therefore all-inclusive. Consequently, even diversity must be conceived as existing within the unity.

But is this not a contradiction of monism? To say that the ground-fabric of the universe is one and undivided, and yet has within it the seeds of division, would seem to imply that it is not a monism after all, but a pluralism of many diverse possibilities. The problem is brought into sharper focus if we translate it into theological terms.

God and Evil.—Let us assume that there is one infinite God —this belief is of course that of theological monism. God, therefore, must be all-pervading, and the Origin and Sustainer of everything that exists. This raises acutely the problem of evil, suffering, pain and the confusion of an ignorant humanity.

We cannot hold another God or devil responsible for these things. They must therefore somehow be embraced within the orbit of God's infinite being.

As at the moment we are not concerned with moral issues, we could concede that the principle of evil exists in the origin of things, but in doing so we postulate dual principles of good and evil, whereas monism insists on non-duality.

The religious consciousness revolts from any conception that a good God can be responsible for evil, and finds it almost equally repellent to postulate two Gods, one of whom is responsible for evil. The problem of evil is of course only one aspect of the problem of multiplicity within that which is conceived to be unity.

The classical attempts at a solution of this dilemma are well known. In the Christian theology the devil no longer plays an important rôle, so the responsibility for evil is laid upon man himself. It is contended that God has allowed man to have free-will, and this implies that he must have liberty to make mistakes, and even deliberately to choose evil as part of his moral growth.

The obvious objection to this view is that God must have foreseen the use man would make of his free-will, and to this extent God must be held responsible for the evil consequences which result from man's free-will. One might almost say, part of man's nature was created evil, which accounts for evil being so often chosen.

Also, mankind has done a lot of wrong things through sheer ignorance. Only in recent times have we learnt the sanitary conditions which must be observed to preserve health. Yet millions have lived in ignorance only to suffer pain and disease. Even moral delinquency is often due to ignorance. The laws of righteous living have not been revealed to us with any compelling force; rather have we acquired our knowledge in slow, stumbling steps, after much confusion and frustration. Free-will we may have, but ignorance clouds its use, and as God is All, is He not the cause of ignorance?

Multiplicity as Illusion.—The other main effort to reconcile monism with multiplicity and all that multiplicity implies in the way of evil and suffering is to conceive multiplicity or the world-process as an illusion.

This view largely prevails in the religions of India.

The world of phenomenal events is regarded as having no real being in the mind of God. The world of appearance is Maya or Illusion, and is the product of Avidya, which may be translated as a deeply-rooted ignorance of the nature of Reality.

A western version of this view is found in Christian Science, which, starting from the premise that God is good, infinite and perfect, proceeds with impeccable logic to draw the conclusion that disease and evil are illusory. Nevertheless, the facts of disease as we experience them have to be traced to some origin. This is done in Christian Science by attributing all imperfections to what is called " Mortal Mind ", which is rather a nebulous and naïve concept, yet has some similarity to the Eastern doctrine of Maya. It could almost be described as the devil in a new guise.

Clearly, none of the doctrines of Maya, Avidya nor Mortal Mind removes evil outside the infinite unity which we postulate as God. Crudely stated, evil must be either within or without God. But as God is infinite it must be within God. This is so even if we regard evil as being an illusion, or due to error.

If we are prone to error it must be because our minds are constituted to think erroneously, and as our minds derive from God, then the capacity for error and illusion are latent within the all-pervading unity.

The Problem of Change.—There is one other variant of the monistic conception which is widely held and should be considered, as it brings into prominence the problem of change. While of necessity the philosophy of monism cannot admit the existence of any outside principle, yet clearly there could not be any manifestation or change within the primal unity unless something happened within the unity to provide the basis for expression.

The pictures projected by a cinematograph would never be revealed unless a reflecting screen were provided.

Similarly, an undifferentiated unity must be conceived to have within itself a principle of resistance, something in fact which, while being part of itself, yet serves as a medium of expression.

Sometimes the analogy of an artist is used. An artist needs some material such as canvas or stone on which to work, otherwise his creativeness is denied expression. All this no doubt is true, but the opponents of monism are not slow to point out that this principle of opposition, even though it is within the unity, involves a conception of something other than unity. Indeed it adds another difficulty in that a principle of change is introduced into a unity which on the hypothesis of monism cannot change.

Reverting again to theological terms we ask, How can God change? God is complete, and a plenum of all that is. The classical statement of this view is represented by Socrates' argument in Plato's *Republic* which, summarized, is as follows: The Divine nature must be perfect in every way, and any change could not arise from an outside cause. Any change therefore must come from within. But if He changes at all, would it be for better or for worse? It could only be for worse because the Divine nature is perfect in goodness and beauty. Consequently it is impossible to conceive that God would deliberately make Himself worse. So Socrates concludes that God cannot desire to change Himself.

Sufficient has no doubt been said to make apparent the difficulties which all monistic philosophies encounter when confronted with the facts of the phenomenal world. Yet the passion of the mind for a monistic solution persists, as there is a strong intuition that in some form monism is true. I will later state my reasons for choosing monism in spite of the intellectual difficulties.

Difficulties of Pluralism.—But we must at least note the even more formidable difficulties which pluralism involves. In the first place pluralism is unsatisfactory because each element in a pluralistic universe is incomplete in itself and requires explanation in terms of something other than itself.

If, for instance, we postulate two principles as the origin of things, say Mind and Matter, we cannot accept these as final and self-evident realities. We find ourselves asking what is the origin of Mind or of Matter.

Mind and Matter are obviously in some sort of relationship with one another, but how can this be conceived?

We have bifurcated the universe into two incompatible principles, but in doing so have made any relationship between them impossible. For according to the hypothesis none of the characteristics of mind can belong to matter. Mind and matter confront one another as mutually exclusive existents. Where one exists, the other is absent. They cannot marry or enter into any productive union.

In fact Descartes (1596-1650) divorced mind from matter so decisively that interaction was logically impossible, and a third principle, God, had to be invoked to account for what seemed to be a relationship.

This indeed is typical of what dualistic or pluralistic theories force us to do. We are intellectually uneasy until we have found some conception to bring diverse elements into a unity.

We may people our firmament with gods, goddesses, powers, principalities, energies, physical objects or sense-data, but we are peopling a firmament!

In other words, all the diverse elements of our pluralistic universe are conceived as belonging to a common background. They are in fact banded by a relationship, and even this relationship is a sort of unifying background.

It has been argued that if we must start from an unknown cause of the universe, we might as well start with two causes as with one.

Those who feel no intellectual need to press beyond dualism will naturally rest here, and logically I see no reason why they should not start from a pluralistic or dualistic basis.

For my part I have a sense of mental unease with dualism, which nags my mind to find a solution in terms of monism in some form.

Temperament and Philosophy.—Temperament plays a greater part in our choice of a philosophy than perhaps we are prepared to admit. In making this avowal the reader is at least put on his guard to make due allowance for my bias.

I should also add that on these ultimate questions reason cannot carry us to complete finality. As we have already observed, all chains of reasoning start from self-evident propositions, and the degree of self-evidence for various propositions differs considerably with different people. The preliminary stage in all discussions is to define one's terms, and it is quickly discovered that what is crystal-clear and self-evident to one can only be acquiesced in by another after long argument. Far more important than our reasoning is our experience of life. Experience is the raw material on which reasoning must work.

Those who experience the world in its surface aspects, who in other words have no doubt that the world of appearance is real, will reason as logically as the profoundest philosopher, but starting from different sets of " self-evident " propositions, the conclusions of the philosopher and ordinary man will be poles apart.

Similarly a philosopher, though his reasoning may be faultless, must of necessity start from a world of his own observations and experience, but if he were favoured with even a momentary glimpse of the deeper level of experience we call mystical, then he would find his experience of the world so different from what he previously thought that he would be compelled to start his reasoning afresh on the basis of his new perceptions and new experience.

I think it is true to say that without exception those who have had mystical experiences have declared the universe to be a unity, and have conceived the realization of this unity to be the supreme goal of human achievement. We will endeavour to assess the value of these experiences later. Our immediate concern here is to consider the difficulty of reconciling unity with diversity.

Our Minds as a Model for Unity and Diversity.—Perhaps the safest procedure is to return to that which is known to us most intimately, namely ourselves. Here, surely, we should find an example of unity and diversity. Indeed this is precisely what we do find.

Our minds are one, yet our thoughts are many. Within our consciousness arise complex patterns of thinking, rich in drama, variety and intensity. We build in our imaginations characters which in the case of some authors even seem to exercise an embarrassing independent influence. Our inner life is a scene of vivid and constant imaginative activity. It is one of plans, plots and mental scenery of every type.

Sometimes in dreams this activity is so powerful as to create scenes as real and apparently " external " as any in the waking state, and only the fact of waking up dispels the illusion.

Although our mind gives birth to all these creatures and situations, yet it remains a unity. Our consciousness is not exhausted, or its unity and integrity impaired, by its unceasing activity and creativeness. It has parts, yet it is not divided. Thoughts which are limited arise within the mind, but the mind remains out of time and space.

Once more we return to the concept of wholes and parts, and here in our own minds we have the perfect model of the undivided and indivisible unity of consciousness yet manifesting in a stream of diversity.

If now we can conceive our minds as embraced within the universal mind, we have a conception that is thinkable in terms of the familiar workings of our own minds.

The unity we are now postulating enables us to understand at least one aspect of phenomenal existence; what we call diversity; but we still are faced with the difficulty of the particular type of diversity we experience.

The universal mind may be conceived to hold within itself all possible and actual worlds. We cannot on this hypothesis exclude what we call evil from the source of things.

Change and Changelessness both True.—But let us consider again what is even more fundamental than evil, namely the problem of change in that which is a plenum, and therefore complete.

Even if we accept Kant's view that Time and Space do not belong to the real world but are categories of our own mind, we still have the problem of the appearance of change.

There are two world-pictures possible, one which William James called the " block universe ", where everything is static, and change is an appearance imposed by the way our minds work.

The other conception is that change is fundamental, or, as in Bergson's philosophy, the only Reality.

I suggest that these views are not irreconcilable. Reality paradoxically must somehow embrace both change and changelessness. If we adhere to our original model and conceive everything as mental, then change would be an act of willing within the universal mind.

Admittedly the question arises, why should that which is universal and complete will or act? We can only return to our own consciousness for a guide, and it is clear that it is a condition for our mental health that our minds should express themselves; that in fact there should be creative activity.

The universal as a whole cannot change, yet it includes change as an ocean includes the waves. When therefore Socrates argues that God cannot desire to change Himself because it would be a change for the worse, we might reply that the question of better or worse does not arise. That in fact God embraces both change and changelessness, and neither of these terms has any meaning without the other. Indeed, changelessness implies change, and God's perfection is revealed in the complete synthesis of all dualities, and not by arbitrarily postulating one term of a pair of opposites as the essential nature of God.

The truth must necessarily be that the universal mind transcends all our categories, but inasmuch as we are aspects of this universal mind we have a guide if we study the workings of our own minds, for on our hypothesis they are mirrors of the greater whole we call God.

When dealing with these ultimate questions we become acutely aware of our feebleness in arriving at satisfying intellectual concepts.

Yet failing more direct intuitive insight, we dare not forsake the path of steady reasoning. It would seem however that simile and analogy may best serve our mental needs.

Assuming therefore that the universe is a whole and that this whole is conceived as mental, then certain questions arise.

Why is There a Phenomenal Universe?—Firstly, how and why has the phenomenal universe arisen within the Supreme Brahman—I choose the Hindu term because it has not the limited personal connotations associated with the word God.

The answers have taken two main forms. Firstly, there are those which insist that Brahman has no knowledge of the created universe. Phenomenal existence is the result of Maya, and is an illusion, not in the sense that it does not exist, but that it is a false view of Reality, due to ignorance or Avidya in the creatures.

The second type of answer is to conceive the universe as an emanation from the Supreme, and therefore the result of a creative act. The motive for this act of creation is variously assessed as being an expression of Divine Love, or as being due to an inherent need for self-expression.

These views, if held with conviction, lead to very different attitudes in practical living. The first causes a world-denying attitude, whereas the second accepts the world as real, although to be transcended.

In the East the illusory aspect of phenomenal existence has been stressed, with a consequent emphasis on world-denying practices, yet from what we have said elsewhere it is clear we can conceive phenomena as the surface aspect of some deeper reality. In this sense the world of appearances need not be denied, but must be re-interpreted in our search for truth.

The real problem, however, is to conceive the need for change in that which is whole and perfect, or, if one denies that Brahman can change, to account for the illusion of change.

We must assume that change within the Supreme is not that of movement in time or space. What happens in the Absolute must be conceived in terms of consciousness. We might imagine the Supreme Self as inventing the not-self in order that Self-knowledge may be complete. Self-limitation thus actualizes some of the infinite possibilities of the Divine.

The Absolute is all that is. Therefore there can be no real change in the sense of becoming other than it is. But as the Supreme is conceived as being of the nature of Mind, the changes are in consciousness and do not involve the introduction of alien elements to break the unity.

Admittedly this is not a monism without some qualifications. It is, in fact, a pluralistic whole in the sense that our minds are pluralistic wholes, or, to change the analogy, the differentiations are those which would occur within a single substance, like the currents and stresses of a universal ocean, although similes which picture Reality in the guise of structureless, homogeneous substance have only superficial relevance.

Brahman is beyond all plurality, yet includes all. It is the Infinite Plenum containing all possible universes, and also the capacity for actualizing universes. We can make no adequate concept as to the nature of the Supreme. It must include a personal aspect, because it embraces ourselves as persons, yet the Absolute transcends personality, and it would be less misleading to describe the Supreme as impersonal and so avoid the tragic misunderstandings which arise from anthropomorphic ideas.

Whatever view we adopt regarding the nature of the Supreme, we are inevitably faced with paradoxes when we consider the world of appearances.

If, for instance, we postulate change as real, we have to explain the appearance of unchanging things in the phenomenal realm. If on the other hand we conceive the Absolute as a changeless Whole, then change, and the apparent creation of novelty become our problem.

The fact is that whatever view of Reality we adopt, the world of appearance has to be discarded. There is something queer about it, and it cannot be accepted at its face value. Even Bergson's conception of change as the only reality turns out to be a peculiar form of change, for the universe is conceived as a continuous stream of perpetual change. There is nothing which changes, but only change itself. When change is thus conceived as universal, one could almost say that change has become changeless. Be this as it may, the contrast between Reality and appearance occurs in as acute a form as it does in the static, changeless conceptions of Reality.

Our problems inevitably arise through the inadequacy of our language forms. If, therefore, we feel that on the whole some form of monism is true, then we must not suffer an undue sense of intellectual frustration if we have to admit that the Supreme is beyond any of our categories of thought. The Vedanta philosophy—which is more a revelation than a philosophy in the western sense of the word—postulates the Supreme as beyond all dualities. This it seems to me is necessarily true, but it still leaves us without adequate concepts to account for the world of appearance as we experience it.

The fact is, the Eastern mystics have experienced a level of Reality which has defeated all their powers of verbal expression.

We will later consider some of these mystic experiences, but for the moment we will still try to form some useful concepts.

Attempts to Explain Evil.—Perhaps the problem of unity and diversity presents itself in its most acute form in connection with the existence of evil.

I will not attempt to catalogue the various types of evil, nor perhaps is it even necessary to define evil. Some may argue that physical pain is not, strictly speaking, evil compared with, say, moral sin. But most of us would I think consider physical suffering evil, and in its extreme form, say as the result of torture or malignant disease, we might sacrifice our eternal life if thereby the pain could be mitigated.

Not only do we find pain and suffering in the human kingdom, but the animals struggle under conditions which cause pain as the price of their survival.

The problem of evil assumes its most perplexing form when it is considered against the background of the conventional God who is conceived as omnipotent, omniscient and good. The ancient dilemma then takes the form that God cannot be both good and omnipotent. A good and omnipotent God would not create evil. He could of course be good, but not omnipotent; or he could be omnipotent, but not good.

I mention this particular form of the problem because it has a wide currency, but it seems to me the problem in this form arises from undefined premises. Omnipotence obviously does not mean the power to do anything. If, for instance, one desires to play cricket, one cannot at the same time abolish the rules of cricket.

Similarly, assuming that an omnipotent God did create the universe, He is limited by the laws of such a universe, even though they are His laws.

The problem of course still remains as to why God created a universe at all, when so much suffering is involved for the creatures. Library shelves bulge with books containing the subtle reasonings of men who have been tormented by this problem.

Two main points of view emerge which briefly are, firstly that Evil is unreal, and secondly that Evil and Good are an inevitable duality.

Under each of these headings many variations of expression occur. For instance, although evil is declared to be unreal, or even an illusion, it is by few writers denied that it is an experienced fact. It is however argued that Evil is a negative condition, and is actually only the absence of Good. Or another variant of this view is to consider Evil as the result of man's free will, which permits him to disobey God's will. In other words, the responsibility for evil is laid upon man.

We have already noted the objection to this view, and also have pointed out that even if Evil is unreal or an illusion, this only transfers the problem to the need for accounting for the illusion.

The second type of explanation, namely that Good and Evil are an inevitable duality, provides a better basis for a satisfactory explanation, although it must be admitted that there seems no logical reason why Good should not exist apart from Evil. Nevertheless, Good and Evil are complementary experienced facts, and we are so constituted as to make it inconceivable that one could be known without the other.

Good and Evil an Aspect of Multiplicity.—Actually the problem of Evil is only one aspect of a wider problem, namely the problem of multiplicity within unity, with which we originally started our discussion.

It should be noted that the facts of Good and Evil are part of that whole category of facts which technically are called contingent facts, that is to say, facts which are purely empirical, or facts which just happen to have been discovered to be as they are, and might very well have been other than they are. For instance, there is no necessary reason why coal should not be pink, and why water should freeze at a particular temperature. We just find out these things by experience.

The other type of facts are, of course, those which are usually represented by mathematical truths, and are perceived by us to be necessarily true without the need for constant repetition as, for instance, that $7+5$ will always equal 12, or that the three angles of a triangle will at all times equal $180°$.

If the universe contained only necessary facts we would be able to deduce the whole of our empirical experience by pure reason, and indeed it has been the persistent effort of many philosophers to do this, Hegel's philosophy being perhaps the most sustained example in the West of abstract reasoning directed towards explaining the universe from first principles, and not based on empirical observations.

But the modern trend is away from this type of philosophy, for the facts of our experience obtrude themselves upon us in a way which pure reasoning would not lead us to expect.

There are, for instance, the facts of Science, which are discovered only by observation and constant experiment. Yet, if monism is true, nothing can exist outside the Supreme —not even a grub on a leaf.

Clearly, our ability or inability to accept this fact depends on the mental imagery we use to depict the Supreme. As we view it, the Absolute is a conscious Whole, and while we have no adequate symbolism to describe the origin of multiplicity within the Absolute, we can perceive that the Universal Self— to use another term for the Absolute—must differentiate within Its selfhood the appearance of not-self as a condition for the realization of Its selfhood.

This so-called differentiation is not to be imagined as a splitting-up process. Rather should it be conceived as a concentration of attention, whereby some of the infinite possibilities are consciously realized. That which was latent becomes actualized, but the actualization is not creation in the sense of bringing something into existence. Rather is it a revelation of part of the Eternal Now, even as the beam of a search-light brings into vivid prominence the features of a dark landscape. Or a more appropriate analogy would be to suppose the universe as emerging from a Divine subconsciousness into a waking focus of awareness. The act of awareness could be conceived as a movement in consciousness, and therefore the origin of what we call time. The search-light of awareness is, as it were, directed sequentially on portions of the universal plenum. There would also be an apparent movement if the phenomenal universe arose out of a Divine subconsciousness. We must be on our guard to avoid pressing analogies unduly.

There is a tendency in our ordinary thinking to conceive time and space as having some independent status. So we speak of "movement in time" and "position in space". Under the influence of these verbal forms we then find ourselves picturing the Supreme as moving in Time, whereas it would be nearer the truth to say that Time and Space are reflections of psychological states. They have no meaning or independence except as expressions of consciousness. For us Time and Space are the mental forms which condition our perceptions, and what is true for us reflects something analogous in the Supreme consciousness. Time and Space do not precede manifestation. They arise with it even as the troughs and crests of a heaving sea, or as pauses and tempo are involved with a melody. That is why the universe cannot have a beginning in Time.

If the Supreme is a unity, then it follows that it includes all that exists, and this embraces all the empirical facts which we appear to discover. When this is expressed in abstract terms we may not feel inclined to disagree, but when we are under the influence of contingent facts and events we find it hard to understand what is meant.

Is it to be supposed that the Supreme embraces fountain pens, the latest model car, or the jet-bomber? Or, as events also must on our hypothesis exist in the Supreme, are we committed to believe that all actions exist in the Absolute— say a cold in the head; war; a picnic by the river; a plane-crash or even our next Sunday's dinner? These are the facts of our daily experience, and if the Absolute is the all-embracing Whole, then these empirical facts and events must be within the cognizance of the conscious Absolute.

Indeed, in theological terms, God's omniscience implies that He knows every detail of our daily lives. Some will find this a difficult idea to accept, for the immensity of the universe as discovered by science has also affected our ideas of God, and it seems trivial beyond belief to postulate that God could be aware of the small events in our little lives. Yet however much the Supreme consciousness transcends our own it cannot be entirely misleading to use our own conscious processes as an analogy of what on a wider scale occurs within the Absolute, for on our hypothesis we are aspects of the Supreme Self.

Dreams.—We have already mentioned dreams as providing an example of unity and diversity.

Some dreams indeed are so vivid to the dreamer as to make them indistinguishable from experiences in the waking life. I have been in dream situations so real and apparently objective that they are included in my memory with the equivalent clarity of many of my normal waking experiences.

Now it is usually assumed that dreams are a purely subjective phenomenon. I do not entirely subscribe to this view because I believe that some dreams indicate that the sleeper is in contact with a common environment or as it is usually called, an objective world. Nevertheless, many dreams are the product of our imaginative processes, and we are accustomed to regard these as subjective.

As we are now using the dream state as an analogy to aid us in understanding the mystery of unity and diversity, we will confine ourselves to those dreams which are clearly imaginative adventures of our minds in the sleep state.

Let us, to make the analogy more effective, suppose that a Rip Van Winkle, instead of sinking into unconsciousness, dreamt continuously. He would lead a life in the dream-state as real to him as is the waking life of the normal man. That is to say, he would appear to live in an external world. He would walk along city streets, traverse a countryside, perceive innumerable objects, travel in all forms of conveyances, meet a great variety of people. Perhaps at times he would find himself sad, and would suffer to the point of tears. At other times his mood would be happy, buoyant and successful in tasks which to him seemed important.

Yet all this complicated stream of experience is purely a product of his mind's imaginative faculty. While he is dreaming he has no means of testing the validity of his experiences.

If, for instance, he happened to meet a philosopher who somehow intruded from the waking state and began to argue that the whole of the dreamer's environment was imaginary, our dreamer with the evidence of his senses so clearly before him would naturally conclude that the philosopher was rather a silly fellow.

There is no need for us to press this point further because we all have our own dream experiences and we know how compellingly real they are while we are dreaming.

A Dreaming Dramatist.—We will now apply the analogy in a somewhat different way. Instead of an ordinary dreamer let us conceive a dreaming dramatist. Imagine the dramatist's mind to be filled with every conceivable plot and dramatic situation. And suppose he has the constructive power to project these dramas into what we call actuality.

Here we have a mind holding within it in rich variety dramas, pageants, tragedies, and comedies. He conceives them as a whole. They are simultaneously present in his mind, but he can only dream them into seeming actuality one at a time.

Can we, without creating too misleading a picture, find in this an analogy of the working of the Absolute or Supreme Self? Up to a point the analogy is helpful. It provides a model of unity and diversity. Our minds remain one and undivided, and yet are fields for complex worlds of ideas, feeling and instinctual urges.

Also it draws our attention to the mind's power to project its contents, so that they appear externalized, a faculty which is even more clearly demonstrated when, under the influence of suggestion, a hypnotic subject is made to see people as present when they are not.

But the analogy of the dream-state, unless it is qualified in certain important respects, leaves us with a very inadequate conception of our existence.

To suppose that we and all creatures are only a dream in the mind of God would strip our lives of all meaning, and leave unexplained our struggles, freedom and individuality. Yet we need not entirely dispense with the dream-analogy. If the universe is a living whole we participate in the consciousness of the Supreme Self, which is the ground-support of our being, and this is similar to saying we are thought-creations within the Absolute.

Unity and Independence.—Does this reduce us to the status of automata within a dream? If we persist with the dream-analogy we shall need to endow the creatures with independence and some freedom.

Some years ago I read a story of which I have forgotten the title and the author's name. In it was a maker of puppets, who constructed his images with fanatical and devoted care. Gradually something of his own life began to manifest in the puppets. They acquired a weird independence and life of their own, taking on in fact the character-rôles for which they were modelled.

Have we in this fantastic story a clue to enable us to make our dream-analogy more appropriate? The puppets lived in the mind of their creator, yet his life had passed into them, and to this extent they enjoyed independence within the limits of their characters.

Actually, if monism is true, we are not separate and independent entities, but are aspects of the Absolute. Yet even so the freedom of the whole permeates the aspects.

Within our own consciousness therefore lies the key to the mystery. Our analogy does at least help us to understand that God is both transcendent and immanent, even as our minds are whole and apart from our mental creations. We may go further and say that once we have produced certain situations, these dramas must continue to work themselves out according to their pattern.

It is indeed part of our daily experience that certain situations get, as it were, out of hand. Authors frequently remark that books sometimes write themselves; the plot and characterization become alive and proceed irresistibly to an inevitable conclusion.

We can imagine the Supreme Mind actualizing in thought the great drama we call the Universe. That which exists out of time as an eternal Now becomes manifest in the sequence we call Time. The Supreme Mind is an infinite plenitude, timeless and changeless.

Time and change appear, we must suppose, as the result of what may figuratively be described as an act of attention within the Supreme, whereby some of the infinite possibilities come as it were into a special focus of awareness, even as a dramatist expresses one plot out of many possible ones.

We should here note that in the actualizing of a drama certain consequences inevitably follow. There is brought into operation a play of contrasts. There is friction, struggle and synthesis. In other words, good and evil manifest as an inevitable result of the decision to actualize the drama. So it comes about that the cosmic drama requires duality in all its forms as a condition for its appearance. And what is more, all creatures participate in the reality of the Supreme. Their individualities are real because the Absolute is incarnate in them.

Here it is easy to get lost in a maze of paradoxes. But the truth of monism is uncompromising. We are not parts of the Absolute, but the Absolute itself. Yet the Supreme Self must project an appearance of real otherness, because otherness itself is paradoxically part of the whole we call the Absolute. The unmanifested and the manifested are embraced within the unity of undivided infinite consciousness.

Because we are infinite and finite we manifest in endless change. Only in this way can the finite reflect its infinity. Time is our awareness of change, and change appears because consciousness, functioning under limitation, can only comprehend infinity in terms of succession.

Finiteness, we must keep clearly in mind, is self-imposed by the Absolute. It is a mode of conscious functioning, and is not due to the influence of some external substance or matter.

Further Examination of the Problem of Good and Evil.—How then are we to understand the experienced facts which compose our practical life—the appearance of evil; the struggle, turmoil and ceaseless change? What also is the meaning of the process of becoming we call evolution, and the whole order of discoveries which comprise scientific knowledge?

If the total pattern of multiplicity is a drama within the Absolute, then can we exclude the ugly facts of evil and suffering as being within the Absolute? Logically, I do not think we can, but in case this idea rather shocks us, we must examine it further.

The truth is that although evil is an experienced fact, it is impossible to label any particular thing or situation as absolutely evil. Situations and experiences which are evil to one set of creatures are good to others. Even disease, which, to the organism attacked, is evil, would not be so to the multiplying germs. The mosquito is evil to us, but is a beneficent host to myriads of smaller organisms.

Throughout nature we find host and parasite, and what is good for the parasite is often bad for the host. Nor can we say in an absolute sense that disease and pain are necessarily evil for man. Sometimes one man's disease is another man's gain, as for instance when it incapacitates a rival, for both the man and his rival are within the Absolute. Also, even for the sufferer, illness, by enforcing idleness, can give opportunities for reflection, and the period of convalescence and recovery often results in a keener appreciation of health and awakens sympathy for others. Pain, of course, is protective of the organism, and therefore assists in its survival.

It may be argued that these physical conditions are not good examples of what we mean by evil, but that evil, strictly speaking, is moral turpitude, or what the Christian calls sin. Even if we admit this we still cannot specify with definiteness moral codes or actions which are evil in an Absolute or universal sense.

Sexual behaviour which is condemned as sinful in one time or place is a normal code accepted as good in others. Even to kill cannot be universally an evil, for those who kill do so in pursuit of what they call good. Cruelty also, which most of us view with abhorrence and feel to be the quintessence of evil, is for the sadist a pleasure which is fascinating and irresistible.

It therefore appears that evil and good are relative terms. Yet it must be noted that the terms are not on an equality, for evil is never committed for its own sake. The evil-doer commits his offence in pursuit of something he thinks good. That is to say, evil is negative and good is positive, or, as it is sometimes put, evil is the absence of good, as a shadow is the absence of light.

There are many who feel that arguments along these lines get rid of the problem of evil and enable us to retain the conception of a good God unconscious of evil, but from what has already been said it will be apparent that the solution lies deeper than this. We must, in fact, realize that the experiences we call good and evil are the inevitable accompaniment of a manifested universe.

If it be argued that good could exist without evil, we might concede this as a logical possibility, but in this event we would be unable to know good. It is only because of those experiences we call evil that we become aware of good. If therefore we postulate good as absolute, we are virtually making it unmanifested. That is to say, it cannot be known in any sense with which we are familiar.

It would be better not to use the word " good " in this absolute sense, for it is a word only known to us as defining experiences contrary to evil or pleasing to ourselves. Plato, as is well known, placed goodness in a special position in relation to all the other Forms. Indeed, the Form of the Good is conceived as the Reality behind all phenomena. It is beyond truth and knowledge, and all the Forms derive from the supreme Good, which is likened to the sun, which makes all things visible and brings them into existence. It is therefore not surprising that, having attributed to Goodness almost the status of the Absolute, Plato refrains from saying anything more, for at this stage knowledge gives way to mysticism.

Here we are faced once again with monism in the guise of universal Goodness, and all the attendant problems of accounting for the experienced facts of evil.

Is God Good?—If we view good and evil as relative facts of our phenomenal existence, and as inevitable consequences of manifestation, we are relieved of the necessity of attributing to the Absolute either good or evil in the form in which we experience them.

Does this mean that we have to discard conventional ideas of God as Good? The answer depends on the meaning we attach to the word " Good ".

The facts of our experience are such that good and evil are linked as inseparable twins. But, like all twins, they have a common mother, which is the universal Matrix, or Absolute.

The only quality we might with the minimum of misrepresentation attribute to the Absolute would be " Wholeness ". The Wholeness of the Absolute reflects itself as the essential element in what we call Goodness.

Although we may not be sure that some particular act or situation is good under every circumstance of time or place, we unhesitatingly recognize that a good act should result in harmony, synthesis or co-operative behaviour.

Where there is love, unity, and the blending of diverse elements in organic harmony, we feel that goodness is manifesting.

This is the law of attraction which expresses itself in the formation of those marvels of sensitive association we call Wholes.

The coherence, mutual affinity and functional endurance of the forms of life point to an inherent principle of Wholeness. Even when energies of repulsion cause forms to disintegrate, this is a phase in the growth towards new forms of integration. Chaos is only a prelude to Cosmos.

Repulsion, disintegration and death seem to us evil, and in a relative sense they are, but from the universal standpoint they break up rigidity, and therefore minister to life's creative expression.

Attraction and repulsion, centripetal and centrifugal energies, together with all similar dualities, are not really in opposition, but can be considered as the complementary light and shade of the picture of life.

They symbolize the conjunction of infinity and finiteness, or that of timelessness and time. On the surface there is the rhythm of cyclic movement; the appearance and disappearance of forms. A heaving tide of life hurls its spray and leaves its pattern on the sand, and then sucks it back into its unity.

Evolution and dissolution, orderliness and anarchy, reveal in time the mystery of Wholeness and multiplicity.

We place our label " good " on the formative creative whole-making tendencies of life, and evil on the destructive, disintegrating elements. But the Hindus worship Kali, a goddess of destruction, because their religious instinct reveals the truth that integration without disintegration would mean frozen forms.

What, therefore, we call " evil ", is essential to good. The goodness of God is revealed in its need continually to oppose evil. This is the ethical expression of the universal law of attraction and repulsion, which are the positive and negative magnetic poles of existence, so that when in theological terms we ask Is God good, the answer is that God is more than good. He is the infinite Whole. That is why the personal pronoun, " He ", is so inappropriate.

To know God is to realize Wholeness in our personal lives. It is something immensely more profound than knowing goodness. The Supreme is neither good nor evil in our sense of the words.

Those who have been tormented by the existence of evil in a universe presumably created by a good God have been wrestling with a wrongly-stated problem, which arises because we have attached our labels, with their relative qualities of good and evil, to the Supreme, which is beyond all duality.

In seeking good we are striving for completeness: indeed, nothing less than the infinite Wholeness. Goodness is only its reflection, which manifests together with its partner evil—a partner eternally to be opposed as the villain in the divine drama of manifestation.

Good and evil disappear in the Wholeness of Divinity. Even our empirical experience of wholes exhibits this aspect of synthesizing diverse elements so that in combination they reveal new qualities, as hydrogen and oxygen in certain proportions become water.

Any terminology which attributes to the Absolute specific qualities to the exclusion of others, denies the Absoluteness of the Absolute. It is beyond duality, yet includes duality—a statement which seems nonsensical to our reason, yet, as we shall see when we come to consider mysticism, may be directly apprehended, even if not understood.

The fact that certain truths are arrived at by insight rather than by reasoning does not disparage reason. Indeed, reasoning is often an essential preliminary to prepare the mind for illumination. Nevertheless, the verbal symbols which are used in reasoning must represent directly-perceived facts which are accepted as self-evident.

Our Perceptual Experiences.—This brings us back to the validity of our perceptions, and the constantly recurring problems of the difference between appearance and Reality.

If we say that what appears to us is not real, it is because certain aspects of our experience seem to conflict with others. For instance, if we described the world as a dream, we could only do so because we had become awakened to another world which seemed to us more real. Similarly, the world of commonsense is discarded because we have obtained an apprehension of a world of more significant ideas, which reveals the world of commonsense to be riddled with paradoxes.

Resuming our dream analogy, we may consider our life experiences as being a series of awakenings to ever higher levels of reality. Each awakening includes the previous dream-state and explains it.

We cannot solve the problems of the dream-state while we accept the facts of our dreaming consciousness as real. The world as presented through our physical senses has also to be transcended in order to be explained.

A strange picture of fragmentation has been created which is a product of our perceptions and not an external physical reality as simple people suppose. We are not just looking out at an external world through transparent windows called senses, but our perceptual consciousness is an interpretative mechanism, translating impressions of a reality radically different from our mental imagery.

Things which seem separate and " out there ", extended in space, may be organic unities, and our perceptions may be as deceptive as those of a blind man who gropingly feels a series of shapes and surfaces which he considers to be separate objects, although in fact they are parts of a single whole.

Our perceptual world cannot be made co-extensive with Reality, and it is the error of naïve realism that it tries to do this. It is as though a man born and confined in a tower, doomed to see the world only through a narrow slit, endeavoured to construct a theory of the universe based on his segmented view.

The philosophic difficulties which arise from accepting our perceptual separateness of things as real is well evidenced in Hume's criticism of the prevailing conception of causality. If events and objects are as separate as they appear to be, it is difficult to understand how the law of cause and effect can operate. Admittedly, we are assured that every effect is traceable to a cause, but when we examine the cause we find it to be a separate event, and the closest examination does not discover any specific quality which we can label " causeness ". There are in fact regular sequences which we feel reasonably certain will continue and so enable us to predict future events. But regular sequences do not constitute what we mean by causality. We are indeed convinced that some events occur *because* of previous events, and do not just follow them. But if this is so, we have to postulate special types of linkage between those separate events we consider to be causes and effects. Consequently, we invent the notion of a " Force " which is supposed to act at a distance. But this hypothetical force, which was only adopted to account for the mysterious attraction of bodies supposedly separate, is no longer needed. Modern theories would account for the movement of bodies such as the planets as being due to modifications of space-time. That is to say, as being due to alterations in the conditions immediately impinging on the body. The effect, therefore, is to close the apparent gulf between cause and effect, with the result that cause melts, as it were, into the effect as a continuous process, as the sound-waves of a thunder-clap are continuous to the point of our hearing them.

If, therefore, we are to believe in the law of causality, we have to revise our notions of the separateness of things. This, according to Professor Whitehead, we must do. In his book, *Science and the Modern World*, he exposes the fallacy which our perceptions impose upon us, that the physical world consists of objects or pieces of matter occupying particular positions in time and space, or, as he calls it, " simple location ". Whitehead's philosophy conceives Reality as an organic whole, where everything is related to and implies everything else. The relationship is a kind of sensitiveness for which he uses the word " prehension ", which he defines as " apprehension which may or may not be cognitive ". (*Science and the Modern World*, p. 86). But actually Whitehead's universe is not a conglomerate of " prehending " things, but an organic whole. It seems therefore that, no matter how varied are the philosophic standpoints, there is agreement that our commonsense world is not a photographic replica of an " out there " reality.

But we must start with our perceptual experiences, for our reason tells us that the final truth will include and explain them. In other words, if monism is true, the Whole that is the Absolute comprises ourselves, and therefore our perceptual experiences. Any conception of the Absolute which falls short of totality would be less than the Absolute.

Why do we seek Reality?—While there is a need in our minds to rest our experiences in some unifying Ground, we can easily get lost in abstractions, so it is as well to remember that they are *our* abstractions. But we can also be lost without a philosophic background, for experience without thought becomes automatism.

If experience were uniformly pleasant, with all our aims constantly realized, and life proceeded with joyous, unrestricted freedom, untouched by sorrow of any kind, it would call for no explanation, and be accepted as ultimate. But our experience does not form a complete, harmonious whole. It exhibits gaps, contradictions, frustrations and pain, and so we are led to look elsewhere for Reality. But it is significant that as long as experience is emotionally and intellectually harmonious, we feel no need to postulate any other order of Reality.

We know that happiness is our natural right. It is an intuitive certainty, in spite of evidence which could point to an opposite conclusion. It follows therefore that joy and harmony exist at the heart of things, and that is one reason why we reject the world of perceptual experiences as unreal. The discordances of our outer lives do not square with a deeper sense of the need for completeness which can only be realized in the greater Whole we call Reality.

The search for Utopias and harmony on earth testifies to a harmony within ourselves which makes conditions in our environment intolerable.

We cannot make a heaven on earth unless heaven is already within us.

Reality and Facts of Perception.—The problem for us lies in reconciling the stubborn contingent facts of perceptual experience with another order of reality which reason and intuitive insight tell us exists.

As we have already noted, it is a difficult task to deduce contingent facts on the hypothesis of monism. What, in fact, we are required to do is to convert contingent facts into necessary facts. That is to say, we must by logical deduction prove that all the perceptual phenomena which appear as arbitrary given data are in fact just where they are and what they are because of *a priori* conditions in the monistic Whole we call the Absolute.

The efforts of the Idealist philosophers to construct by pure reasoning metaphysical systems from which all phenomenal facts may be deduced have not achieved the finality desired. Modern philosophy tends towards technical discussion of specific problems, and the adherents of certain schools known as philosophical analysts or logical positivists are little more than the analysers of verbal forms.

But we may be sure that philosophy will never relinquish the effort to embrace the universe as a whole within the scope of reason. Analysis, however, of the nature of our perceptual experience renders contingent facts less difficult to explain even on a basis of monism.

The world of our sense experiences is a mental construct, and this is so regardless of whether we adopt a Realist or Idealist interpretation.

There are certain objects which even to commonsense appear as being extensions of ourselves. This comprises our technological creations, such as houses, cars, pens, furniture, and so on. They represent an externalization of our psychological needs.

So we might logically argue that these objects are not of the class of facts we call arbitrary, inasmuch as a super-psychologist, endowed with a genius akin to clairvoyance, could forecast the coming into existence of these technological forms as the inevitable expression of the nature of man.

The house is a psychological reality before it is externalized. Questions of its subsequent endurance and the materials from which it is made do not enter into this particular aspect of the problem, for as we know, the so-called material is itself a perceptual construct.

If, therefore, our technological environment is a projection of our racial psychological needs, a similar principle may underlie the phenomena of nature. That is to say, there is a mind in nature and the forms we perceive are the outward expressions of psychological needs. Nor need we exclude mountains, and the whole range of solid, enduring things, for they, too, are aggregations of atoms, and on our hypothesis the universe is a living whole, the totality of nature being an organic expression.

But underlying all our problems as to the nature of the external world is the need to establish the validity of our perceptions.

Our difficulties arise from mistaking our perceptual world for the real world.

If, through some freak of geographical position we never directly saw the sun, but only its reflections in numerous pools of water, what strange philosophies we would invent to account for the multiplicity of suns! Should someone wiser than the rest arrive at the conclusion that there was only one sun, those who never doubted that the reflected suns were real would ask: How can one sun become many suns?

Similarly the question, Why does the Absolute manifest? involves assumptions based on our perceptual experiences of Time and Space.

The Absolute is not in Time or Space, and manifestation therefore does not involve change in the form of outcropping into an external space. We can only surmise that Time and Space are forms under which we view reality. To this extent we may say that the Absolute is cognizant of Time and Space, because the Absolute is one with ourselves.

Multiplicity, with all the attendant phenomena of good and evil and the contingent facts of nature are embraced within the Whole. Plato's theory of eternal archetypal forms provides, even for modern minds, a fruitful concept of Reality.

We summarize.—The conclusions which may be drawn from our discussions in this chapter can be summarized as follows:
1. We conceive Reality in terms of monism, which is of the nature of mind and consciousness.
2. The Whole, or Absolute, is an Eternal Now of infinite possibilities.
3. We surmise an act akin to will and imagination, whereby one set of possibilities becomes actualized as a manifested universe. This implies a Self-imposed limitation—but only a limitation in thought.
4. Although the Absolute is beyond duality, it must be cognizant of multiplicity as a result of Its own thought-creation, and we, who are aspects of the Whole, register this in our perceptual experiences. Metaphorically speaking, our private dramas are acts within the Master-play of the Whole.
5. Good and evil, and all the contingent facts of an apparently external nature may be compared to a dream.
6. The Absolute is not a static Eternal Now in a spatial sense. The conception of Its totality implies both change and changelessness. But these concepts are to be understood after the model of our own minds, which remain unchanged though the ground of our changing thoughts.
7. This produces on the periphery of our experience the appearance of life emerging from an unmanifested state and evolving in Time in series of forms of ever-increasing complexity. In other words, the facts of evolution.
8. All is life, and the limits which we observe as bodies are equally forms of life.
9. There is real freedom for ourselves, and in fact, within the limits of their forms, for all creatures, as all participate in the Absolute freedom of the unifying Ground which some call God.
10. It also follows that, while nothing new can be added to the Absolute, novelty must manifest in the experienced world of the creatures, for the infinite world of possibilities is ever impinging on the limited forms of expression.

11. This results in an eternal rhythm, akin to in-breathing and out-breathing.

These speculations are no more than a few guiding lines to aid our thought. We are compelled to use words which were not designed to convey abstract meanings. But if we can go beyond the words, these speculations may lead us to a real insight as to the nature of Reality.

Actually, no reason can be given for the Reality which is the source of reason. As Professor Whitehead expresses it: " No reason can be given for the nature of God, because that nature is the ground of rationality". (*Science and the Modern World*, p. 222). Consequently, no reason can be given to account for the limitation which produces particular things.

If, then, by reason we cannot enter the heaven of final truth, are we doomed to grope in the semi-gloom of intellectual abstraction which mocks our efforts to achieve certainty and mental peace?

If our consciousness were confined entirely to the plane of rationality, such scepticism would seem to be inevitable. But there are deeper levels of our being on which something akin to direct contact with Reality can be achieved.

The words we use in reasoning are symbols for a particular type of experience, largely that of commonsense.

A race of blind men would still reason, but their language-symbols would be different because their perceptions were different. If their organs of sight developed, then problems which were insoluble in terms of blind-language would cease to be problems. The facts of the blind world would not have been changed, but explained in the light of a wider perception and more fundamental experience.

Already our reason has disturbed our faith in the simple testimony of our sense-experiences on which so much of our reasoning is based. We are therefore almost being forced to turn into a new dimension of Reality. Indeed, there have always been some among us who have testified to perceptual experiences which brought them into relationship with a Reality behind the scene we call normal.

Religion has consistently proclaimed that there is such a world, and mystics insist they have directly experienced this deeper reality. And this experience has occurred not only to those normally described as mystics. Often for quite ordinary people the outer pageant disappears, and although the experience may be only momentary, the sense of an inner reality satisfying and beautiful, survives all subsequent evidence to the contrary.

A note on terminology should perhaps conclude this chapter. I have used the term monism which has associations with various philosophic systems. René Guénon warns us against confusing the Hindu doctrine of "Non-dualism" with monism, " which, whatever form it assumes, is, like ' dualism ', of the merely philosophic and not the metaphysical order . . ." *Man and His Becoming*, p. 53.

Actually the non-dualism of the Vedanta cannot be expressed in terms of any philosophic system. Nevertheless I have not discarded the term monism as the context in which it is used serves to define it, and I hope makes it clear that it is not a monism arrived at by exclusion of an opposite.

It will be noticed that René Guénon draws a distinction between philosophy and metaphysics. This distinction is contrary to prevailing usage, where metaphysics is considered to be a branch of philosophy.

Metaphysical knowledge however, by some writers, is regarded as the equivalent of actual and direct apprehension of the Ultimate Reality which is the ground and cause of the Universe.

In later chapters we shall consider the testimony which exists for such direct apprehension.

CHAPTER XIII

" THE FUTURE " IN THE LIGHT OF PRECOGNITION

"There Pandava beheld the whole universe divided into manifold parts, standing in one in the body of the God of Gods."
Bhagavad Gita XI.

"And if a finite consciousness can know what card is going to be turned up three seconds from now, or what shipwreck is going to take place next week, then there is nothing impossible or even intrinsically improbable in the idea of an infinite consciousness that can know now events indefinitely remote in what, for us, is future time."
ALDOUS HUXLEY, *The Perennial Philosophy.*

Precognition—A Definition, and some General Comments.—I do not propose to review the evidence for precognition. I shall indeed assume that it has been demonstrated to occur, and the reader who is unfamiliar with the evidence is referred to the Journals and Proceedings of the Societies for Psychical Research both in England and America.

Briefly, precognition is the ability under certain circumstances to become aware by paranormal means of events which have not yet occurred; in other words, of events which are normally regarded as being in the future, and which could not be inferred by reasoning.

Precognition is a crucial example of the whole range of paranormal (or Psi) phenomena which clearly cannot happen if the universe is precisely as it appears to commonsense. Consequently their occurrence is one more challenge to the naïve realism which we have criticized in previous chapters.

Suppose, however, the universe is as we have argued, a product of mind: that, in fact, philosophical Idealism in some form is true; then have we a better world-frame to accommodate these Psi phenomena? Most probably we have, but no intellectual formulations are likely to satisfy us at our present level of experience. Should the experiences now called paranormal ever become numerous enough to be normal, then the higher perceptual slant on the Universe, we suppose, would disclose new facts of existence and much that is now obscure would appear as self-evident, and therefore need no support from reasoning. In other words, Psi phenomena would be accepted as in the nature of things even as science to-day accepts the external world as given.

Problems of course would still exist, but these would only arise for a minority whose minds were reaching out to new levels of apprehension.

What actually we are now doing is to bring two systems of experience into some kind of relationship. Each generation lives within its own peculiar mental frontiers. The frontiers are composed of sets of assumptions, propositions and dogmatisms. When the frontiers are guarded by a priesthood, the psychological limits are rigid, but they are equally rigid when materialistic postulates present a ring-pass-not. There is always a difficulty in assimilating foreigners within a nation, and ideas can also be aliens.

Psi phenomena are aliens which if they are to be admitted to our society seem inevitably destined to be disturbing elements, and many would wish them good riddance. But others would rather study the aliens and eventually grant them certificates of nationalization, even if it means a re-orientation of the existing population of ideas. The problem, therefore, presented by paranormal phenomena is not so much to establish proofs of their occurrence—the evidence is abundant that they do occur —but rather to find some way of assimilating these facts into the respectable society of our accepted notions about the Universe.

Many efforts are now being made to do this, but we must be prepared for fantastic hypotheses, for it is clear that if the physicist feels it necessary to resolve the world of matter into a set of mathematical propositions in order to explain the atom, then any hypothesis which purports to explain Psi phenomena will offend equally our notions derived from commonsense.

It is not my intention to hazard a hypothesis in the technical sense. This is a task for experts engaged in the practical work of investigation, and those who can test the hypothesis according to the normal procedures.

A Philosophical Background Propitious for Precognition.—However, a certain general attitude emerges as the result of our discussion in previous chapters, so it may not be without value if we examine the phenomenon of precognition in connection with our view of an " Eternal Now ". Actually the term " Eternal Now " is implied in the concept of the Absolute, which is usually conceived to be a universal plenum.

When stated as a theoretical proposition it is not difficult to acquiesce in the idea that the whole we call the Absolute, or in theological phraseology God, is the origin of all that exists. But this purely abstract notion needs to be expressed in more concrete terms if it is to be useful as a guiding idea or hypothesis to explain precognition.

When we say that all things exist in the World-Mind, or Absolute, what do we mean?

Almost inevitably our minds tend to build up an imagery based on our normal sensory experiences. Those who are not accustomed to abstract thinking would be inclined towards a concrete picture of the World-mind as a gigantic museum which contains all the objects that have existed, and do exist, together with those which will be known in the future. Analogies indeed are frequently used which picture an observer carrying a lantern through a vast dark building and as he passes through the rooms and galleries of the immense edifice the light from his lantern reveals one group of objects after another. The objects in the immediate glow of the light would be described as existing in the present, but as the circle of light moves forward objects sink into the darkness and become the past, while objects in the more distant rooms would be regarded as in the future and come into present existence only when the light of the moving observer illumines them.

Analogies of this type do aid our pedestrian efforts to arrive at some general concepts regarding the Eternal Now. But most analogies are more confusing than helpful if pressed too literally.

Eternal Forms.—Clearly this World Museum picture is our old friend naïve realism back on a cosmic scale. In other words, having rejected physical objects as external realities we must be on our guard when using analogies which depict the Cosmic Mind as being filled with these objects. While the concept of an Eternal Now is a valuable key to the mystery of precognition we must not imagine that there is some department of the Cosmos holding replicas of all the objects of the phenomenal world. Yet there is a sense in which even the phenomenal world must exist in the cosmic mind, for have we not postulated a monistic Whole as a universal Ground?

How then are we to conceive this cosmic plenum? It seems too great a concession to our commonsense notions to suppose that pens, writing desks, toothpicks and similar phenomenal objects exist precisely as they appear to us in some universal plenum.

Yet Plato's theory of eternal forms fundamentally leads to this conclusion. For Plato the real world consists of archetypal ideas or forms in which all the objects of our phenomenal world participate. In other words, our world of sensory objects exists only because of the prior existence of their eternal archetypes. A bed, for instance, is only an expression of what we might call an eternal idea of " bedness ".

The theory of the independent reality of universals, such as whiteness, triangularity, beauty and similar abstract ideas is as old as philosophy, and still excites the keenest discussion, but Plato's theory of the eternal forms extends universally to particulars.

Admittedly the theory, like all philosophic theories, raises its own crop of problems, particularly as we seem to have on our hands almost two phenomenal realms of experiences without any very clear explanation of their causal relationship. All however that concerns us at the moment is to note that the conception of what for purposes of exposition we might call a realm of eternal objects or archetypal ideas is one supported by centuries of keen philosophical debate, and more recently we find Professor Whitehead advancing with considerable cogency the theory of Eternal Objects, although with different characteristics from those of the Platonic Forms.

This conception of eternal patterns is in essence only another variant of the problem of change and changelessness which we considered in Chapter 12.

We have already noted that a monistic Whole or Absolute is necessarily changeless since it is infinite, and therefore beyond our categories of time and space. Consequently our problem reduces itself to giving some account of the appearance of becoming or change in the world of phenomena.

By conceiving monism in terms of Mind we have expressed the view that the World Mind retains its unity, the appearance of change being described as a manifestation of infinity in terms of forms.

In this chapter we are endeavouring to apply this concept of a changeless Whole or Eternal Now as an hypothesis to interpret a particular phenomenon, namely that of precognition.

The theory has plausibility when stated in general terms, but as usual we meet our real difficulties when we descend to the concrete empirical facts.

Consider, for instance, some of the types of events which are foreseen. They range from major events, such as train disasters, sickness, murder, sudden reversals of fortune, both national and personal, to cases of the precognizing of events sometimes trivial to the point of banality, as, for instance, J. W. Dunne's precognitive association test related in his book, *An Experiment with Time*, where he saw a folded umbrella " upside down, handle on the pavement just outside the Piccadilly Hotel ". The next day the vision was verified when he saw an old lady, freakishly dressed in a very early-Victorian black costume, and using a closed umbrella" as a· walking-stick, grasping it pilgrim's-staff fashion ". But she had it upside down, holding it by the ferrule end, and " was pounding along towards the hotel with the handle on the pavement ".

I refrain from the temptation to cite numerous cases of precognition.

How can the Future Influence the Present?—By what means does an event which we regard as being in the future, yet influence a cognizing mind in the present?

The usual view is that the future is non-existent; that in fact we are in process of making the future by our activities in the present. If this view were correct then clearly precognition would be an impossibility, for we cannot become aware of a non-existent event.

In the light of the evidence therefore we are forced to postulate that an event cognized prior to its occurrence in the normal manner must have had some existent status when it was cognized.

There are certain cases of precognition where an explanation suggests itself without unduly straining normal psychological principles.

Many events have a prior incubating period in the sub-consciousness of a person or persons.

A strong antagonism, for instance, could be so thoroughly repressed and blocked by the censor that the normal consciousness displayed no outer sign of the conflict. If, however, the conflict were dramatized in the subconscious it might be possible, in view of what we know of telepathic rapport, for some sensitive to become aware of this dramatized conflict.

Should an occasion subsequently arise where this conflict bursts to the surface in murder, the original statement of the sensitive would appear to be precognitive, whereas it was really a diagnosis of a person's present state of consciousness. Of course all conflicts do not result in murder, so we must suppose in the above example the psychic ferment was at the point where precipitation into action was inevitable, and the sensitive we presume sensed this and so foresaw a murder.

Actually the recorded cases of precognition are far more detailed than the above hypothetical case. Also, geographical and time details are foreseen.

However, a simple case of the type we have related illustrates a general principle which gives at least a clue towards an explanation of some cases of precognition.

A deduction from the view we have expressed in previous chapters is that the Universe is a product of Mind, and that the process we call becoming is not creation, but manifestation.

Therefore it follows that events have in some form an eternal existence.

The Nature of Time.—The problem of precognition is usually supposed to involve some mystery in the nature of Time. We are now becoming familiar with theories which confer on Time new dimensions. Instead of conceiving Time as uni-directional, on the straight line of past, present and future, we are asked to conceive the possibility of time having a past, present and future along a line at right angles to our familiar time; thus time becomes an area instead of a line, and events which are future, say along the line of our familiar time, would be perceived as past if we made a right angle turn into the second dimension of time.

Then we have conceptions of time such as Dunne's Serialism, which involve an infinite regress of times.

Another approach to the problem of precognition is that of C. H. Hinton in his book *The Fourth Dimension*. In this book by means of ingenious analogies and diagrams he seeks to demonstrate dimensions of space other than the familiar three of length, breadth and depth. Starting with analogies based on hypothetical two-dimensional creatures, he shows how the third dimension of space would appear as motion to such a two-dimensional consciousness. Similarly a fourth dimension would be represented in our three-dimensional consciousness as motion or time.

Ouspensky, developing the same idea, considers that an animal sees only two dimensions, in other words, a flat world. He bases his view on the fact that we ourselves see objects as flat, but later experience corrects this optical illusion through our mental concept of three dimensions. As, however, animals have not the capacity to form concepts, they must accept the world as it usually appears to them, viz., flat. They have of course three-dimensional bodies, but do not know this. For animals, therefore, the third dimension would appear as motion.

"The animal", says Ouspensky, "can see an angle of a three-dimensional object only while moving past it and during the time it takes, the object will seem to the animal to have turned—a new side has appeared, and the side first seen has disappeared, or moved away. . . . Could the animal think about those phenomena which have not yet entered into its life (i.e., angles and curved surfaces) it would undoubtedly imagine them *in time only*. . . . The angle of a house past which a horse runs every day is *a phenomenon repeating under certain circumstances, but nevertheless a phenomenon proceeding in time*, and not a spatial and constant property of the house." (*Tertium Organum*, pp. 105-6.)

These analogies and examples, while helpful up to a point, do not reach to the heart of the problem of time.

Even if we accept the theory of a fourth dimension of space and agree that our apprehension of this fourth dimension would be in terms of time, we have virtually shelved the problem of time by making it into a dimension of space.

The apprehension of the fourth dimension implies motion in the three-dimensional observer and this process will continue indefinitely for observers on any number of higher dimensions. The fifth dimension will be cognized as Time by a fourth-dimensional consciousness. Always an observer must be supposed to experience motion which is the essence of our awareness of time.

Time is our consciousness of change, and although inseparably associated with space, it remains a primary datum of our awareness, with its own characteristic problems.

We must also be on our guard against promoting time into an independent existent. Statements such as "events happen in time" or that "time flows" encourage us to think of time as a sort of medium in which events occur almost like a river carrying its craft towards some unknown destination.

Actually time is no more than our awareness of the sequence of events from which arise our notions of past, present and future.

Time should not be abstracted from Events.—The problem of Precognition is not primarily one of time abstracted from events. Rather is it one concerning the order in which happenings occur in the phenomenal world.

In other words, the fact that an event we call " future " can be cognized in the " present " challenges our ideas of normal sequence, including the law of causality.

We have taken it for granted that the future is nothing at all. We instinctively regard events in the past and present as determining or even causing future events. Time's arrow points in one direction, from the past to the future.

Is this an illusion imposed by our perceptual limitations? This may very well, in the light of precognitive experiences, be the case. There seems no reason—except normal experience —why we should regard causality only in terms of events along a straight line labelled past, present and future. We can, without doing undue violence to commonsense, surmise that the phenomenal plane is not strictly speaking a causal plane at all, but for the most part a plane of effects. In other words the process of becoming which includes the whole pageant of evolution and historical sequences is an unfoldment of causes lying as it were vertical to our horizontal plane.

The drama is a whole on the spool of a cinematograph film. But when it is projected on the screen we see a sequence of cause and effect as the characters play their parts and the final scenes seem to be the inevitable effects of earlier events in the drama. But we know that no law of cause and effect was operating on the screen. The play as witnessed was a total effect of causes outside the flat surface of the screen.

We can imagine a primitive man, unaware of the mechanism involved, sitting with attention riveted on the screen and becoming identified with the drama, as children do. To such a man it would be incomprehensible if we spoke of the screen sequences as existing as a single whole in the present.

The conception of a Cosmic Mind or Absolute, we repeat, implies that in some sense it is an all-inclusive Whole.

How are we to conceive the term " All-Inclusive "? Our difficulty is to formulate an intelligible statement as to the meaning to be attached to the phrase " all-inclusive."

We have noted above that it is not intended to build up a picture of the Absolute as a cosmic museum containing among other things all our familiar objects, nor as a cosmic theatre projecting an infinite variety of dramas.

Reverting again to the cinematograph analogy, on the screen there are emotion-evoking situations; clashes of personality; the scene we witness is alive; crowded with action and sequential incidents.

How different this is from the same scenes on the film-spool stationary in the theatre store-house. Yet even in this static form the pictures are visible in miniature on the film. At an earlier stage, however, after the film has been shot, but before it has been developed, nothing is visible to the naked eye. Nevertheless the scenes are there, buried in the emulsion. Still earlier, the drama was a series of isolated shots in the studios, and before this it was only a series of actors' scripts marked with the professional jargon of the stage. Originally of course the drama was an idea in a single mind.

The point of this analogy is to illustrate the metamorphosis of an idea in its journey towards actualization. Also it provides an example of timelessness and a time-sequence. We may say that the Drama as an idea is timeless, although its unfoldment requires the sequence we experience as time. If therefore this were a fair sample of our phenomenal experience, prevision would be explicable, for although an observer chained to his seat would be compelled to wait for each scene to come into the focus of his present awareness, and the later scenes would be in his future, another observer free to move could see the future of the chained observer if he had access to the film as a whole.

Hinton's higher space-dimensions basically imply the same conception, for the higher dimensions are described as appertaining to physical objects. Thus we are asked to accept a sort of changeless universe of eternal, multi-dimensional objects which are perceived as motion because of the limitations of our three-dimensional perceptions.

Perception therefore of the future, according to Hinton, would amount to an extension of our consciousness so as to embrace a higher dimension of space; in other words, to contact a stratum of reality in which our future exists as an eternal present as in a sense the film drama is a present unity.

I do not disagree with the basic idea which these analogies struggle to express, but they are helpful only if treated as symbolic expositions.

It is not sufficient for our purpose to postulate the existence of such universals as Truth, Beauty and Goodness nor even those of Whiteness, Triangularity, etc.

It may even be true that all things phenomenal participate in the eternity of their universal archetypes, but such a general statement needs bringing much closer to earth before it can be useful as a basis for understanding the fact of precognition.

"*The Future*" *is not Cognized.*—First, let us be clear that precognition does not mean "seeing the future." The "future" is an abstraction based on conceiving time as though it were independent of events.

What is implied in precognition is that an event is cognized twice. Firstly we experience the event in the present, then later the same event occurs, or one with features that are sufficiently similar for us to declare that we have experienced it previously.

Normally, B follows A and C follows B, or in terms of causality we say that B is caused by A and it seems sheer nonsense to state that B can be cognized before it has been caused to occur. If however the relationships A.B.C. are those of a logical nature as, for instance, mathematical formulae or geometrical relationships such as the angles A.B.C. and A.C.B. being equal if the sides of a triangle A.B. and A.C. are equal, then we are dealing with non-temporal relationships. In such cases although the relationships will take time to be worked out they are really non-temporal and therefore can be said to exist as eternal truths. To perceive one or more of the factors in such an inter-related logical or mathematical system implies the co-existence of the other factors.

When, however, these purely logical or arithmetical relationships are applied to actual events, predictions lose their certainty and become only probable estimates depending on the nature and number of unforeseen intrusions which may intervene to distort the purely logical inferences. If we know that a car is travelling at 30 miles per hour and that another car twenty miles behind on the same road is following at a speed of 40 miles per hour we can calculate precisely how far the following car will travel in order to draw level with the first car.

Arithmetically these are a set of fixed relationships, and the answer is included in the premises. But when the calculation is applied to actual events, prediction is at the mercy of innumerable empirical occurrences. A driver may faint at the wheel; a tyre may burst; or a dog run under the wheels. Bridges may collapse, thus causing a detour or an accident.

It is precognition of events of this unexpected and unpredictable type that constitutes our problem. Our normal experience is that these events must happen in accordance with a law of Causality.

In spite of the fact that it is by no means certain that the so-called " law of causality " is a law in the sense that events called effects are the *necessary* result of prior events labelled causes, we most of us find sufficient practical evidence to feel confident that certain sequences are not just *before* and *after*, but that there is some necessary connection which justifies us in describing one event as occurring *because* of a previous one.

If therefore A.B.C.D. is a causal series, our commonsense expectation is that D has no existence until after the occurrence of the antecedent events, A.B.C. What then are we to conclude when an event is cognized out of its turn, as it were, or as we have expressed it, the event occurs twice?

Actually the phrase " the event occurs twice " needs some qualification because if it really is *the same event* it cannot strictly speaking " occur twice ". In any case the fact of its occurring later means that it bears another date and consequently occupies a place in a different sequence.

For the purposes of my present exposition I will assume that the event at the time cognized has the same content as the event which later occurs and is described by us as a fulfilment of the precognition.

This being the case we can say that it is one event, but has been cognized twice. If this conclusion is valid, then precognition is less puzzling, for the cognition is not of a " future " event, but of a present event which is recognized later in a different setting which we call Actualization.

But we still have to form some conception of the status or mode of existence of this so-called " present event ".

The Subconscious Latency Theory.—Our task would be considerably lightened if we could bring all the contingent and unexpected circumstances which are precognized into the category of latent or subconscious energies in process of manifesting. That is, reduce them to the type mentioned above where a murder might be precognized if a sensitive became telepathically aware of a complex of subconscious energies.

I am inclined to the view that a theory along these lines could lead to an explanation.

There are indeed certain types of precognition which fit neatly into a theory of subconscious latency. These are those which foresee an individual's personal future.

Dr. Osty even goes so far as to say that: " Every human being knows his own entire life according to laws that are still to be discovered, and metagnomic subjects are psychic instruments of variable quality that reveal what each human being knows concerning himself without being aware consciously, or even subconsciously, that he has this knowledge." (*Supernormal Faculties in Man*, p. 185.)

Dr. Osty based this conclusion on the experimental evidence of many years of investigation during which he recorded the results of supernormal cognition by numerous sensitives of both past and future events in the lives of large numbers of people.

Admittedly, many of Osty's cases, and indeed other records of prevision of personal events, do lead to the conclusion that events in our personal lives have some existence prior to their occurrence in the normal manner.

But this general statement conflicts so radically with our experience of freedom of choice, and also carries with it implications fundamentally at variance with the usual conceptions of the human personality, that Osty's generalization will not readily be accepted without interpretation.

Yet I think that a theory of what I call subconscious latency can be usefully employed as an explanation of precognition. Particularly is this the case where important events are foreseen, such as a serious illness, death, or a major crisis.

We may reasonably postulate in the light of a theory of multi-existences that we are born into a matrix of psychic influences which form a sort of general life-map and determine the main sequences we are destined to experience. This would imply that determinism rules the general pattern of our lives yet permits freedom regarding the details. On such a view the only events in a personal life which could with certainty be precognized would be the crucial ones, together with the minor ones which lead inevitably towards the major experiences even as the most important towns or ports on a journey may be foreseen once a certain direction is taken, but not the many contacts with persons and circumstances which, while they may cause deviations or delays, yet cannot affect the final end of the journey, or even the sequence in which the chief ports or towns *en route* would be experienced.

Unfortunately such a theory, while it embodies a valuable general principle, requires a different expression if it is to accommodate some of the actual facts of precognition.

In my book, *The Superphysical*, I advanced this latent subconscious view, and pointed out that " such an explanation assumes greater plausibility in the light of modern conceptions of the unconscious as being the seat of energies which determine much of our conscious thinking and activities. Events, then, can exist in the psychic world before they are projected outwards, and some prevision may be telepathic sensing of thoughts and complexes before their manifestation on the material plane." (p. 111.)

And the fact that, ordinarily, the future seen by sensitives is a personal one, and not the future in general does strengthen this theory.

Dr. Osty illustrates this point by examples from his records showing that the 1914-18 war was precognized by many sensitives, but only in relation to the individuals who were to experience the war. He cites the case of M. Leon Sonrel " who, on July 21st, 1869, in a kind of spontaneous ecstatic state, seized upon the whole future development of the life of his friend, Dr. Amadel Tardieu, and announced to him the second great war in its relation to an episode of Dr. Tardieu's life. It was in relation to an individual life that Sonrel took cognizance of the war still far distant in time. It would seem that if Dr. Tardieu had not had to live through the war, Sonrel would have had no knowledge of its coming." (*Supernormal Faculties in Man*, p. 178.)

This aspect of precognition is also illustrated by Dunne's precognitive dream that the number of lives lost in the Martinique volcano disaster was 4,000, whereas the actual numbers bore no relation to 4,000. But a press account he subsequently read printed the number as 40,000, which Dunne actually misread as 4,000, only discovering his mistake years afterwards. The fact is, therefore, that he perceived the future as he would experience it, and not as it occurred. (*An Experiment with Time*, pp. 34-8.)

Even so we can hardly agree that to some extent the future in general was not cognized. Clearly both the war and the volcano disaster were future events of a non-personal character, and although they were perceived as part of a personal experience yet the general events of war and volcanic upheaval were part of the precognition.

In any case, there are many records of public events which have been foreseen.

Even, however, if we confine our attention to the precognition of events in a personal life, the theory of subconscious latency needs clarifying. Consider, for instance, the case related by Dame Edith Lyttleton in her book, *Some Cases of Prediction*, p. 106 *et seq*. Mr. Calder was in 1928 appointed headmaster of the Holinforth Secondary School in Yorkshire. Previously he lived in Middlesex, and while there his wife, who had never been in Yorkshire, dreamed " of an old house built of grey stone, situated in a lovely valley through which ran a shallow stream of black-looking water ". Eventually in the course of house-hunting they saw the house of the dream and went to live in it, or rather in half the house, for the other half was tenanted. The stream was there as foreseen and was "frequently discoloured from the waste-products of the neighbouring dye-works". If these were all the details foreseen the dream could be interpreted as only partially precognitive inasmuch as the dream itself could have influenced the eventual taking of the house. From the details reported I do not think this was the case. However, there follow other details which make this dream clearly precognitive.

In the dream Mrs. Calder saw that outside the other tenanted part of the house was "a barrel being used as a dog-kennel for a black retriever."

The half house was indeed occupied, as in the dream, but there was neither a dog-kennel nor a dog. And here is the curious fact: a year or two later new tenants arrived, and "they brought with them a black Labrador retriever and placed a barrel by the door for its use".

One further example will illustrate small details which are often foreseen. A woman dreamed that she saw her carpet burnt in *five patches*. Subsequently the dream was fulfilled. A housemaid in carrying live coals from another room, spilled some which burned the carpet in *five places*. (*S.P.R. Proc.*, V. 343.)

If precognitions were only of crucial events of deep concern to a person or to a nation we might conceive some theory in terms of personal or cosmic cycles. There are, of course, rhythmic sequences. History may never repeat itself precisely, although certain basic conditions seem to recur which cause the appearance of personal and national behaviour-patterns very similar to previous ones. Surely, however, no law of cycles would embrace the repetition of the humble trifles which sometimes are the content of precognitions. Actually the published accounts of precognition cover almost every type of event from inconsequential details to major disasters.

Some of the precognitions relate to accidents considerable periods before they occurred. As, for instance, Dunne's dream in the autumn of 1913 that a train going North had fallen over the embankment. He saw several carriages lying towards the bottom of the slope, large blocks of stone rolling and sliding down. He got the date on which this accident would occur as

"THE FUTURE" IN THE LIGHT OF PRECOGNITION

"somewhere in the following Spring; March or April". He also knew in the dream that the place was just north of the Firth of Forth Bridge in Scotland. On April 14th, the following Spring, "The Flying Scotsman" jumped the Firth of Forth Bridge, and fell on to the golf links 20 feet below.

Those of my readers who are familiar with the literature of precognition will realize how easy it would be to fill many volumes with examples.

Close study of the actual evidence leaves one with a sense of bewilderment, and it becomes clear that we are in the presence of facts which are not only a challenge to philosophy but also carry implications for practical life.

A Recapitulation.—It may be useful at this point to summarize the lines of approach to the problem of precognition which we have so far discussed. They fall into four main groups of theory.

Firstly, we have the concept of an Eternal Now which is a Plenum of infinite possibilities and actualities.

This type of theory is the one I favour, but it is hard to state it in a form to make it fit the actual facts of experience.

Secondly, there are those theories which require a revolutionary change in our views of the nature of time.

Some of these theories are highly technical and difficult to follow, as they postulate new dimensions of time, and they leave me with a feeling that the solutions are verbal and are too divorced from the actual facts. Also I feel they are based on a substantialized view of time, that is a conception of time as though it existed independently of the happening of events.

Thirdly, we have theories based on a fourth dimension of space. The concept of four or more dimensions of space is plausible and on many points illuminating. However, it carries with it a whole crop of difficulties and tends to create an image of a static Universe. Also, it suffers from the defect of the theories based on time-dimensions in that space becomes substantialized, instead of time.

Fourthly, there is the concept of what I have called subconscious latency; precognition being explained as the ability to detect events in a latent form in their progress towards actualization.

This last theory departs least from our commonsense notions of causation, and if it were adequate to explain the actual facts it would be welcome, as it is sound practice not to desert the world of commonsense except under compulsion.

Probably no single theory will prove adequate to cope with all the facts of precognition, but as that of subconscious latency stems naturally from the general view of the Universe outlined in previous chapters it might be worth while to examine it further.

Let us state precisely what actually occurs in precognition.
1. A "future" event is in the present when it is cognized.
2. The fulfilment when it occurs is the same event or more precisely we should say it has a content which is the same or with features similar enough to be recognized.

This causes us to ask what is the distinction between the event when first cognized and the event which is the fulfilment?

We must note that in both cases the events are experiences in someone's consciousness, but the latter event becomes one which is shared with others, that is to say it becomes a public event. This process of converting a private experience into a public one we may call actualization.

When however the event was originally experienced, say in a dream or waking vision, it had just as much reality for the person dreaming as it had when it occurred later as fulfilment. The only difference between the dream and actual events which we described as verifying the dream is that other people become witnesses.

Thus we are brought back to our old problem of the nature of the world we call external.

We have already been compelled to discard the commonsense notion of an external world existing " out there ", precisely as it appears.

The problem therefore of dreaming an event is part of the general one of perception in the normally accepted meaning of the term.

If we keep in mind the fact that all events are experiences in someone's consciousness we have a better basis for understanding the problem of precognition.

Should also we accept, as does Osty, that "every human being knows his own entire life . . ." then precognizing events in an individual's life would be less mysterious, for it would imply that, within the depths of the psyche lie the causative factors which determine the external experience of a person's life, exerting an influence not unlike that of the hereditary factors which control the physical organism.

However, this view seems to imply that the sense of choice in our daily lives is illusory, inasmuch as events are already determined at some deeper level within the soul. Also, when confronted by the actual facts of precognition we are baffled to conceive in what form events of the type mentioned above may be said to exist before they occur in our normal consciousness.

Memory and Precognition present Similar Problems.—We should here note that a similar problem is presented by the existence of past events. We are accustomed to regard the present as constantly becoming the past, and ordinarily describe past events as existing in our memories. But what is Memory?

I have in my book, *The Superphysical*, discussed the problem of memory. My purpose then was to demonstrate that no materialistic theory of memory could account for the actual facts of memory. The arguments there advanced I need not repeat, but certain points have relevance for our present discussion.

If we believe that past events still exist and may indeed be recalled in memory, then in what form do they exist? The plain man nurtured on commonsense and mechanistic notions will reply unhesitatingly that past events only exist in memories and memories reside in the brain.

But this is only another variant of our old epi-phenomenalist theory which we considered in Chapter 3.

No one has ever observed a memory in a brain. The brain when it is observed by a physiologist exists in the mind of the physiologist, or if the materialistic myth must be preserved, in the brain of the physiologist.

He is in fact observing sense-data from which he infers the existence of the physical object called the brain. However legitimate it may or may not be to postulate the independent existence of physical objects let us at least be clear that such an independent world is the product of inference and that we are directly acquainted only with sense-data. If there is a wide divergence of views as to what may be legitimately inferred to exist independently of our conscious states, it is rash indeed to dogmatize about one section of the supposedly external world called the brain and declare that it is the seat of thought and memory.

We must draw a line of distinction between the sense-data which are experienced when observation is made of the brain and the theories based on these phenomenal sequences. There are in fact two bodies, one the body as perceived and another one which is inferred as the result of a process of translation of a series of code signals. We call the latter the physical body and naïve commonsense assumes that it exists precisely as observed, but this cannot be the case, as the physiologist is in the same position as the rest of us and has no direct access to the physical world.

But even if we accept at its face value the usual text book description of the brain, we learn nothing which can assist us in understanding the mystery of memory. A memory is not just in the brain. Neurones and nerve-impulses are transmitters of signals which consciousness interprets, even as Morse code signs are interpreted.

But the plain man will ask if memories are not in the brain, where are they? It will be noticed that this question could be considered illegitimate inasmuch as it implies that memory must occupy some space. Memory is a psychological phenomenon and spatial concepts are inappropriate.

We could say that memories are in the mind and leave it at that. There are of course psychologists who insist that no one has ever observed a mind directly, and therefore we are not entitled to say mind exists. However, linguistic usage rather than psychological fact is the basis for such statements. It no doubt might be better to say we *are* minds or psyches, and not that we *have* minds. Exercises in Semantics can be fascinating, but they lead to puerility if words are allowed to masquerade as the facts for which they are only the labels.

No one can doubt that he is conscious, and memory is a function of consciousness. Remembering an event implies that this past event has continued to exist and exercises an influence in the present. This may seem to be stressing the obvious, but our familiarity with the word " memory " tends to make us miss the significance of the phenomenon.

An event remembered is one that is experienced again in the present, but how can it be recalled into present consciousness unless it endures in some form?

A great deal has been written on this subject and various theories have been advanced. Some of these theories depart radically from the usual materialistic assumptions. For instance, Dr. Bousfield in his book, *The Basis of Memory*, states: " The basis of memory is not a record of protoplasmic structure but is an immaterial psychical structure. Such a structure involves a conception of a substance of which it is built . . . this substance we shall call psychoplasm, a substance which we postulate as consisting not of material protons and electrons, but of some other modification of the ether. This substance which we call psychoplasm is as hypothetical as the ether, and no more so." (p. 40).

The Psychic Ether Hypothesis.—This idea of a psychoplasmic substance is fairly widespread.

Frederick Myers, one of the founders of the Society for Psychical Research, has also used this hypothesis under the name Metetherial. More recently this theory has been developed and applied to certain problems of psychical research by Mr. C. A. Mace in a lecture to the Society for Psychical Research (Vol. XLIV., November, 1937), and later Professor H. H. Price discusses the same theory under the title " Haunting and the Psychic Ether Hypothesis ": Presidential Address, Vol. XLV., December, 1939. Both these writers are fully aware of the philosophical and theoretical objections which may be raised against such unorthodox speculation. But the facts themselves are unorthodox and therefore must be studied by radically new methods.

However, this theory of a psychic ether is really only a variant of a very ancient one. Those who are familiar with Eastern philosophical systems will recognize at once the similarity of psychic ether with that of *Akasa*, which is also conceived to be a sort of universal medium retaining a record of the entire history of the cosmos.

Professor Price pays his tribute to the eastern wisdom and indeed points out that " It is well to remember that in India and the Buddhist countries men not necessarily inferior to Europeans in intelligence have been devoting themselves for very many centuries to the deepening and extension of human consciousness." (*Ibid.*, p. 317.)

Those trained in an atmosphere of academic caution are apt to appear rather ponderous and circuitous in their expression of a particular theory. But it must be remembered that this cautious approach is a valuable discipline, and the psychical researcher in particular is only interested in theories to the extent that they promise to be useful tools for the investigation and explanation of his strange field of enquiry.

I am not writing for the specialist, yet the theme of my book does require that I outline some general framework of the type of universe in which we are living.

The application of the Psychic Ether hypothesis to our present discussion is that it provides a basis for understanding how thoughts or psychic energies can continue to exist and exert an influence in the present although according to conventional views of the mind thoughts are transient products and have no existence except as the contents of a thinking mind. Also thoughts are supposed to have no location. How then are we to explain the phenomena of haunting and also the strange influence which objects and certain places exert on sensitives to evoke clairvoyance?

There are many well-authenticated instances of whole chapters of past history being re-experienced by people who have become *en rapport* with what might be described as the " spirit " of a locality.

Perhaps the best known example is the experience in the Petit Trianon at Versailles, published under the title *An Adventure*. Although this experience does not measure up to the full evidential standards required by the S.P.R., nevertheless it is typical of a large category of similar experiences, and taken as a whole the evidence is convincing. Also object-reading or psychometry compels us to postulate that articles handled by people seem to act as vehicles for their psychic influence.

Clearly it is not in the physical properties that we can find this strange character of retaining psychic impressions. A Psychic Ether however which *ex hypothesi* was somewhere between mind and matter might serve to explain hauntings and similar phenomena. The reader interested in a detailed application of the theory of Hauntings should read Prof. H. H. Price's address (*S.P.R. Proc.*, Vol. XLV.).

All that concerns us here is to note that even to account for the phenomenon of ordinary memory we have to postulate some form of endurance for past events—events being of course past psychical experiences.

A Psychic Ether is an attractive theory because it is near enough to our normal conceptions to make it thinkable. We are inevitably prone to think in terms of substances and if the logic of the evidence compels us to reject the brain as the seat of thought then we are grateful for even a nebulous Psychic Ether to function as a vehicle for our psychical nature.

Provided we treat the Psychic Ether strictly as a hypothesis it can aid our thinking about these difficult matters. But there is always the danger of the Psychic Ether becoming substantialized and regarded as having an independent existence. The problem for which it is invoked as an explanation may be summarized as follows:

Material things are supposed to be discrete, and occupy particular positions in space. They are conceived as being linked with other material things in various ways, the most important, of course, being the linkage we call Cause and Effect.

Minds however are supposed to be non-material and to have no position in space except for their relations to bodies.

As we have already noted, this relationship of an immaterial mind to a material body is most mysterious if we insist that mental and material phenomena are fundamentally different. The problem then becomes one of accounting for the empirical fact that there is some relationship between these incompatible phenomena. The assumption is that there is nothing which has the characteristics of both mind and matter.

It is this assumption which the advocates of a Psychic Ether challenge. The Psychic Ether is supposed to be an intermediary existent capable of registering both mental and material stimuli. Thus it can act as a bridge between purely material and mental phenomena.

A Psychic Ether Unnecessary on our Assumptions.—The point to note for our present discussion is that this hypothesis of a Psychic Ether emphasizes the bankruptcy of conventional commonsense theories of mind and matter and the relationship between them. If it is assumed that mind and matter are incompatibles, as they appear to be, then they can only be brought theoretically into relationship by adopting ingenious hypotheses and goodness knows how many new entities will have to be invented in order to preserve the assumptions of commonsense!

From what I have said in previous chapters it will be clear that I prefer to adopt the Mentalist position and regard the whole Universe as a product of mind.

Theoretically therefore I do not require the Psychic Ether hypothesis. All that I need is the basic postulate that Mind transcends the physical body, and that the physical body is also a phenomenal expression of another order of consciousness. If for the purpose of explaining specific phenomenal experiences, including those of Haunting, we need to postulate that mental images possess location, then we may do so without I think introducing new hybrid entities.

It is merely an assumption that an image in my mind ceases to exist after it has passed out of the focus of my attention. Clearly in the case of memory-images this is not the case, otherwise they could not appear again in our minds and be identified as memories. Nor can we assert without reservation that images are originated in our minds.

Anyone who has attempted what is called creative thinking will be aware of the strange invasion of ideas to which his mind becomes subjected. Often indeed it is after effort has ceased and a mood of passivity has intervened that the mind seems to be a little more than a clearing-house for ideas and images which come from who knows whence.

Also the phenomena of telepathy act as a caution against the theory that the mind is a private idea-factory.

In this connection it is perhaps relevant to mention that modern theories of a collective-unconscious imply some independent status for racial memories and ideas.

Some philosophers also postulate that sense-data have an independent existence. It may seem fantastic to imagine patches of colour, sounds and tactile impressions as existing without substantial support. But serious philosophers do not regard such notions as nonsense, nor therefore is the assumption that images may also persist apart from being the content of a particular mind.

We have already noted that this idea while comparatively new to the West is a very ancient doctrine in India, and it has been popularized in Western countries by the Occultists and Theosophists. The term " thought-form " is now in current use by the members of various occult societies.

What is more, these " thought-forms " are, it is claimed, cognizable by clairvoyants.

All these diverse speculations lead to the conclusion that we are surrounded by a psychic atmosphere of thought-forms, images, sense-data (sometimes called sensibilia), and a collective unconscious region of racial memories.

Each of these theories has its special application to particular problems. It is not necessary for our purpose to discuss them in detail. What interests us is the independence which most of these theories concede to psychic elements.

I prefer to avoid conceptions which postulate a sort of substance such as a Psychic Ether as a vehicle for these images or psychical elements.

If the evidence points to the transcendence of mind, as I believe it does, then we need not invent strange entities as carriers of psychic energies.

Why does it seem so queer that a thought-image should persist when we are not thinking it? The reason is, we are accepting almost unconsciously the notion of commonsense that thoughts are ephemeral reflexes of processes in the brain—that in fact the brain is an organ producing thought.

How then could a thought exist without a brain?

Once however this unwarranted assumption is discarded and the full weight of evidence for the transcendence of mind is realized, then we can perceive that thought must exist independently of the embodied mind.

I use the term "embodied mind" but I emphasize that body is not matter. Body is a living aspect of a wider self or consciousness. Mind has location when it thinks in terms of location.

It is my view that the whole phenomenal universe can be likened to a dream and our individual lives are a dream within the greater dream of the creative imagination of the Supreme.

If this is the case for phenomenal experience in general then it applies also to those particular phenomena we call paranormal. A haunted place is a persistent set of images in some consciousness, and its location in our space may simply be accounted for by supposing that the images include the idea of the particular place concerned, say a house or other area. These composite images may be conceived to exist even when features in the district have changed or a house has been structurally altered, or perhaps destroyed.

If in some cases these images may be postulated as actual ingredients of a disembodied consciousness, then such a consciousness can be regarded as being subject to an obsessional dream.

There is a further conception which bears more directly on our present discussion. I will describe it as the doctrine of aspects. By this I mean that nothing phenomenal is complete in itself. This is more than mere interdependence, which implies separate existences in a linked system.

I have already referred to the body as an aspect of our total personality and our search for meaning in living inevitably drives us towards a greater unification of our experience by a realization of deeper relationships. In other words towards an apprehension that particular phenomena are aspects of wider Wholes.

The view I now express is that the Universe as we perceive it is a broken aspect of a deeper layer of conscious existence. According to this conception our day to day experiences would be only a more concrete expression of events occurring on a deeper causal level.

I hope that by now the reader will find a reasonably clear picture building up of the Universe as a living Whole. At the moment however we are considering the phenomena of precognition.

If we assume that the " future " exists " now ", then the problem of precognition resolves itself into an examination of the *modus operandi* of paranormal perception.

This brings into prominence the modern conceptions of the hidden or unconscious regions of the human personality. What therefore is present in one part of consciousness is future for another part, say the waking self. There is nothing at variance in this statement with modern psychological doctrine, for it is a familiar experience for submerged elements to be active in a human consciousness—and therefore they can be considered as present facts—yet to become known to the surface consciousness only at some later date.

Precognition, Causality and Freedom.—However, the baffling, and I think crucial, feature of precognition is not the mere time-sequence, but the outrageous disturbance of our notions of causality, and this in turn gives a jolt to our conception of freedom. On the basis of our ordinary experience we conclude that what we do to-day often causes certain events to happen to-morrow.

For instance, in the example given above, where Mrs. Calder found a house, we would, if it were not for the dream, assume that the actions and decisions made in the normal course of house-hunting would be the antecedent events or causes which eventually determined the finding of the house. But this could not be the case, for the house was seen previously in a dream, even to the trifling detail of the dog in a barrel.

There are indeed cases where houses have been precognized before they were built!

How are we to reconcile this conception that in some form the " future " exists, with our deep faith in the law of cause and effect? As I have already hinted, we can only do so by postulating a new direction, as it were, for the law of causality. Instead of regarding it as a horizontal sequence on a unidimensional line of time, we must conceive the outer place of normal waking experience as largely one of effects. The true causal plane would then be an interior one.

In popular parlance we do not " make our dream-house come true ". The " dream house " is an archetypal reality which the process of living " objectifies ". We of course should not take the word objectify too literally. What we have already said about sense-data or sensibilia will put the reader on his guard against the existence of any objects existing " out there ", precisely as we " see " them.

Whatever may be our views regarding the independence of sensibilia, it is clear on either the Realist or Idealist views that the apparent external objects are mind-constructions, partially so to a Realist philosopher and completely so to an Idealist.

If therefore we can conceive a plane of consciousness where events are in process of maturing, as it were, we have a thinkable basis for understanding precognition which only requires a modification of our commonsense notion of causality.

Nevertheless we must admit that this theory conflicts with the sense of freedom which most of us would insist is an experienced fact of our daily lives. No matter how formidable may be the arguments for determinism, no one lives and acts as though determinism were true.

I am convinced that I can stop writing this very instant and proceed to some other task, or can even just lie in the sun. And such decisions carry with them whole trains of consequences. The determinist, of course, will insist that these decisions are not arbitrary acts of " free will " but that they are governed by other prior decisions and in general all our activities stem from the nature of our character and the environmental conditions which surround us.

What in fact the determinist aims to do is to fit human beings into the mechanistic pattern of causality which on his assumption rules in nature. When therefore psychological behaviour seems at variance with a determinist scheme of things, he can always resort to the plea that failure to predict the course of human behaviour is due to insufficient knowledge. If, he would claim, we knew precisely all the psychological and environmental factors, together with the hereditary history of the individual, we could predict human behaviour as exactly as we do an eclipse of the sun.

Having postulated a mechanistic monism, the determinist on his own assumption cannot tolerate exceptions, consequently he is unmoved even if human beings act as though they were free, and although legal and moral codes are based on the ability of people to choose.

This is one more example of the power of background-assumptions regarding the nature of the Universe.

If on general principles it is accepted that the Universe is a product of mechanistic forces, then such an assumption assumes the power of a dogma and governs all our interpretations of life.

My background assumptions however are not mechanistic but are conceived in terms of life and organism. We are therefore not committed to pursue the will-o'-the-wisp of seeking the detailed factors which would reduce human behaviour to a mechanistic pattern. But we need not go to the opposite extreme of denying mechanistic sequences, although I would prefer to call these habit-patterns.

Actually all behaviour when observed as an external phenomenon seems determined. Even human beings when studied as systems of conditioned reflexes after the model of Pavlov's researches seem little more than adaptive mechanisms.

Fortunately however we have access to another type of investigation, namely, that provided by introspection. Naturally the doctrinaire behaviourist disparages this mode of examining human nature.

Psychology in the western sense is very young, and is only just emerging into respectability. There is therefore an earnest effort to make psychology into a science. Consequently, as with all parvenues in polite society, the emphasis is on correct behaviour, and the psychologist tends to discard introspection as unscientific and instead copies the methods of science by studying the human being from without by means of instrumental gadgets and statistical analysis. This type of approach to the study of the human psyche can result only in superficial knowledge.

There is sure eventually to be a swing away from this modern fashion, and we may then not disdain to learn something from certain Eastern techniques for self-exploration. What we are now considering however is the relationship of human freedom to the facts of precognition.

It is an undoubted fact of introspection that we *feel* free. Is this an illusion? The determinist would say, yes. We must admit that the determinist case is a strong one. Often when we think we are free it can be demonstrated that our conduct is determined by pre-existing conditions and behaviour-habits.

It is true therefore that we cannot accept our sense of freedom at its face value. An example of illusory freedom is provided by post-hypnotic suggestion.

For instance, a person under hypnosis is told to perform a certain act after awaking, say, open a cupboard and remove an article. The subject when awakened does not remember the hypnotic suggestion, yet carries out the order given. When asked why he did so, it is not unusual for some quite reasonable explanation to be given. But everyone present knows this to be a fictitious reason; in other words a rationalization. The same process of rationalization occurs in the justification of behaviour which is due to complexes and subconscious motivation.

Yet in all these cases the person has a belief in his freedom of choice. Even when after the event the evidence points conclusively to the fact that the circumstances prior to a particular act made that act inevitable, we still feel we could have chosen otherwise. Almost every act can be traced to antecedent environmental or psychological conditions, and when hereditary and subconscious influences are added there seems little scope for freedom. This becomes even more apparent in modern complex societies which impose codes, customs and occupational patterns.

Confronted by this vast pressure of determining causes what do we mean by freedom?

We certainly do not mean arbitrary or motiveless behaviour. Our actions are governed by motive, but provided we can choose our motives we can claim to have freedom. The point is, what determines our motives, and here the determinist repeats his arguments to prove that even our motives are determined by the causal factors of our environment. But if the determinist wins his argument he leaves us unconvinced.

If we are creatures whose every act and thought are only the product of mechanistic laws, how can we explain the fact that we feel free? Our conviction that we are free to choose is a fundamental fact in our life, and it is indeed curious that we should feel free when so much evidence seems to point to the reverse. If the universe were as the determinist supposes, I would suggest that the psychological sense of freedom could not arise.

It may be true that for large portions of our lives we are in the grip of external and internal pressures which make us creatures of habit, living in predetermined grooves. But we know beyond the need for argument that somewhere within the core of our being there is a power of free choice. That in short, there is an unpredictable element in human nature.

It is my view that the sense of freedom derives from the ultimate nature of the living Whole we call the Universe. Absolute freedom belongs only to the Whole in which we live and have our being. So, while we are bound in our pursuit of limited purposes, we are free because we participate in the Infinite. In Bergson's phrase, " We are liberable rather than liberated."

It is clear that if we were wholly determined it would be easier to account for precognition. Or at any rate we should not so resent the fact of precognition.

What disturbs us about seeing the future is the uneasy feeling that the prediction will be fulfilled in spite of anything we can do about it!

Many cases of precognition undoubtedly do point to this conclusion. But in other cases the event foreseen has been avoided by taking appropriate action. For instance, in a case which Flammarion quotes, a mother distinctly heard an " inner voice " warning her against allowing her little girl to play on a certain strip of land. The voice said: " Send for her at once or something frightful will happen to her!" The child was recalled, and " it was precisely at that point that the locomotive and the tender ran off the track, breaking the walls and crashing against the very rocks on which the child was accustomed to go and sit ". Camille Flammarion, *Death and Its Mystery, Before Death*, p. 306.

However, warnings and unfulfilled predictions are not genuine precognitions, although it will be noted that even a warning, to be justified, must relate to some future event. Admittedly, the mother in the above case did not foresee the train accident, nevertheless it was this accident which in some sense caused the " inner voice " to give the warning.

The problem of genuine precognition however is to reconcile it with our belief that the future does not exist until we create it by our actions in the present. The foreseeing of future events in the lives of persons is, I think, more explicable than that of precognizing public events such as earthquakes and train accidents. These accidents of course often involve persons, but there is an impersonal element in their occurrence which makes it hard to understand how they can be cognized before they happen.

In the case of foreseeing events in a person's future we may invoke two hypotheses. Firstly, we can assume that although our lives are not entirely determined, we are nevertheless under influences which form a general pattern and compel a certain future. The element of compulsion or destiny would differ greatly between individuals. Some would live according to stereotyped patterns, easy to foresee. In others, the future would be less certainly determined, creative intrusions perhaps altering or cancelling a future which might otherwise have been inevitable.

This view can be reconciled with our commonsense conception if we are prepared to accept a doctrine of pre-existence which makes our present life only one of a linked chain.

In other words some events in our future are inescapable, others just possibilities, while a large number are perhaps only probabilities.

This is more or less what commonsense assumes, and the doctrine of multi-existences merely explains why some events in the future must be experienced. We would still need to supplement this hypothesis with the conception of the independent status of thought-images which we have already discussed.

Assuming these postulates we could set about explaining precognition of events in a personal life somewhat as follows: Firstly, we conceive the individual as incarnating, surrounded as it were by an " atmosphere " of thought-images, many the result of previous existences. Secondly, some of these images exercise a compulsive effect on the individual's present experiences. Thirdly, some of these image-forms may be cognized or may become revealed in dreams.

The images, strictly speaking, are " out of time ", but may be conceived to represent a simultaneous pattern which the individual experiences sequentially. To what extent these images may be changed or erased need not be considered, as our present concern is to account for those cases where a " future " event is cognized in the present.

If we conceive the individual as existing on another plane of consciousness, expressing himself in a medium of thought-images, then this region of consciousness may well be one of causality and that of the normal waking state largely one of effects.

An individual's life-span therefore may be considered as the unrolling of an inner pattern in the deeper strata of consciousness.

The Precognition of Public Events.—But although these principles might, if expounded in more detail, provide a basis for explaining some cases of precognition in personal futures, how could they apply to the prevision of impersonal events?

Are we to suppose that earthquakes, sinking ships, train derailments, fires and other similar physical happenings, exist on some inner plane as eternal events?

The records of precognition show that events of this type are foreseen, and this being the case I am afraid we must follow the logic of the data and concede that such events must have some status at the time they are cognized.

Our imagination baulks at this idea because physical things seem so solid and permanent, and to suppose them as existing elsewhere than outside in an external space seems nonsense.

But if we assume that the Universe is a mind-creation, and indeed is not unlike a dream, then we can conceive all things as expressions of mind on various levels.

This is obviously the case with technological objects such as trains, ships and the whole range of man-made things. We would usually describe these things as a product of man's creativeness. That is to say they first existed as mental structures.

The words we are compelled to use are a product of normal sensory experience and inevitably arouse a concrete imagery. What however we have already discussed regarding the independence of sensibilia will no doubt indicate sufficiently that whatever exists independently of our consciousness is entirely different from the sensory images we call objects.

Similarly any sphere of eternal forms might better be regarded as a Cosmic shorthand, needing to be translated into the forms necessary for individualized consciousness. In terms of phenomenal existence there may be many degrees between the eternal shorthand and its eventual presentation we call (say) " bridge ". At some intermediary level the bridge may well be almost an image of the ultimate physical bridge.

In order to understand precognition of, say, the collapse of a bridge we would need to postulate that the complete history of the bridge was inherent in its foundation idea. Consequently on the interior plane on which it is paranormally cognized its beginning and end are perceived as an ever-present fact. I do not know what merit there may be in these speculations, but it seems to me that the facts of precognition do at least require that we conceive future events as having some type of existence in the present.

Any technological construction, we may assume, is a sequential manifestation of an archetypal form. The idea obviously must precede the construction. A locomotive, for instance, is first conceived. Then follow blue prints, specifications, assembly of material and so on until there emerges the completed structure. All these processes however can be regarded as merely the disclosure of a mental concept. Up to this point we have said little more than is usually accepted. But we will press further than commonsense notions and suggest that the locomotive existed in a realm of ideas prior to its becoming part of the conscious awareness of any man. This may seem rather a fantastic assumption, but we are driven to unusual theories when faced with such topsy-turvy facts.

If the phenomena of telepathy and memory require us to postulate an independent status for ideas, then it becomes logical to concede a similar independence to the ideas of technological objects.

We may even conceive the whole pattern of our civilization as existing on some inner plane of consciousness. The imagination of a Jules Verne therefore might have been the result of a psychic contact with this " eternal pattern in the sky ".

It is not however to be supposed that ideas exist in the form of a cosmic picture gallery, although the conception of an " Eternal Now ", or Absolute, implies that phenomenal appearances are aspects of a non-temporal reality.

For practical purposes we seem to be creating something new. Yet if our view of the Absolute is valid, then originality is not creativeness in the strict sense of the word. More appropriately might it be described as a process whereby definition is given to some of the infinite possibilities and eternal ideas of the Absolute.

From our point of view there is trial and error, change and creative effort; but what really is occurring is a process of actualization of archetypal ideas.

On this view it is always theoretically possible for us to perceive what is for us the " future ".

The application of the above general principles to the actual facts of precognition would involve us in an exhaustive study of the evidence, which is beyond the scope of our present purpose.

In broad outline however we may summarize by saying:
1. That the " future " must have some existent status in the present, i.e., at the time it was cognized.
2. I therefore conclude the existence of a realm of ideas in process of manifesting.
3. This view does not necessarily mean determinism. Rather can we conceive the realm of ideas as our true " creative or causal " sphere of consciousness. If therefore some of these ideas are of a type which renders their manifestation inevitable, they are *our* ideas either individually or collectively.
4. An individual's life may exist as a complete pattern to be worked out sequentially in the time-sequence of our sensory awareness.
5. Public events including volcanic disturbances, train derailment and similar incidents, which have been frequently foreseen, must be conceived to take place in the causal world above mentioned.
6. Technological constructions, such as trains, ships and bridges exist in some ideological form including their complete history as it is subsequently revealed to our exterior consciousness.
7. The defects in technological structures which ultimately cause what we call " accidents " are inherent in the intermediate design which translates an archetypal form in its process towards actualization, and therefore theoretically can be foreseen.

The general key to guide us in our understanding of precognition is the conception that our physical sphere of consciousness is chiefly one of effects, the real causal plane being an interior one.

I am fully conscious of the inadequacies of the above exposition, but my aim has been to offend as little as possible against our commonsense notions while at the same time providing some thinkable basis for understanding the baffling facts of precognition.

CHAPTER XIV

THE INFLUENCE OF MIND ON PHYSICAL THINGS

" Strange and true, that paradox hard I give, objects gross and the unseen are one."

WALT WHITMAN.

Modern Experiments in Psychokinesis.—In my book, *The Superphysical*, I devoted a chapter to the consideration of the evidence for those phenomena usually called Materialization and Telekinesis.

The belief that objects may be moved in some supernormal manner is one that is persistent and widespread. In fact, reports of hauntings and poltergeist phenomena are by now almost commonplace.

It is not my intention to repeat what I have said elsewhere. The evidence is on record and is continuing to accumulate. The time has long passed when these phenomena can be brusquely dismissed as being due to mal-observation, fraud or superstition. I must indeed emphasize that those who have not studied the evidence, or have not personally experimented, are unqualified to express an opinion, no matter how eminent they may be in other fields of knowledge.

In recent years special attention has been devoted to a study of this phase of supernormal phenomena.

The term now in current use is psychokinesis or P.K.

Experimental examination of these phenomena is comparatively new, in spite of the long history of their occurrence. Perhaps among some races they occurred more frequently. However it is not the mood of our generation to take these facts for granted, especially when they cannot be fitted into the frame of prevailing assumptions.

The earliest consistent experiments of which I am aware are those which were conducted by Dr. Rhine of Duke University, somewhere about 1934, and eventually published in 1943. Since then, accounts of other experiments have been published, notably those of Dr. R. H. Thouless, *Proc. S.P.R.*, XLVII, 1945, pp. 277-81, and more recently Dr. Thouless has given a further account of experiments under the title, "Report on an Experiment in Psychokinesis with Dice and a Discussion on Psychological Factors Favouring Success." (*Proc.* XLIX, 1951, pp. 107-130.)

We are sure to hear a great deal more about these and other types of experiments, for their significance is very great. The experiments so far have been conducted with dice and coins in an effort to influence the falls in accordance with the intention or willing of the thrower. Mechanical devices have also been constructed to avoid unconscious muscular intervention, and needless to say every ingenuity is exercised to eliminate all normal interference and so leave direct mental influence as the only explanation. The results are then tabulated and subjected to the normal mathematical procedures to determine the odds against chance coincidence.

I should however here interpolate that as far as the experimental evidence has so far proceeded there is a possibility that some of the P.K. results could perhaps be interpreted as examples of precognition rather than of psychokinesis. That is to say, it could be argued that the dice-thrower paranormally cognized the future positions of the dice faces, and did not mentally influence their falls.

It is indeed extraordinarily difficult to eliminate the possibility of precognition in P.K. experiments. We must bear in mind that once a particular phenomenon has been demonstrated to occur, it is sound scientific practice to apply the accepted hypothesis to the utmost limit. For instance, telepathy is now the most generally accepted type of Psi phenomenon, consequently the aim is to press the telepathic hypothesis as an explanation until its limits become known by experiment.

Similarly, precognition was recognized experimentally prior to psychokinesis, therefore it is quite natural that the precognitive hypothesis should be invoked as an explanation of some P.K. experiments. The reader who is interested in the technical problems of this research should refer to an article by C. W. K. Mundle entitled, " The Experimental Evidence for P.K. and Precognition," *S.P.R. Proc.*, Vol. XLIV, pp. 61-78, July, 1950.

Considerable ingenuity is being devoted to the devising of experiments which will succeed in isolating the effects of precognition and so demonstrate the occurrence of P.K.

However, apart from these specialized lines of research there is a wide range of paranormal phenomena which imply the influence of Mind over material objects. Poltergeist phenomena are instances of these.

Psychometry.—But I make particular reference to the phenomenon popularly called psychometry or object-reading.

I have experimented with a number of sensitives, and they all declare that articles touched by people carry the impress of their psychic influence. The article in fact seems essential to enable the sensitive supernormally to cognize events in a person's life. When psychometrizing an article a sensitive is not usually in a trance, or hypnotized. The article may be held in the hand, placed against the forehead, or in some cases held in the region of the solar plexus.

In successful experiments the history of the article may be given, together with evidential character-delineations of the owner, and incidents in his life. Still more strange is the fact that a good sensitive is not confused by the different contacts to which an article may have been subjected. In some manner the article enables the sensitive to distinguish a variety of impressions relating to different people who at various stages have impressed the article.

Sensitives who are gifted with this faculty have their own way of describing their sensations and speak of the " fluids " or " magnetisms " of objects and these " magnetisms " or " fluids " are supposed to correspond with those of the people who have owned or contacted the article. It seems possible to detect these different " magnetisms " almost as a radio receiver selects the various wave-lengths.

We of course must not take these descriptions literally. Rather are they an effort to express the psychological sensations which arise from psychometrizing an article. Nothing that is known about the physical constitution of objects could justify the assumption that they contain " magnetisms " or " fluids " which are capable of receiving psychic impressions.

Nevertheless, an article does seem to be necessary in order to evoke the psychic faculty, and in some way to place the sensitive *en rapport* with the person or situation to be cognized.

The ideal type of experiment for demonstrating psychometry is one in which those participating have no knowledge concerning the article given to the senstitive, thus eliminating telepathy between sitters and sensitive.

A good example of psychometry is given in S.P.R. Journal, Vol. XXI, p. 219, and quoted in *The Superphysical*, pp. 126-7. It relates to an experiment by Dr. Pagenstecher with the medium Senora Maria Reyes de Z. In this experiment Senora Z. merely by holding a sealed envelope derived information unknown to all present until after the sitting, when the envelope was opened and disclosed a hastily written note which was found in a bottle picked up off the coast of the Azores. Enquiries led to the conclusion that the note was written by a man who disappeared in 1916 and was believed to have perished when the *Lusitania* was sunk. Senora Z. gave a description of the man, including a scar over the left eyebrow.

If it were my purpose to marshal the evidence I could from my own experience cite many examples where the article submitted to a sensitive seemed to be the determining factor which evoked the psychic faculty. Assuming therefore that physical objects are focal points for psychic influences, what hypothesis can we adopt to explain their function?

In *The Superphysical* I discussed three hypotheses. I will repeat them here because I wish to add some further views.

The hypotheses are:
1. That objects possess no occult characteristics. The sensitive obtains his knowledge from an article because his senses are more acute or are in a state of hyperaesthesia.
2. That objects may retain photographically, so to speak, the impress of events.

3. That objects, though impressible by psychic energies, are not the source of the visions, but serve to place the sensitive *en rapport* with the event or the persons who have contacted the article.

The first two hypotheses I rule out for reasons which I have already given in *The Superphysical*.

The third hypothesis is the one which most closely fits the facts. Sensitives derive information by means of objects, but often the sensitive cognizes events in which the article has not participated. As, for instance, when Dr. Osty's sensitive, Mme. Morel, traced the body of an old man who had disappeared in the estates of Baron Joubert and could not be found in spite of long and active search. The sensitive cognized the location of the body by means of a scarf belonging to the old man. We here note that the scarf which was given to Mme. Morel was " taken from a wardrobe and not from the corpse ". *Supernormal Faculties in Man*, pp. 104-9.

This case therefore disposes of any theory which implies that articles are impressed in some photographic manner. Nevertheless physical objects are in some way carriers of psychic impressions, and the latest P.K. experiments are designed to prove that mind can influence the movements of objects.

Why Psychokinesis Seems Unbelievable.—The statement that thought, without normal means of contact, can influence the movements of physical things startles the plain man into a robust protest against such an absurd notion.

Once again we find ideas derived from sense-impressions fighting against knowledge of the Universe derived by other means. It appears so obvious that physical objects are solid, dead, substantial things which exist " out there " independently of anything we may think about them.

Accepting this world of sense-objects at its face value, it seems preposterous to the point of lunacy to suppose that our thoughts can have the slightest effect on the way in which dice fall, except of course by manual or other physical means. And it seems still more incredible to suppose that an article can retain psychical impressions.

Should we however be forced by the evidence to accept psychokinesis, our normal tendency is to strive for some explanation as near as possible to commonsense conceptions.

In *The Superphysical* I attempted an explanation, using mostly mechanistic terms.

Naturally, we first turn our attention to an examination of the nature of physical objects in an effort to detect if there is anything in so-called Matter itself which could account for its being influenced by thought.

Immediately we are impressed by the fact that the atom is for the most part empty space, in which the electrons occupy relatively about as much space as would a few grains of dust in a cathedral.

Seizing upon this fact, we feel we may have a clue to understand the influence of thought on matter and we ask whether this " vast " space within the atom is empty after all.

The next step along this line of thought is to postulate that the intra-atomic space may be filled with an ether or medium for electronic waves of some kind which might be modifiable by thought.

In other words, we conceive that the space within particular physical objects may not be undifferentiated, as ordinary conceptions usually suppose.

We then proceed to build up an hypothesis in terms of vibrations, and suppose that objects possess a characteristic vibration which can be affected by external stimuli. On such premises we can make psychometry thinkable without unduly departing from mechanistic terms.

We can suppose that an article is a form within which certain vibrations occur in the intra-atomic spaces which comprise the article. These vibrations, we may assume, can synchronize and cause responses in the human body, and particularly in the bodies of those people we call sensitives. The sensitive then interprets these vibrations in terms of thoughts and events.

By this means a sensitive could be put in touch with events which have been " experienced " by the article. Also on the assumption that past and future events have some independent status, we can suppose that the vibrating structure of the article can connect the sensitive with these events. Thus the sensitive does not derive information from the article but by means of it.

It will be noted that this conception of a sort of etheric structure within material substances is virtually the psychic ether hypothesis which I discussed in the last chapter. I do not wish to deprecate any view or hypothesis which aids our thinking, but it is my present opinion that this approach is superficial, and whatever appeal it may have is due to the fact that it preserves a mechanistic way of thinking about paranormal phenomena. Also, such theories carry the implication of a basic and irreducible duality of mind and matter. Thus we are forced to seek for some bridge between these two incompatibles. Hence the invention of a psychic ether, or, if we are not prepared to go so far, we concentrate on the least material aspects of matter and seek an explanation in terms of vibrations and energy-potentials. However, if we do persist in probing what we take to be material substance, we find it dissolves into an abstraction, or in the words of Professor Whitehead, " The Atom is transforming itself into an Organism." *Science and the Modern World*, p. 149.

In seeking to solve the mystery of matter we come face to face with Mind; thus extremes meet. This is what we should expect if the Universe is a thought-creation. The problem of psychokinesis is not one of mind influencing matter, but is one which concerns the relationship between different orders of mind.

Psychokinesis within the Body.—We may take as an example the mystery of how our thoughts affect the movements of our bodies. I describe it as a mystery because that is precisely what it is on mechanistic principles.

We normally regard the body as being governed by physical, chemical and electrical causal sequences. Perception, we suppose, starts with an external stimulus which affects one or other of the sense-organs. The external impulse is conducted by the afferent nerves to specialized centres in the cerebral cortex which can be likened to a telephone exchange switching the nerve impulses to another set of nerves called efferent, which discharge their energy to various muscles, tissues and organs. Thus there is completed a circuit describable in mechanistic terms, except for a strange and unaccountable break in the mechanical linkage. All goes well, mechanically speaking, until in the brain the material sequence suffers the intrusion of a mental event. This is indeed a mystery on the assumption that up to this point every link in the chain has been physical.

Then a further mystery occurs when the outward efferent impulses are controlled by a volition.

So we are posed the problem of how an intangible thought or volition can affect the purely physical, chemical and electrical sequences?

I decide to raise my arm, and instantly it moves in obedience to my will! In other words, we have an example of psychokinesis, but it excites in us no sense of wonder. Yet it should do so if we accept the purely material sequences of the physiology text-books.

It is altogether inexplicable within the limits of classical theory that a thought should move my arm. And of course it is equally inexplicable that a thought or volition should move or influence the behaviour of an object outside my body.

The point to note however is that we have two inexplicable phenomena, one which we accept as commonplace, and the other which provokes our incredulity.

But it is most probable that psychokinesis in the paranormal sense may be only a special example of a more general phenomenon. Or perhaps it might be more accurate to say that what we regard as normal, viz., the psychokinesis within our bodies, may be the specialized expressions of more generalized aspects of the same influence. Moreover there are good reasons for supposing that those aspects of consciousness we describe as paranormal are actually only specialized manifestations of consciousness in general. Having evolved particular organs and specific behaviour-patterns, consciousness has lost its diffused character and has become canalized through the focusing points we call organs. Consequently we might expect to find a wider incidence of telepathy and other Psi phenomena among primitive people and animals, and there is some evidence that this is the case.

Analogous Processes Regarded as Normal.—Psychokinesis therefore can be regarded as normal in a generalized sense, but is classified as paranormal in those cases where exosomatic effects occur, i.e., movements of objects external to the body.

A most interesting application of a theory along the above lines has been developed by R. H. Thouless and B. P. Wiesner, *S.P.R. Proc.* Vol. XLVIII, Dec., 1947, pp. 177-196.

Also Dr. Geley in his book, *Clairvoyance and Materialization*, has given lucid expression to the theory that there are normal processes in nature which are analogous to those phenomena of the seance room usually called materializations. The term materialization refers to manifestations of form-building, generally supposed to be due to an extrusion of a substance from the medium's body which possesses ideoplastic properties. This makes it capable of assuming a variety of forms. The forms may become visible and be photographed; also they can develop an apparent materiality dense enough to affect the movement of ordinary objects, and there is evidence to show that a complete manifestation of the human form sometimes occurs.

In *The Superphysical* I reviewed the evidence for this type of phenomena, and since this book was written I have found further evidence, but the collection of data must cease somewhere, and personally I am now prepared to accept the occasional occurrence of materializations as a fact, and must endeavour to assimilate these facts into my philosophy for living to the best of my ability. The bibliography at the end of this volume will provide some useful references for the reader who has not studied the subject.

In the meantime research is continuing, and although experiments with dice may seem trivial, it should be remembered that Psychical Research Societies are endeavouring to present the evidence in a form acceptable to those trained in scientific methods. This implies the development of controlled experiments and although the phenomena obtained under such test conditions are usually minor in character, the research-worker prefers to demonstrate even a trivial paranormal event under controlled conditions rather than rely on the much richer data which spontaneous cases provide. But it should be strongly emphasized that it was the multiplicity of spontaneous cases which originally drew attention to the subject. In fact, most psychical researchers know in their hearts that paranormal phenomena occur, otherwise it is inconceivable they would devote so much of their time to investigation.

Psychical research journals are often very dull reading because of the effort to present proof to those who are recalcitrant and on *a priori* grounds have already decided that paranormal phenomena cannot occur.

A useful approach, I suggest, to the study of paranormal physical phenomena is to realize that similar processes occur in nature. As Dr. Geley pointed out, we have analogous processes " in the histolysis of some insects in the chrysalis, their organism being partly reduced to an amorphous magma and then reorganized into new forms ". He cites six natural processes which are similar to those of materialization in the seance room, his final example being "with normal generation, the highly complex organism developing from simple protoplasm emanating in the one case from the medium and in the other from that of the ovum . . .", pp. 180-81.

I have discussed this and other aspects of materialization in my previous book. All that concerns us here is to consider the general implications which follow from the fact of psychokinesis. The point I again stress is that psychokinesis presents a problem whether we regard it as normal—as in the movements of our own bodies—or as paranormal, as when objects outside our bodies are moved by the psychological processes of thought or volition.

The Duality of Incompatibles.—The essential nature of this problem is the ancient one of how to bridge the gap between matter as ordinarily conceived, and mind.

This problem does not arise for those who accept monism as true. As we have seen in previous chapters, monism has its own special problems, but a relationship between incompatibles is not one of them. At least in theory we have a better basis for explaining psychokinesis if we assume that it is a phenomenon concerning the relationships between different orders of life-functioning, and not one of life and matter.

Clearly our bodies are organic wholes, and not just combinations of carbon, oxygen, hydrogen, nitrogen, sulphur, phosphorus, etc.

These chemical ingredients may seem to us material enough, nevertheless the body as a whole is a living entity. In fact it represents *some order of mind*.

Consequently it is theoretically to be expected that it can be affected by other types of mental functioning. And of course, empirically, we know this to be the case.

We can therefore proceed to account for the relationship between our mind and body in psychological terms instead of having to resolve the puzzle of a marriage between the living and the dead.

Admittedly the body can still be regarded as in the main an automatism, but it is not the automatism of a machine. Rather is it an organism governed by habit. And habits, being products of life-functioning, can be changed, and what is more, changed by mental means! Metaphorically speaking we can " talk " to our bodies, and they will understand the right " language ". This " language " is usually in terms of emotional impulses, and to reach the deeper habit-patterns it is often necessary to get rid of the rational layer of consciousness by means of hypnosis or reverie techniques. Those who are familiar with the Indian Hatha Yoga system, whereby many ordinarily automatic bodily functions may be altered, will be aware of the extraordinary power which can be obtained over the body. Some of the fakirs are able at will to produce a cessation of breathing, prevent bleeding though the body be pierced with knives, and arrest the heart's motion, thereby simulating a bodily state indistinguishable from death. See, for example, Dr. Hereward Carrington's account of the phenomena of the fakirs, Rahmen Bey, Tarak Bey, and Hamid Bey in *The Story* of *Psychic Science*, pp. 183-91, also *A Search in Secret Egypt*, by Paul Brunton.

These phenomena are not on our principles basically mysterious in the sense that they are examples of Mind influencing Matter. What we are witnessing is the capacity of an individual to become *en rapport* with lower orders of life within the bodily organisms.

The impulses, starting with volitions in the conscious mind, become translated into " orders " which modify the normal automatisms of the cells and organs.

The methods practised to achieve these results do not concern us here. Our present need is to make psychokinesis thinkable by removing a false conception regarding the nature of the phenomenon. The relationship we have with our own bodies is admittedly a special and intimate one. But in the light of our discussion in previous chapters, where matter is shown to be an abstraction based on sense impressions, we have at least removed a barrier to our understanding of how mind can influence external objects.

The key to the problem is to realize that the whole phenomenal realm is a form of mind-expression. The word mind, unfortunately, has too narrow an association with our normal rational thinking.

Mind in the abstract however can be conceived as a general term for many levels of conscious functioning. The forms we call minerals seem devoid of life or consciousness, but this appearance is due to our accepting sense-impressions at their face value.

We may say, paradoxically, that materiality is a form of life. It can be regarded as a principle of resistance which enables form-building. But fundamentally matter arises as a thought of limitation in the cosmic whole. It is the means whereby the abstract infinity becomes expressed in the appearance of diversity, and concreteness. On this view all phenomenal objects are, in the broadest sense of the word, mind-objects. Therefore they can be influenced by mind.

These conclusions, which are based on deductive reasoning, admittedly will not carry the same conviction as the results of induction. However I think it can be claimed with some justification that the facts of psychokinesis and other allied paranormal phenomena do lend evidential support to a monistic conception of a living Whole.

From this point of view it matters little whether we regard a mineral as a sleeping form of life or man as an awakened mineral. As we have said previously, if we probe matter deeply enough we find a life behaviour-pattern.

Psychokinesis therefore is no longer a theoretical impossibility, as it must be on conventional views.

It is always theoretically possible to establish a relationship with those orders of mind which we regard as external objects. This of course may be regarded as a return to a primitive animism, when all objects were supposed to have souls. Perhaps, however, primitive people had intuitive contacts with nature which enabled them to sense the hidden life in things we regard as dead.

I should interpolate here that the above conception that things are forms of life is not necessarily an expression of philosophical Idealism. In fact it can be regarded as Realism to the extent that it implies the independence of sense-data. That is to say, independent of ourselves as particular observers. The external world is one which is the product of a collective mind, and therefore is independent of any individual mind. Nevertheless, it is a mind-phenomenon and not the product of an alien and incomprehensible dead substance.

What I have to say in the concluding chapters will give further point to the above statement. In this chapter however my aim has been to provide a basis for understanding the experimental phenomena of psychokinesis. These phenomena are inexplicable largely because we have bifurcated the universe into two irreconcilable realities, one of which is governed by an iron law of mechanical causation, and the other by psychological or as it is sometimes called, teleological causation. We cannot rest content with this duality, and the evidence from many fields shows that it is the mechanical concepts which must be scrapped.

Universal Sensitivity.—As we study paranormal phenomena our conviction grows that classical and conventional views of the Universe, based on sense impressions, are almost certainly fallacious in important respects.

If these facts are to be accommodated within the frame of our general views it is clear that it is the frame which will have to be altered and not the facts. For instance, in our efforts to understand the phenomena of psychokinesis, the abstract conception of dead matter is not our only obstacle. Although we discard the dualist assumption, there are other notions based on abstractions and derived from appearances, which must be revised. One in particular has relevance for the subject-matter of this chapter.

Even granting that things are thoughts, we still regard them as being isolated concrete phenomena. Chairs, pens, trees, animals and so on are viewed as independent realities separated in space. We suppose they can be understood and described in their lonely separation without regard to their relations with other things.

The idea of the separateness of things creates many difficulties when we come to explain the action of one thing on another. We have already noted that the observed relations we call cause and effect are particularly difficult to understand if things are *really* separate. Similarly the notion of spatial isolation clogs our efforts to understand psychokinesis. Accepting the appearance of spatial separateness at its face value, we necessarily create the need to invent notions of " force " and other connective influences to account for the empirical evidence that things act on one another, as for instance in the orderly motions of the planets.

I have previously quoted Professor Whitehead's strong criticism of the inherent separateness of things which he calls the Fallacy of Misplaced Concreteness, but I do so again because his views are particularly relevant to psychokinesis. To continue in his words: " To say that a bit of matter has *simple location* means that, in expressing its spatio-temporal relations, it is adequate to state that it is where it is, in a definite finite region of space, and throughout a definite finite duration of time, apart from any essential reference of the relations of that bit of matter to other regions of space and to other durations of time."

This notion he rejects: " I shall argue that among the primary elements of nature as apprehended in our immediate experience, *there is no element whatever which possesses this character of simple location.*" (My italics.) *Science and the Modern World*, p. 72.

Whitehead, as we have already noted, develops a philosophy of Organism in which everything in the universe is connected with everything else because of an inherent sensitiveness. No thing can be defined apart from its relationships with other things. These relationships therefore may be considered as constituting its nature.

But the connectiveness of things lies deeper than a set of external relationships. The relationships are inherent because they belong to an organic process, and manifest the principle we have expressed elsewhere as particulars within a Whole. Whitehead expresses himself in terms reminiscent of Plato in his exposition of a theory of Eternal Objects.

It would take us beyond the scope of our subject to pursue Whitehead's ideas further. In any case, much of his writing is not easy reading because of his unusual terminology.

His term, " Prehension ", I think, gives the key to an understanding of the organic unity of things.

He attaches great importance to a passage from Francis Bacon's " *Natural History* " which states, " It is certain that all bodies whatsoever, though they have no sense, yet they have perception . . ."

He construes " perception " as meaning taking account of the essential character of the thing perceived, and for this not necessarily cognitive awareness, he uses the term " Prehension ". Prehension is akin to feeling, which is a kind of universal sensitiveness which links the whole of phenomenal existences.

The image which arises as I read Whitehead is that of a sea of psychological sensitiveness which permeates and makes all things prehend or take note of everything else. Fundamentally this arises because the Universe is an organic process, therefore, the Whole ingresses into the spatio-temporal flux.

I may be wrong, but it seems to me that a philosophy such as Whitehead's could provide a number of basic conceptions for making psychokinesis thinkable: at any rate it is a corrective to mechanistic views and relieves us of the necessity for inventing connective agencies in order to account for the influence at a distance which both animate and inanimate existences exert on one another.

As I have said previously, it is our background set of assumptions which is in need of revision.

CHAPTER XV

MYSTICISM AND ALLIED STATES

"You ask, how can we know the Infinite? I answer, not by reason. It is the office of reason to distinguish and define. The Infinite, therefore, cannot be ranked among its objects. You can only apprehend the Infinite by a faculty superior to reason by entering into a state in which you are your finite self no longer—in which the divine essence is communicated to you. This is ecstasy. It is the liberation of your mind from its finite consciousness."

PLOTINUS, Letter to Flaccus.
Quoted from DR. BUCKE: *Cosmic Consciousness*.

"But these feelings are incommunicable. We have no words to express a thousand distinctions clear to the spiritual sense. If I tell of my exaltation to another, who has not felt this himself, it is explicable to that person as the joy in perfect health, and he translates into lower terms what is the speech of the gods to men."

A. E., *The Candle of Vision*, pp. 113-4: "Intuition."

Direct Apprehension.—It will be widely agreed that a great deal of what we accept as true is not due to a prior chain of reasoning. In fact, often, the reasoning only succeeds in making clear something which we apprehended in the first place. What we take for granted is usually more significant than our reasoned conclusions. Reasoning may lead to new apprehensions which in turn become postulates for further chains of reasoning. But at each stage there is a sort of intuitive leap and the realm of the self-evident has become enlarged.

In Chapter 12, under the sub-heading, "Temperament and Philosophy", I warned the reader of my bias. My espousal of a particular philosophy or viewpoint is the final result of innumerable inferences, acceptances, rejections and long brooding on the evidence, combined with certain experiences. Thus a general "response-pattern" has arisen which determines the premises which for me seem self-evident, although they may not be so to the reader. Conscious effort to understand has of course preceded the ultimate acceptance, but now a certain viewpoint arises almost unconsciously, and awakens a peculiar response. It is as though an inner voice said, " You are on the right road and need not be unduly troubled if the map is badly drawn and includes a few irrelevant and even misleading features ".

This total response of a personality to a particular viewpoint is a psychological phenomenon of fundamental significance. The causes which are usually cited to account for this are well known. Heading the list is " wishful-thinking ", but it is not difficult to avoid this, or at least to be aware of its influence. But even wishful-thinking is not necessarily wrong thinking. The " wish " itself may be a significant pointer to a truth. Then, of course, we know how powerful is the effect of early teaching, prestige-suggestion and egoistic identification with views towards which we adopt a possessive attitude. I think once we are alerted to the dangers, most of us feel capable of detecting our bias.

Still more deeply there is the basic psycho-physical type to which we belong, such as whether we are predominantly introvert or extravert.

All these and many other personality-patterns largely determine our response to and acceptance of particular philosophies and views of life.

Later, I shall have something to say about psychological types in relation to certain disciplines, but my point here is that although reasoning of necessity must ultimately be traced back to some set of postulates which seem self-evident to the reasoner, the selection of these postulates is determined by fundamental personality-responses.

Reason is dependent on words, and these are symbols representing experience at various levels. On the simplest levels of sense-experience words mostly represent things seen, heard, smelt, tasted, or touched, and the movements of these things; that is, nouns and verbs. It is a long journey in the history of thought before words are coined to represent abstract truths. However, words expressing abstract truths are meaningless sounds unless they are linked in our consciousness with some particular experience, and many arguments used in philosophical discussions abound in such words.

There are some truths which are immediately apprehended and do not arise as the result of an analysis of particulars. The values, for instance, of Goodness, Beauty and Truth. It is direct intuition of these as realities which indeed confers value and meaning on particulars. The degrees of our response to these values does not depend on our capacity for reasoning. These realities may be reasoned about, but are perceived apart from reasoning. Even as reasoning about concrete things is preceded by direct perceptions, so our response may be equally direct to abstract existents, describable by such words as " whiteness ", " justice ", " goodness ", " wholeness " and so on—all words which collect into one concept qualities which are shared in common by a multitude of particular objects.

The empirical philosophers of course argue that these concepts are merely derived from our sense-experience of the qualities of particular things. Other philosophers with equal cogency contend that Universals are independent entities. In Chapter 12 we have already glanced at this perennial cleavage in philosophical discussions.

No amount of subtle reasoning is likely to reconcile schools of thought which start from different interpretations of basic experiences. Experience is the raw material of reasoning. If therefore we were able by some enhancement of interior perception to experience the Universe at a deeper level, the whole process of interpretation would start with a new set of postulates derived from our altered experience.

Levels of Consciousness.—Before considering the specific state of consciousness called mystical, some further general remarks should be made about the psychological complexity we call our personality. We know that our ordinary waking consciousness is not a full expression of ourselves. We use such terms as subconscious, subliminal, superconscious, and so on, to describe various aspects of awareness which have been uncovered or revealed by the different psychological techniques. Increasing importance is being attached to these under-regions of consciousness, and it would seem almost as though the self of our waking awareness is as a point of focused light against a vast background of possible levels of consciousness.

When studying psychological records, especially those concerned with trance states, it becomes apparent that some people are able to slip easily from one state to another. But none of us, not even the most prosaic, is immune from intrusions from this wider consciousness. We speak of levels of consciousness, but this is only a spatial imagery which exposition imposes on us. Consciousness is described as being on higher or lower levels according to our assessment of the quality and type of experience. We have many " windows ", but what we see depends firstly on the quality of our mind, and secondly on the degree of distortion in our window of awareness. We can regard the " windows " as capacities for conscious focusing. It is only the state on which we are focused which seems real, as the other realms of awareness sink into the background. This, of course, is our normal experience with sensory impressions, but I see no reason why the same principle should not apply to our shifts of awareness between the various levels of consciousness. Very often these shifts of consciousness are accompanied by trance. That is to say, the outer sensory level sinks out of focus in a kind of sleep.

Strictly speaking, a consideration of trance states has only an incidental relevance for mysticism. Admittedly, the mystical experience is often accompanied by a withdrawal of outer attention, but there is usually no break in consciousness, as is the case with the typical trance.

Yet trance-states do provide evidence of the complexity of the psychological fields of experience. There are, indeed, many minor upsurges from deeper levels, whether as the result of trance or not, which produce effects on the lower consciousness akin to the genuine mystical vision.

Religious conversion seems to be one example, and even a genuine falling in love can, for some people, effect a major personality transformation. There are, of course, spurious imitations of this experience which, although popularly called " falling in love ", are usually mere symptoms of libidinous urgings. The genuine experience is one of quite a different order.

There is often a complete abandonment of one's self-interest and a sudden identification with the interests and welfare of another person. Sometimes this experience extends far beyond the particular person who first evoked the love-attitude. The hard core of egoic self-interest seems to have been split open, and there is an acute sensitiveness for the welfare of others. But even when the experience does not enlarge itself to this extent there is always in cases of genuine love a profound change of attitude, and the sense of unity with another shadows to a limited extent the wider unity we call mystical.

There are also experiences which can be described as moods of exaltation. The stimulating cause varies for different people. It may be music, visual beauty or any manifestation of harmonious unity, particularly in literature or in nature. The moods evoked by art-forms are unique experiences which colour a person's total interpretation of life.

These experiences are facts as definite and real as any so-called perception of an external world. A friend of mine who experienced one of these moods of exaltation suddenly found new meanings in everything she read. It was as though layers of meaning had previously been hidden and were revealed in the light of her new mood.

Most of us I think must at some time have had our " high moods ", which at least temporarily have transformed our interpretations of life.

It is difficult to make clear in any precise way the peculiar quality of an aesthetic experience. Speaking for myself I would describe it as an experience in which conflicting impulses and desires suddenly are resolved in a new synthesis or unity. For the most part we are creatures governed by a multitude of cravings, appetites and desires which often pull in opposing ways. We are in a condition of chronic dissatisfaction. Now and again we reach periods of satisfaction, but they are brief and quickly give way to new restlessness as our cravings assert their sway. It is a pitiless turmoil to which we are subjected. Desire is never permanently satisfied. The illusion persists that our craving will cease as each new object is grasped. What it is we are seeking we do not know, but most people would say they want to be happy. Yet happiness escapes us because of our desires. Often even our desires are not consistent with one another, and the nature seems a ferment of opposing elements, which in extreme cases split the personality.

But somewhere in our depths there is a knowledge profounder than that of reason. We know we are whole; that we are a unity, and that the diversities which so disturb us are only manifestations on the periphery of our being. And this slumbering intimation from within is suddenly confirmed in what we call an aesthetic experience which for the time being unifies us and grips the personality in its entirety, making it whole. Nothing is left outside the moment of rapt attention. We are complete.

There are other personality-transformations which, although they are unusual, are not regarded as abnormal. I refer to those which occur under the influence of some drugs. For instance, there is a persistent belief that under the influence of nitrous oxide and ether certain people may experience a remarkable transfer of consciousness to a new plane of meaning. In fact, William James even goes so far as to state: " I know more than one person who is persuaded that in the nitrous oxide trance we have a genuine metaphysical revelation ", and he cites several examples. (*The Varieties of Religious Experience*, pp. 386-92). I also notice that Dr. J. R. Smythies in *S.P.R. Journal* Vol. XXXVI Jan.-Feb. 1952, considers that ". . . the phenomena produced by Mescalin are of absolutely fundamental philosophical importance ". See also Aldous Huxley's recent book, *The Doors of Perception*, which relates his personal experience after taking Mescalin. More recently, experiments have been and are being conducted with Lysergic Acid Diethylamide (L S D) and also with Psilocybin, the active principle of the Mexican mushroom.

One significant physiological feature should be noted, namely, that in the deeper forms of trance the consciousness achieves the maximum lucidity when the body is reduced to a state of abnormal quiescence. In the case of the Samadhi trance the body may almost have the aspect of death.

This phenomenon alone is enough to discredit the dogma of epi-phenomenalism, or even psycho-physical parallelism.

Consciousness, surely, on any theory of its being a product of brain-causation should be most vivid when the body is functioning with vigorous normality! For our ordinary intellectual processes this indeed is usually the case, but not so for many types of Psi phenomena. Even the retentiveness of the subconscious memory is not subject to the same laws as those which apply to normal memory. If we wish to memorize a piece of poetry it is necessary that we concentrate our attention on it and practise frequent repetition. In order to pass an examination we keep our minds alert, and read and re-read our text-books. But how different it is with the subconscious memory! Below the threshold of our outer awareness there exists a meticulous record of details which were hardly noticed at the time they were observed. Nothing seems to be forgotten; both trivial and major events retain equal vividness regardless of the degree of intensity with which they were originally recorded. In my previous book I gave examples of sub-conscious memory, including that of a friend who was almost drowned and when at the point of death re-experienced his past life. I repeat the account as he wrote it for me.

" Only for a few seconds was I conscious of sinking. Then dropping ever so rapidly through a pale green world through which hazily and with terrific speed all the events of my life seemed to whirl around me. Crowds of people hurried about me. All I had ever known was flung into this great whirl. The green was gradually fading and a golden light came suddenly and clearly illuminated each particle of the memory.

" Here the memory of events became so clear that they were re-experienced.

" Yet all the time even in episodes unconnected with them, there were all the crowds of people. The final images before regaining consciousness were amazingly complete with a wealth of detail, even to sunlight on a blade of grass, the willows in bloom, the hum of bees among the catkins, and the acrid dampish odour of the black earth covered with decaying willow twigs. These were details of my life when I was five years old.

" I remember as particularly vivid the impressions of a nurse with whom I had lived for two years at this time."

Here, as in cases of trance, we gain access to other levels of consciousness by imposing quiescence in various degrees on our physical organism. We pass over the threshold of reverie, sleep or deep trance in order to awaken " elsewhere ". But merely to close the door on our outer life does not necessarily mean that we enter into a state of illumination. The fact is, our surface selfhood is not as stable as we imagine it to be, and is subject to various types of intrusion from the wider area of consciousness in which our individual selves are rooted. These interior psychological changes are most important, because they constitute the stream of experiences which determine our individual universe, and therefore provide new axioms for our reasoning.

When the consciousness is directed to what is usually regarded as an external environment, we seem to be dependent on sense-data for our knowledge, but when our consciousness is focused internally, we discover truths equally valid, and in fact interpretative of the knowledge apparently derived from external stimuli. What emerges from a study of personality-transformations is that they cause an altered perception of the supposedly real external world.

The implications of this statement are far-reaching. Man has made all kinds of tools for the conquest of his environment, but has not devoted enough attention to his master-tool, the personality. Indeed, it does not appear to be a tool, but rather is taken to be himself. Admittedly the word " person " is derived from the Latin *persona*, a player's mask, but for the most part we are so closely identified with the mask that we regard it as our only self. Yet we are not quite consistent, because in our moral precepts we imply that man may change his nature, alter his character, and that, in short, a " bad " man may become a " good " man if he takes sufficient pains and exerts his " will ".

Clearly if man were only the psycho-physical personality, these injunctions to alter his nature would be largely meaningless. Man must be more than his personality if he is to alter his personality.

Thus injunctions towards " self-control " and the doctrine that we have " free-will " to modify and change the inherited and environmental habits of the personality are virtually appeals to some higher self.

We are now approaching one of those frontier-regions where distant horizons lead us to explore, but without the aid of familiar landmarks.

It is useless at this stage to marshal further arguments to prove the existence of a transcendental self, or more precisely a state of expanded self-awareness. We must appeal to experience for an answer. There are two signs at the cross-roads to which we have come. They point towards different disciplines. One leads to continued attention to the external world, using the methods usually described as scientific. Along this path the nature of the observer is largely ignored, and reality or truth is sought in an objective study of phenomena. This can lead to power through the conquest of nature, but as man still remains " the unknown ", we have psychological pygmies liable to be destroyed by the Frankenstein monsters of their mechanical creations.

The other path leads to self-knowledge, inner poise, and unification with a wider whole, which gives meaning and purpose to the outer life. This path also has its dangers, for it can lead to escapism, delusions, and neglect of the experiences provided by the sensory life.

We, however, are now faced with a situation where we must appeal to the testimony of experience on a profounder and more illuminating level. We are seeking more than knowledge and conquest; we crave for the meaning of the state in which we find ourselves.

Trance Utterances not Necessarily Authoritative.—No special authority is conferred on a teaching merely because it comes through a trance-state, or is a product of visions. Some of the most fantastic utterances have been the result of " voices ", visions and trances. There are many regions of consciousness from which these queer teachings can emanate, and it is usually not difficult to detect the personality-distortions which cause these aberrations. Actually voices, visions and similar manifestations are only psychological devices and symbols to interpret awareness on some vaguer level.

In some cases a "voice" may be the means of conveying veridical information, and in other instances be only a tormenting symptom of derangement. Presumably Socrates listened to his Daemon with good reason, because it was accompanied by deeper confirmatory intimations. The prophets may say " Thus spake the Lord ", and Mahommed had his visions, but these abnormal settings add nothing to the truth of the teachings. The Ten Commandments would be a sound code of behaviour even without the dramatic incidents of Sinai.

This is not to decry revelation. We would be in a parlous state without the testimony of illumined spiritual teachers. These great ones have always spoken with authority, and often could only declare without qualification or reasoning that such was the truth.

But a revelation is not a revelation unless it reveals! And it has been the tragedy of religious history that revelations have crystallized into Scriptures which become rods of authority over men's minds when used by the unenlightened.

It is a curious paradox that at the stage when an individual is capable of realizing the full content of a scriptural revelation he is no longer in need of any written account of another's inspiration. He has achieved his own inspiration, and it is in the light of this that he can detect the true and the false in Scriptures.

The Masters of the spiritual life cannot transfer their inner experience to others by mere words and philosophical teachings. Their influence is that of a mysterious power which awakens in us those responses which lead to a direct participation in Their life. It is not what They say but what They are which starts new eras of religious impulse. The disciples and followers do the writing and formulate the doctrines, sometimes to the point where only a meaningless ritual remains.

I have frequently used the following parable when speaking on this subject. I imagine it was my own invention, but I cannot be sure of this because it is the sort of illustration which might occur to anyone thinking along these lines.

There was once a Yogi who gathered about him a band of disciples. He meditated deeply for long periods. Now it so happened he owned a cat of which he was very fond. The cat formed the habit of jumping on the holy man's shoulder and this disturbed him during his meditations. So, very sensibly, he tied the cat to a post and continued undisturbed with his meditations and teachings to his disciples, who noted with reverent attention everything the Holy teacher did. There were some who perceived the inner meaning of the Yogi's teachings and there were others who only heard the words and studied the Yogi's actions.

In course of time the Yogi died and left his disciples desolate. For a while the teaching continued undistorted but as only a few had had " ears to hear " when the Teacher was alive, there soon arose different interpretations and dissensions. Eventually the time came when the more enlightened disciples died, leaving behind them what had now become a substantial organization. The organization grew in strength and numbers, and with the numbers came a multitude of sects led by men well-versed in the texts and tradition, but without vision or comprehension of the original teaching. Their differences from one another were acute and acrimonious. But in one procedure they were united and harmonious: they agreed with one voice that in all their ceremonies it was of paramount importance that *a cat should be tied to a post*!

Mystics.—We will now proceed to examine and assess the value of that order of experience usually described as mystical. It is unfortunate that mysticism has in the popular mind become associated with a condition of vague unpracticalness, or worse still, is confused with psychism, mediumship and mystification in general. This, of course, is remote from the true meaning. The Oxford dictionary defines Mysticism as " concerned with direct communion of the soul with God; seeking absorption into God or the Infinite; believing in the spiritual apprehension of truths intellectually incomprehensible."

Mysticism therefore represents an order of experience of a type entirely different from that commonly classified as psychism.

The characteristic of the mystical experience is that of universality. It is a vision from the heights, whereas psychism is merely a slightly increased sensitivity to the phenomena of the valleys. The mystic's selfhood becomes expanded to embrace infinity. His soul is overwhelmed with a joy and peace beyond expression.

In previous chapters we have outlined a conception of the Universe as an organic Whole or Absolute. This, as we have stated, is one of the forms of monistic philosophy. We have been fully mindful of the intellectual problems which arise from this view, and in fact have virtually come to the conclusion that intellectual formulations, based as they must be on normal perceptual experience, will never penetrate beyond the basic assumptions from which they start. The philosophy stems from the philosopher, and is often only his intellectual biography.

Although reasoning, and particularly philosophic reasoning, is a scarifying flame dispersing the miasma of credulity, confusion and ignorance, nevertheless it is chained to its subject-matter. What we reason about is more important than the reasoning. When therefore we experience life at a new level we must still reason, but we cannot establish proofs of our premises. These premises are already given us in our new experience. This then is the experience of the mystic. What he knows he must of necessity reason about, but only to clarify in terms of his familiar concepts the nature of his strange experience. The experience itself derives no authority or support from reason.

We shall see in a moment how grotesquely inadequate normal concepts are for translating the mystical experience.

The main features of the mystical consciousness may be summarized as follows:
1. Consciousness is expanded, and there is an immediate awareness of the universe as a Whole. This experience is variously described as union with God, with the Infinite or Cosmic consciousness.
2. There is a sense of unity with all that exists. Self-consciousness is transcended into an entirely new order of self-awareness which embraces all other selves as " ourself ".

3. The whole nature is illuminated and drenched with a sense of interior light and joy.
4. It is known beyond doubt or need for argument that the universe is a living presence. This seems final truth, complete and self-evident.
5. A conviction of immortality, which is not based on belief but arises from a realization of man's identity with the Universe.

The above is very much the " bare bones " of what I think are the chief characteristics of the Mystical Consciousness.

Needless to say, no exposition such as I am now giving can be expected to convey the positive quality of this profound experience. Few people, I think, will fail to be impressed when reading the testimony of the mystics. Their accounts bear the impress of a burning sincerity and conviction that their experience pierces the veil of our deceptive outer consciousness.

An Assessment of the Mystical Testimony.—Nevertheless those who have not even a faint intuitive glimmer to guide them will naturally ask how can we possibly be sure that the mystics are not deluded? Their unshakable certainty in the truth of their vision is of little help to those who are not privileged to share the experience. This is true enough, but I think we can apply some useful intellectual tests which will at least predispose us to treat the mystical experience with respect.

Firstly: we note the long historical record for the occurrence of this experience. *Secondly*: a study of the accounts will reveal that in spite of great differences in cultural or religious background, and regardless of geographical position or historical period, men and women have clearly shared the same state of unified consciousness. *Thirdly*: those who have had this experience are recognized as among the greatest of our race. *Fourthly*: the testimony of all religions confirms the basic elements in the mystical experience.

Those who stand four-square for the world of commonsense feel their view reinforced by the fact that this world represents a shared or common experience. They would point out that this is what distinguishes it from the delusional worlds of the insane. If, for instance, any one of the delusional worlds became common to the majority of people it would cease to be considered delusional. The fact therefore that the world experienced by the mystics is one which is shared by so many is at least presumptive evidence of its reality.

This argument alone however is not enough to compel acceptance of the mystical experience as having a status superior to that of everyday consciousness. It can still be contended that the common features of mysticism are due to a form of degeneration wherein there is a weakness in the links of association, thus producing sensations of vague significance. Or, without necessarily implying degenerative features we might argue, as does Leuba, that the mystical experience is the result of a mental simplification, and regard it as similar to the effect produced by certain recent psychotherapeutic methods. So he states, " We are thus led to regard the mystical method of soul-cure as an approximation to the present day, more or less scientific, methods of psycho-therapy." (*The Psychology of Religious Mysticism*, p. 331.)

The plausibility of arguments of this type depends on turning a blind eye to those aspects of Mysticism which do not conform to the theory one happens to be espousing.

However at least there is agreement that we are dealing with a state of consciousness with clearly recognized features, and capable of being experienced by many people.

As to whether this is a higher or an inferior state of consciousness must, failing personal experience, be decided by an assessment of the contents of the mystical state, and above all by the characters of the people to whom this experience has come. In many cases the experience has been partial and temporary, but even so it can still be identified as the same as that experienced more fully by the saints, seers and illumined thinkers of our race.

There is nothing negative and vague about the mystical state. It is a stupendous statement on the nature of reality. It comes to the percipient sometimes with suddenness and the shock of a revelation. The truth is almost blinding, and is such as could never have been imagined. Invariably the experience testifies to the unity of man with the Cosmos.

But in studying mystical literature we must not take too literally the forms in which the mystics express themselves. The experience itself is clearly recognizable as the same, but the mode of expression is of very uneven quality, and often indeed the literature makes boring reading. The interpretation will inevitably be in terms of the symbols, imagery and language to which a mystic is accustomed. The Christian mystic therefore will struggle to interpret the vision as union with Christ, The Trinity, or God. So Saint Teresa writes, " . . . it was granted me to perceive in one instant how all things are seen and contained in God."

In other cases the expression is paradoxical to the point of nonsense. Jacob Boehme's language, for instance, is in part most obscure. Yet there is not the slightest doubt about the profundity of his experience. Sometimes Cosmic-consciousness is realized by men who are able to give a more lucid account of it. Edward Carpenter, for example, who experienced this illumined state, was an educated man, a Cambridge graduate, and possessed of literary ability. His book, *Towards Democracy*, is an attempt to express something of what this enhanced form of consciousness means. In a note to *Towards Democracy* he writes, " I became for the time overwhelmingly conscious of the disclosure within of a region transcending in some sense the ordinary bounds of personality . . . an absolute Freedom from mortality, accompanied by an indescribable calm and joy. I also immediately saw, or rather *felt*, that this region of Self existing in me existed equally (though not always equally *consciously*) in others " (p. 512). He then adds as a footnote to his own experience the following: " I do not know any description in its way better than one attributed to Tennyson—" All at once, as it were, out of the intensity of the consciousness of individuality, the individuality itself seemed to dissolve and fade away into boundless being, and this not a confused state, but the clearest of the clearest, the surest of the surest, utterly beyond words, where death was an almost laughable impossibility, the loss of personality—if so it were

—seeming no extinction but the only true life. I am ashamed of my feeble description. Have I not said the state is utterly beyond words? " (Footnote, p. 515.)

Always in the genuine mystical experience there is this sense of a melting of the frontiers of limited self-hood and a flooding of the Whole into the part. This is the hallmark of the true vision, and the symbols used to express it are mere incidental trappings.

Consider, for example, the following account of what was obviously the same experience of unity, yet how differently expressed. The account is from my private records: " I had been reading Bhagavan Das's *Science of Peace*, at a part where he was expounding the Hindu conceptions of Pratyag-Atma (the collective self) and Param-Atma (the Supreme Self). I was completely confused. I made a strenuous effort to understand but put the book away feeling incapable of extracting any meaning from the words. Next day I took the book up again, determined to succeed. I opened it at the same page, and a ' miracle ' happened! Instantly my surroundings disappeared. I was in the midst of a boundless ocean. Around me were innumerable columns of water, arising from the water below, and uniting in a misty unity overhead.

" I knew the columns of water to be human-beings, who sprang from a common source, and re-united after their temporary separation in a richer unity. But the essence of the experience was this: the water-columns were people. I was one of them, and they were myself. Many of these people I recognized, and understood their natures. All these individuals were simultaneously present in my consciousness. I knew that I, with all the other beings in my vision, had arisen from a common source, and would reunite after our temporary apparent separation. The essential point of the whole experience was *unity*—that in reality all are one.

" The next moment I was ' back ' in my room, with the book in my hand. I looked at the clock and knew that the experience had occupied scarcely any of our time.

" At this particular period of my life I was feeling very happy, and full of love for my fellow-beings. The experience filled me with joy and exhilaration. Some aftermath of the increased sensitivity remained with me for about ten days, during which I felt a frequent urge to throw out feelings of love over the entire neighbourhood. I felt as though I were walking on air. Also, when I read such writings as those of Dante and Omar Khayyám I was able to sense depth upon depth of meaning in the lines. This was almost as phenomenal an experience as the vision itself, and I felt very bereft when the faculty left me."

Clearly in this case the " water columns " were purely a symbolism to enable the experience to be registered in the lower consciousness. I draw particular attention to the intrinsic quality of this experience. Firstly, it interpreted a difficult intellectual problem; secondly, it illumined the mind in a general sense; thirdly, there was a deepened capacity for love —not, be it noted, love in a narrow personal sense, but love and understanding for all, even towards people who normally were uncongenial. And finally the memory of the vision remains as an abiding one although not as yet repeated. But never has it been doubted that the vision represented " Reality ". This latter point does not appear in the above account, but I know it to be the case.

The positive and permanent elements in experiences of this type surely justify us in deciding that mystical experiences represent a higher order of awareness than our normal consciousness.

What impresses us is the ubiquitous distribution and persistence of the testimony. This transcendental experience occurs to men and women under the most diverse circumstances, and regardless of their religion or lack of religion in the conventional sense of the word. We can recognize the essential symptoms of mysticism in the testimony of the unlettered as well as in that of the cultured. Jacob Beilhart, for instance, was an uneducated working man, consequently he writes in simple and direct language every sentence of which reflects his inspiration and gives evidence of the mystical consciousness. He writes, " I have no way of my own, no personal interests; for the Life I am is equally interested in all things, and is not centred anywhere." His teachings have been privately printed in a series of papers under the title *Spirit Fruit and Voice.*

Sometimes mystical experiences seem to be a product of asceticism, but as often as not they occur quite unexpectedly to people living normal lives. There are examples where a keen aesthetic enjoyment suddenly changes its character and becomes a mystical experience. For instance, Warner Allen in his book, *The Timeless Moment,* writes, " It flashed up lightning-wise during a performance of Beethoven's Seventh Symphony at the Queen's Hall. . . . The swiftly flowing continuity of the music was not interrupted so that what Mr. T. S. Eliot calls ' the intersection of the timeless moment ' must have slipped into the interval between two demi-semi-quavers " (p. 30). He described the experience as " Union with God ", which was accompanied by illumination. In seeking to describe his experience he writes, " Something has happened to me—I am utterly amazed—can this be that? (*That* being the answer to the riddle of life)—but it is too simple—I always knew it—it is remembering an old forgotten secret—like coming home—I am not ' I ', not the ' I ' I thought—there is no death—peace passing understanding—yet how unworthy I——."

Mr. Warner Allen is a cultured man. But even with his capacity for beautiful writing he feels unable to express the simple directness of the original experience. Nevertheless the vision has compelled him to write, hence his most interesting books. The result is one more interpretation.

How differently does the same experience take shape in a scholar's mind and in that of a mind filled with naïve religious symbology! Plotinus, who several times realized mystical unity, was a philosopher, and the vision for him becomes the illumined core of his metaphysical system. But for an active nature like St. Paul the vision inspires a doctrinal expression in terms of the person of the Christ. I live, yet not I, but Christ liveth in me.

It is however to the East we must turn for the most lucid and sustained expression of the illumined consciousness. " That art Thou " is the challenging statement of the Upanishads. " That which is the finest essence—this whole world has that as its soul. That is Reality. That is Atman. That art thou Svetaketu." *Chandogya Upanishad*, R. E. Hume's translation.

Professor Max Müller in his Preface to the *Sacred Books of the East* writes: " The Individual Atman or self was with the Brahmans a phase or phenomenal modification only of the Highest Self, and that Highest Self was to them the last point which could be reached by philosophical speculation. It was to them what in other systems of philosophy has been called by various names, the Divine, the Absolute. The highest aim of all thought and study with the Brahman of the Upanishads was to recognize his own self as a mere limited reflection of the Highest Self . . ."

The monism of the Upanishads and the Vedanta is not a mere product of elaborate reasoning. On the contrary, the reasoning is only a progressive attempt to express the original Truth as perceived by illumined Seers. " The seer sees not death nor sickness, nor any distress. The seer sees only the All, obtains the All entirely." (*Maitri Upanishad*, Hume's translation.)

The revelation is that of our identity with the Brahman, the Supreme and only Reality. So we read in the *Bhagavad Gita*: " He who seeth Me everywhere, and seeth everything in Me, of him will I never lose hold and he shall never lose hold of Me." (Sixth Discourse, V. 30. Translation, Annie Besant and Bhagavan Das.) This reminds us of a parallel mystical statement in Matthew xxvi, 40. " Inasmuch as ye have done it unto one of the least of these my brethren, ye have done it unto Me."

In China, mystical experience appears in the quaint and paradoxical language of Lao Tzu. His book *Tao Teh King* consisting of 81 short chapters, is written in such a way that the words themselves often make nonsense, nevertheless to the intuitive they reveal one more expression of the transcendental consciousness which in intellectual terms is inexpressible.

" Looking at it, you do not see it, you call it Invisible. Listening to it, you do not hear it. You call it Inaudible. Touching it, you do not grasp it. You call it Intangible. These three cannot be described, but they blend, and are One." (*Tao Teh King*, XIV. Translation, Isabella Mears.)

I think it will be apparent even from the few examples here considered—and literally hundreds could be cited—that no matter how varied are the expressions and interpretation, the testimony relates to an identical state of consciousness. The literature of mysticism is very extensive but the reader can obtain an excellent survey from the following: *The Perennial Philosophy*, Aldous Huxley; *The Varieties of Religious Experience*, William James; *Cosmic Consciousness*, Dr. R. M. Bucke; *Tertium Organum*, P. D. Ouspensky. Other books will be found in my bibliography.

Aldous Huxley well named his book *The Perennial Philosophy* for the mystical experience lies at the root of all the great religions, and if the spiritual geniuses have entered into this consciousness fully we would expect that to a lesser degree it can be, if only fitfully, the experience of others. It is as though, to use an analogy, we are enveloped by a radiant sea of which we become aware as our localized opaqueness melts into translucence.

An interior effulgence has expanded the circle of our direct awareness. That is to say, the area of " the given " has been extended.

The characteristic of our perceptual sense-world is that it is one presented to us. It imposes itself upon us as an external reality which we discover. We do not argue a patch of colour or a sound into existence. The impression on our consciousness is that these sense-data are there for us to observe. I am not here reviving the discussions of previous chapters as to precisely what it is we are observing. All that I draw attention to now is the peculiar characteristic of " givenness " or " otherness " which accompanies sense-knowledge. " Seeing is believing " is a popular expression of the independence of an external world. We now know this to be an unsophisticated view, and that it is by no means clear what is given to us in sense-impressions. Nevertheless, no matter how philosophical and subtle are our reasonings, we always seem to be arguing about a series of experiences which come to us from without.

It is irrelevant for my present point whether " within " or " without " has any ultimate meaning. I am now drawing attention to the psychological fact that we make a clear distinction between the perceptual data of the senses and the truths based on reasoning.

The perceptual data come to us with a peculiar authenticity, and even if later they have to be modified we still feel something has been given us in a more direct manner than is the case with the truths of ratiocination.

It is precisely this sense of something being given to consciousness which confers a conviction of authenticity on the mystic vision. It comes as a revelation or disclosure of reality waiting to be known.

Some Implications of Mysticism.—What conclusions may reasonably be drawn from the facts of mystical experience? Firstly, let us consider their significance for philosophy. We have here centuries of speculative thinking and every conceivable attitude towards the universe has been formulated and subtly presented in the many philosophies. No one of them has ever commanded universal acceptance, and now almost in despair we retreat from the effort to construct by abstract reasoning a view of the universe as a Whole. To-day constructive Metaphysics in the tradition of Plato and the great German idealists is out of fashion. Instead, we have speculation devoted to the clarification of special problems of an empirical nature. Philosophy is becoming mainly analytical. It is clever but uninspiring; more concerned to define clearly the meaning of words than to think in bold sweeps which might provide significant glimpses of the nature and meaning of the universe. The philosophical mirror of the " whole view " is being shattered, and in the broken bits we see the reflection of Logical Positivism and other analytical schools struggling with technical problems in Semantics.

But speculative philosophy can never die. We yearn to see things whole, and not piecemeal. If it remained for the intellect alone we might well despair. For the cynical could always point to the history of philosophic speculation and sneeringly show that philosophy has for the most part only been seeking for reasons to justify what was already believed.

So those monuments of metaphysical effort represented by the philosophies of Plato, Hegel, Fichte, Kant, Spinoza and others are slickly relegated to the plane of elaborate rationalizations.

It is all very plausible if we confine ourselves to an empirical approach, that is, if we take sense-data as our subject matter. Suppose, however, we start from the top instead of the physical empirical bottom. Here also we have a world of data and it is supplied by a perception deeper than that of the physical senses. Admittedly it often emerges in the form of beliefs, and perhaps at times philosophy may only supply bad reasons for these, but let us look deeper into some of those " beliefs ". As William James states, " What reader of Hegel can doubt that that sense of a perfected Being with all its otherness soaked up into itself, which dominates his whole philosophy, must have come from the prominence in his consciousness of mystical moods like this, in most persons kept subliminal?" (*The Varieties of Religious Experience*, p. 389.)

I will not presume to speculate to what extent any future philosophy will succeed in constructing a rational system of thought in terms of the mystical experience. The effort will surely be made, as man must clarify his intuitions into intellectual terms. Yet where Plotinus and the writers of the Vedanta have failed, who shall succeed? Each generation must find its own statement. But the mystical experience inevitably eludes a final statement in terms of the intellect. We are overstraining our intellectual mechanism in striving to make it do work for which it is not designed. Words are the tools in trade of the intellect, but words are only symbols of our experience. So we are caught in a vicious circle. Experience will always coin its own symbols and throw them to the intellect to play with. Yet the intellect must be used to the full, and as experience expands it will be supplied with an infinitely subtle range of abstract formulations which, if illumined by intuitive intimations, can ease the strain of frustration in the presence of the ungraspable.

A point may be reached where the intellectual horizon fades into a world of another dimension. It could happen that the mind in a poised peace will be illumined. Then it will have performed its highest function in bringing us to the threshold of a new mode of apprehension, and should this culminate in a mystical experience we would become one more of those, lit from within, striving to express the inexpressible. " For thought is a bird of space, that in a cage of words may indeed unfold its wings but cannot fly." (Kahlil Gibran, in *The Prophet*.) But even if our thought may not fly within its cage of words it must at least " unfold its wings ". So, we ask, does the mystical experience point clearly towards any particular philosophy? More specifically, does it imply monism rather than dualism or pluralism?

I think we must credit philosophers with sufficient ingenuity to graft the facts of mysticism on to almost any philosophy they have a mind to. Nevertheless I feel that if one approaches the data of mysticism without preconceptions, and so enables the testimony to speak for itself, we will conclude that it predisposes towards a monistic philosophy.

The heart of the experience is that of complete identity with the Whole. This is made clear by Plotinus when he says, " Such logic is not to be confounded with that act of ours in the vision; it is not our reason that has seen; it is something greater than reason, reason's Prior, as far above reason as the very object of that thought must be.

" In our self-seeing There, the self is seen as belonging to that order, from which we are merged into that self in us which has the quality of that order. It is a knowing of the self restored to its purity. No doubt we should not speak of seeing; but we cannot help talking in dualities, seen and seer, instead of, boldly, the achievement of unity. In this seeing we neither hold an object nor trace distinction; there is no two. The man is changed, no longer himself nor self-belonging; he is merged with the supreme, sunken into it, one with it: centre coincides with centre, for on this higher plane things that touch at all are one; only in separation is there duality; by our holding away, the supreme is set outside. This is why the vision baffles telling; we cannot detach the supreme to state it; if we have seen something thus detached we have failed of the Supreme which is to be known only as one with ourselves." (*The Enneads of Plotinus*, VI., 9, 11. Translation by McKenna and Page, p. 251, Vol. V.)

Always in the mystical statement our intellectual head bumps into some hard core of unintelligibility. There are many pitfalls for those who seek to translate a deeper experience into the terms of a lower one. " TAO that can be expressed is not Everlasting Tao. The Name that can be named is not the Everlasting Name." (*Tao Teh King*, Book I, Isabella Mears' translation.)

Yet even as blind men must give some expression of the world of light which affects them though they cannot perceive it, so we make our choice for monism as embodying most nearly the essential feeling of the mystical vision. We have in Chapter 12 outlined a conception of the Absolute as the Infinite and Supreme Whole. If such a view does represent Reality, then mystical experience would be the reflection in our lower consciousness of its truth.

In previous chapters we have wandered into many fields in our search for the meaning of life. We would gladly have stayed in the familiar world of particular things, but always we have had to look beyond them for their explanation. The particulars were not self-supporting. Our sensory experience needed interpretation and gradually it became apparent that it was presenting us with a misleading picture of an apparently external world. The phenomenal world is an appearance, but this implies something more fundamental to account for the appearance. So we found ourselves involved in the age-long search for the final Ground of the universe which, when perceived, is clear beyond all doubt as a self-evident Reality, in need of no further principle to explain it. The yearning to discover this Reality is evidenced in the history of philosophy. But inevitably the search has led beyond the screen of the obvious. It has been a long journey from the Greek Thales to the present abstract speculations. Those early efforts to find a sure foundation for the appearance of things led their authors to postulate water or fire as the ultimate origin of the world. But whether it was water, fire, or a primordial cosmic matter which was postulated, the effort was to discover a single reality appearing in different forms, although at times the search rested in pluralistic conceptions. Eventually the early cosmologies based on one or other of the elements were superseded by more metaphysical interpretations, as in the Platonic theory of ideal forms. In our generation we have witnessed a similar refinement of conceptual background in the transition from the eighteenth century postulate of a universal matter to the present-day theories of physics, which, as we have already noted, lead directly to mental abstractions.

Along the twin paths of speculative thinking and empirical research we shall continue, towards the ever-receding goal of final certainty. In intellectual terms it always must be a receding goal. " It was Plato's belief," writes Professor Burnet, ". . . that no philosophical truth could be communicated in writing at all: it was only by some sort of immediate contact that one soul could kindle the flame in another." (*Greek Philosophy*, Part 1.)

This implies that at some stage the intellect must be illumined from above, and eventually transcended. The final truth is beyond knowledge, yet may be directly apprehended. So we return to the claim of the Seers, Mystics, and those who are illumined that they have experienced the Divine and Ultimate Ground, indescribable, yet known. An eternal truth given to us " Through the treasured teaching of inspired ones—never lost and never wholly given to the world, but always emerging." (Edward Carpenter, *Towards Democracy*.)

CHAPTER XVI

THE MEANING OF LIVING

"... We shall not cease from exploration
And the end of all our exploring
Will be to arrive where we started
And know the place for the first time."

T. S. ELIOT, *Little Gidding*.

"The religion which does not cry out: 'I am to-day verifiable as that water wets or that fire burns. Test me, that ye can become as gods.' Mistrust it. Its messengers are prophets of the darkness."

A. E., *The Candle of Vision*, p. 20.

Recapitulation.—We set out to discover the meaning of our life. This has forced us to examine some of the backgrounds against which our lives are lived. Quite early it became apparent that the physical world was not just "out there", registering itself on us photographically through our senses. We realized instead, that it was more in the nature of a mental projection based on our interpretation of sense-data. Nevertheless we agreed that we existed in a shared world, that is to say, a world which is independent of us as individuals. This so-called external world on examination presented many puzzling features and was by no means self-explanatory. In fact we have been forced to seek for some unifying principle or ground to account for even our sensory experiences, which consciously or unconsciously has been the age-long search of both philosophy and science.

A universal matter at one time promised to serve as the unifying ground, but the closest scrutiny has failed to reveal it, and at the best it was only an hypothesis to account for our sense-impressions.

Instead therefore of assuming an unknown matter as the ground of the Universe, we postulated mind. The concept mind has of course had to be enlarged, but even in the form of " Universal Mind or Self " we are not dealing with a reality of which we have no experience, as is the case with a universal matter.

As a commentary on our general argument we have considered certain types of paranormal phenomena which implied a transcendence of mind over normal sensory awareness. Gradually a view has emerged of ourselves as being rooted in the mysterious depths of universal consciousness which in the mystical vision may be directly apprehended, so we find ourselves confronted with the need to reconcile two groups of experiences which seem to point to different and opposing conclusions.

Two Orders of Experience.—We have the experience based on our normal sensory responses, which present us with a universe of discrete things and ourselves as separate psychological entities, in short, the world of multiplicity with the appearance of change, and of becoming, or evolutionary development. But the other set of experiences represented by the mystical vision forces upon our attention a view of the universe radically different from that of multiplicity.

If we accept both views as facts of experience—and facts they obviously are—we must find some way of bringing two worlds into relationship. The mystic certainly will not recant; the experience is too profound for doubt. Neither can ordinary men doubt their experience of the commonsense world in which they have to conduct their innumerable practical affairs.

There is a temptation to reject one or other of these worlds. The contemplative under the impact of his vision often tends to reject the sensory life and adopt a world-denying attitude, whereas the man without any experience other than outer concreteness proceeds on the assumption that his world is all that is.

Yet these worlds refuse to be separated. The mystic cannot escape from the world of multiplicity even if he wants to, and the man of commonsense is eventually forced to look beyond his circumscribed sphere in order to understand many things which happen to him. So we are brought back to the view outlined in Chapter 12 which reconciles all differences within the Absolute or Supreme Self, but this purely intellectual concept is now reinforced by the facts of direct perception which we considered in the last chapter.

The Supreme Self, Param Atma or Brahman, is both Infinite and Finite. Therefore The Supreme is present at every moment of finite time. This truth can only be expressed to the intellect by means of analogies and we have to some extent done this in Chapter 12. Many types of analogies are frequently used to express the relationship of the One to the Many. When examples are taken from physical phenomena, the Sun naturally suggests itself as a symbol of Unity and its rays are pictured as representing us as individuals. Or we may imagine a universal fire and ourselves as sparks within an omnipresent flame. Then again, the Infinite is sometimes likened to a sea on which we live as wavelets upon its surface. The great truth which these and similar analogies seek to convey is the fact of our identity with the Supreme.

"Just as a spider spins forth and unwinds, as plants grow on the earth, as hair and down from man, so from imperishable (That) comes forth this all." (*Mundako Upanishad*. Translation, G. R. S. Mead and J. C. Chattopadhaya.)

Although we are driven to use analogies, they can easily defeat their purpose and cause the formation of confusing and contradictory concepts, whereas the Vision itself reveals a truth, simple and obvious.

The Reality of the Finite.—In this chapter we are concerned with the practical application of the views we have discussed in previous chapters. We must therefore anticipate a possible wrong interpretation. When emphasis is laid on the Infinite and analogies are used likening it to a universal sea, there is a danger of ignoring the equally important truth that Multiplicity and Unity are two apprehensions of the same Reality. We are both one and many. This truth is exemplified by the concept of organic Wholes which are diversities within a unity. Indeed, as we noted in Chapter 7, a description of organic wholes involves as many paradoxes as does the attempt to describe the unity and diversity of the Absolute. Yet we witness the mystery in the case of living organisms without bewilderment.

If we conceive the Absolute as a kind of infinite sea, we must guard against the false concept that it is a sea into which we are absorbed. If there is any process of " absorption " it would be our own Self which absorbed the Absolute! I make this apparently nonsensical statement because it brings home to us the futility of all analogies if pressed too far.

According to the Vedanta and the Mystical Vision the Absolute is ourself. There are not two selves, an Absolute and a particular self, but only One Self. Yet it is misleading even to say this, for the idea " One " is a term which contrasts with " Many ". The truth is non-dual.

As the " One " and the " Many " are aspects of the non-dual Reality, this will reflect itself at every point in our individual lives. Individuality does not mean separateness in the sense of spatial and temporal isolation. The distinctiveness we associate with individuality is better conceived in terms of quality, say as a musical note within a harmony. It is the harmony which confers significance on the note. Yet the note is real and indispensable. We therefore are as necessary to the Absolute as the Absolute is to us.

Indeed, individual uniqueness is an essential part of the concept of the Absolute, and it is this which gives meaning to our experiences on the sensory plane of apparent multiplicity. The whole pageant of the Universe and the meaning of existence are within ourselves. The " pilgrim's progress " is a psychological one.

The Formula of I and Not-I.—At the highest metaphysical level the process which we apprehend as manifestation can be summed up in terms of a formula of identification with apparently external phenomena and a repudiation of this identification. This may be expressed in terms of the formula I—Not I—Not Am, which being interpreted means that the Supreme Self affirms the pseudo-existence of a Multiplicity or Not-Self. Thus there occurs what may be described as an act of identification. But the identification is followed by repudiation. The Self knows itself as the undifferentiated. This identification with an external phenomenon is illusory because the "Not Self" is within the Self, so the next stage of the formula occurs. " I am not this." Those who have a liking for pure Metaphysics will find in *The Science of Peace*, by Bhagavan Das, M.A., a subtly reasoned exposition of the first principles of the Science of the Self in the light of the Vedanta. He quotes the great hymn, Pushpadanta's Mahimastuti, referring to the Supreme in these words:

" Thou whom the dazzled scripture doth describe
As being negation of what thou art not."

Here we have an epitome of the process of definition by negation. By knowing what we are *not*, we know what we *are*.

The key to the understanding of our life in form is to realize that the individual self is an aspect of the Universal Self. The macrocosm is reflected in ourselves as microcosms. We find evidence of this truth in every aspect of phenomenal existence. The atom, for instance, is a miniature cosmos. The finite expresses its infinitude by endless change. Omnipresence becomes in the finite the successive efforts to encompass all Space, and Eternity manifests as a rhythm of perpetual dying and being born.

The Supreme Self's affirmation of the Not Self and its negation is apprehended by us as a law of involution and evolution. The mythological story of creation is that of God descending into the forms of limitation and ascending again, not of course becoming entirely immersed in His creation for, as it says in the *Bhagavad Gita*, " Having pervaded this whole universe with one fragment of Myself, I remain."

This and other statements in the form of Myths which describe the death and resurrection of a God, embody in pictorial language the truth of the supreme identification and negation which can never be expressed except by symbols.

Here we have the metaphysical basis for the law of cycles on every level of manifestation, expressed for us by the rhythm of births and deaths called reincarnation.

Reflections of the Infinite in Normal Life.—How then may we sum up the meaning of living in terms of our normal experience? Firstly, we note that our experiences are broadly either painful or pleasurable. The painful experiences are those which cause what might be described as a contraction, or sense of " lessness ". In the case of physical pain the area of our awareness is restricted almost within the limits of our physical organism. Also with frustrating circumstances of any kind the sense of limitation is accentuated. We feel these conditions to be " wrong " and cry out for an explanation, whereas conditions which cause us to feel " expansive " and " full of life " are unhesitatingly accepted as natural. Thus the Infinite Self reflects itself in the individual self.

This principle may be expressed in endless ways. It enables us to understand why we attach value to the conquest of space by the restless striving for faster movement: why business measures its success in terms of expansive and ever-increasing control over resources. And even in our educational aims we proclaim the value of knowledge for its own sake, which represents our conscious efforts to expand the area of our awareness. Also the supreme truth of our Wholeness discloses itself in our passion for order and symmetry in our lives. Apart from this principle there seems no reason why we should not be happy in disorderliness, but it is a fact of our experience that disorderliness registers as ugliness. We may hold differing views as to what constitutes orderliness and symmetry but their absence arouses a sense of unease in the normal person. When therefore the housewife imposes order in the domestic sphere and a balanced sense of unity to the decorations, the principle of universal wholeness is manifesting.

Wherever and whenever we identify ourself with some aspect of the phenomenal world we achieve a definition of ourself, but as it is infinity we are seeking to express in terms of the finite, the process of identification and rejection in ever-widening circles of self-awareness is endless. So our normal life swings between the two poles of attraction and repulsion, symbolized by the phrases " I want this " and " I am tired of this ". Everywhere in manifestation there is duality, but all the phenomenal dualities are a reflection of the primary metaphysical duality of *I this am, I this am not*. But it is important to realize that the act of identification on whatever level it happens confers *reality* on that with which the identification occurs.

The Absolute is beyond duality, but in manifestation it necessarily assumes the aspect of duality. The One confronts and opposes the Many. To use the Sanskrit terms, The Pratyag-Atma or the Abstract Self confronts the Universal root-matter or manyness called Mula-prakriti. But although The Self is the only Reality, the Not-Self shares the reality of the Self because it is the assertion of the Not-Self which enables the Self to define Itself; that is, to become manifest.

In the light of this general principle we may deduce a value for every aspect of our phenomenal experience.

In this chapter we are concerned with our experiences as individuals. Does it seem contradictory to talk of " individuals " when we continually insist that there is only one Self? The truth is that individuality is not a contradiction of the Self, but is its definition. Universal and particular permeate all manifestation. Nothing stands isolated. Every particular has its universal aspect. A single leaf exemplifies a genus, and an individual man is only an aspect of mankind.

The individual and particular are always definitions of some wider whole, and the totality of manifested existence is only a definition of the One Self. Again we must guard against interpreting the above exposition to mean that we individuals have no ultimate value. Our ultimate value derives from the fact that the Universal embraces our particularity. Not only is this our assurance of immortality in some abstract sense, but it also implies the immortality of every phase of our phenomenal experiences, including personal and even bodily aspects. All these characteristics have been cognized by the Self and therefore are Eternal. How could it be otherwise if the Supreme and the individual self are identical?

On the surface of life as we experience it there is everywhere manifested the reflection of the Eternal Oneness and Manyness. In our own lives we seem to be enduring personal selves manifesting in an ever-changing environment. At first the environment imposes itself upon us and masquerades as reality, that is, we become identified with it and in our later years a process of withdrawal occurs; our mood becomes retrospective; we are assimilating our experiences. This process continues after the death of the body, and through endless cycles, and in the popular sense is called Metempsychosis or Reincarnation. From the deepest metaphysical view we as individuals do not reincarnate. As Ananda K. Coomaraswamy expresses it, "The Lord is the only transmigrant. That art Thou—the very Man in everyman." (*The Bugbear of Literacy*, p. 125.)

However, from the phenomenal aspect there must be a rhythm of identifications and withdrawals and reincarnation is as "real" as is the experienced fact that you and I are functioning under the guise of separateness. Indeed the Universality of the Absolute lends validity even to separateness.

Meaning in Living—Another Expression.—Although I believe the mystery of our existence is locked up in certain key metaphysical principles, this is not a language congenial or helpful to many people. I would therefore fail in my purpose if I did not re-express the basic principles in more familiar terms.

Many of us may be inarticulate when asked to express the meaning of living, but our actions themselves speak for us.

What are we seeking? We attach many labels to our goals, such as "Money", "Freedom", "Security", "Independence", "Family"; and we espouse social aims which will achieve these and similar benefits for others. But not one of these goals can be accepted as of value in its own right. We can always ask the further question, "Money for *what*?" And even freedom, security, independence and desire for family are not ends in themselves. Of course in a general vague sense we all agree that we want to be happy, but we do not pursue happiness in a specific sense. Always we desire particular things or circumstances which we believe will create that sense of satisfaction we call happiness. The objects and conditions we may desire are almost infinite, and we are not deterred from seeking these things even when we know others possess them and yet are not happy. We feel there must be something wrong with such people for we are sure we should be happy with economic security, ample possessions and freedom to do as we like. The craving is never satisfied. Each period of satisfaction is only a respite before desire again asserts itself. Nor indeed is there a lack of craving in the apparently lethargic and those who claim to be satisfied with very little. Their laziness and lack of ambition only disguise a craving for security by avoiding normal obligations. We would be pursuing a will-o'-the-wisp if we attempted to catalogue the multitude of things and situations which at various stages are supposed to be indispensable for happiness.

The truth experience eventually teaches us is that we have to look beyond phenomena for the meaning of phenomena. It is an advance towards an explanation when we perceive the values of Truth, Beauty and Goodness expressing themselves in our lives. But the final explanation lies in the juxtaposition of Infinitude and Finiteness, and it is this paradoxical association which explains the world of appearances.

In this world everything seems to exist for something else.

We work in order to feed, clothe and house our bodies, but even the most ardent physical-culturist does not regard the body as an end in itself, but only as a means for living. Indeed hypochondria is the penalty for making the body an end in itself.

Similarly sex, if indulged in for its own sake, becomes physically unsatisfying and this is so for all the appetites. Their gratification always leads beyond themselves. Even our economic activities are means to an end. Our houses not only protect us from the elements but become centres for our social expressions, and the whole complex fabric of a civilization is in its turn a means towards the end that man may achieve not only sustenance, but security and a fuller life.

But what is a " fuller life "? And so we start once again asking *what are we aiming at*? We mostly agree that man cannot live by bread alone, and in various ways we proclaim our intellectual needs, so universal education becomes a panacea for all ills. But education for what? Technical education, of course, is largely an adjunct for our physical necessities, but education in general is supposed to be a passport to a " fuller life "—again this vague phrase " fuller life ", although it is sometimes interpreted as education for citizenship. The aims of education are very much under fire, and it is not even certain that literacy and education are synonymous, but what interests us here is this " fuller life " that education is supposed to promote. Education as an end would be as stultifying as physical culture would be. The goal is always in the future, but our aims are not clear, and for the most part we live because we must.

I have asked many people such questions as " Why are you here? " and, " Having been born, what meaning do you attach to living? "

Alternatively I have asked, " What do you consider should be the main aims of living? "

Unsophisticated people usually do not see the point of the first question. Clearly they are here for better or for worse, and there is nothing they can do about it. When asked the further question as to the meaning of living the answers usually imply that " progress " in the sense of an increase in economic welfare justifies our living. Replies to the question " What should be our aims? " vary considerably. Some answers are mere clichés such as, " Everyone should try to improve himself " or " We should live so that we are respected, and enjoy friends." Others without finesse frankly are ambitious to gain particular positions which confer power and prestige.

But when pressed to take a less personal view and answer what aims are generally desirable, most people seem agreed that " we should do good to others ". People who have well-formed views in terms of some particular religion have little difficulty in answering " We are here to do God's will and serve our fellow man ", a satisfactory enough answer providing it is properly comprehended. Unfortunately it is often little more than a conventionalized phrase.

If these replies are reasonably typical of the " man in the street " we can see that in substance they indicate a predominantly utilitarian attitude. This is what we should expect from people who are convinced that the world of commonsense is the real and only world.

It is inevitable, and indeed logical, to live according to the laws of the world we know. Preaching and exhorting can make humbugs of people if they merely provide sets of religious phrases which have no obvious connection with the world as experienced.

There is deep wisdom in not casting one's " pearls before swine ". Were the swine to become men they would know how to use pearls, and when we are spiritually awakened we shall need no exhortation to live in accordance with the laws of the world as then apprehended. That is why Esotericism is inevitable; not because of a desire to retain a secret teaching for a privileged few, but because the light is too strong for weak eyes. The seers proclaim laws of the spiritual life which to them are only statements of fact.

When however we are urged to live lives of complete unselfishness we find such an injunction confusing and even liable to set up painful moral conflicts. The average man is therefore compelled to compromise. In other words, he does not take the Sermon on the Mount seriously. To live selflessly does not make sense. He feels he owes something to himself; that in fact he has certain rights as well as duties. If each one of us is supposed to live for the sake of others, then applied universally, everybody would be minding everybody else's business. Commonsense eventually must assert itself, so communities devise practical rules of conduct which sanction selfishness within limits. Therefore we fight to defend legitimate interests, acquire enough property to maintain ourselves and dependants, and endeavour to become good citizens within the laws and customs which have stood the test of time.

Consequently we continue our prosaic ways, and if the Prophets sometimes stir a response within us, the facts of our commonsense world soon re-assert their influence over us. Thus we develop a " Sunday religion " which leaves our normal lives largely unaffected. We need not feel censorious towards ourselves because of this. We are not to be blamed. Our conduct is quite logical and sensible according to the facts as we experience them. Occasionally, as we saw in the last chapter, a sudden shift of awareness occurs; perhaps we love someone, and then we have a glimmer of the meaning of selflessness. But for the most part the separate self represents our centre of interest.

Yet it will be clear from what has been said in previous chapters that the meaning of living is not to be found in our exterior normal life. This realm is only a partial view, consequently even our mundane activities will reflect the truth that the Absolute is the supreme Reality.

It is from this fact that Love and Compassion derive their authority. They speak the language of our universality, whereas hate and cruelty are products of the illusion of separateness. Men cannot love because they are exhorted to do so, but they love in spite of themselves. Love shatters the frontiers of egoism and pours out joyously without regard to self-interest, and in its purest form it embraces all persons and creatures. Intellect tempered by love is wisdom. The wisdom to discriminate, to help where needed, and refrain where " help " might hinder. Yet love is not a state to be cultivated. It is not under the control of the conscious mind. Love is the manifestation of unity under the guise of form. It is not necessarily emotional in character. In some natures it becomes a passion for universal justice. The virtues, whatever may be our labels for them, testify to our underlying unity, and the vices to our separative tendencies. Yet it should be observed that in practice it is not easy to place our labels " Good " and " Bad ". The cyclic swing from unity to diversity and from diversity to unity requires that on the downward curve accentuation of the separateness of forms may be " Good ", yet " Bad " on the return cycle.

We will later comment further on this law in connection with " attainment ". We are here endeavouring to detect the signs which indicate our infinity manifesting under the guise of our normal activities. It is not only the accredited virtues which symbolize infinity. What can insatiable desire be other than the search of the limited for the unlimited? It is our " Hound of Heaven". As Pope expresses it, " Man never is, but always to be blest." Caught by the illusion of the time-sequence, desire lures us everlastingly to seek for our rewards in the future. Endless " pasts " lie behind us and a future without end lies ahead. But only the " present " is experienced, and this for barely a moment of duration before it melts into the past. Desire compels us to live for the future whereas it is only the present we possess.

Is it not apparent that the psychological state we call desire is an expression of Eternity spread out on what might be described as " the plane of time "? But the hunger which our desire indicates is never satisfied in time, and at some stage of our journey we have in the words of the Bhagavad Gita to " renounce the formative will ". This leads us to a realization akin to a revelation that Eternity exists in the present moment. We are at the point of emancipation. Our consciousness is withdrawn from the periphery to the centre of the circle. But the periphery does not vanish when we are at the centre. Periphery and centre are one. How may this liberation be achieved? Must we wait for " God's grace "? These are questions we will now consider.

CHAPTER XVII

THE ATTAINMENT OF ENLIGHTENMENT

"I tried to obtain by effort that which I could only obtain by ceasing all effort."

MADAME GUYON,

Quoted from A. Wyatt Tilby, *The Quest of Reality*, p. 369.

"He who would be serene and pure needs but one thing, detachment."

MEISTER ECKHART.

"He whose mind is free from anxiety amid pains, indifferent amid pleasures, loosed from passion, fear and anger, he is called a sage of stable mind."

THE BHAGAVAD GITA (ii., 56).

"Him that overcometh will I make a pillar in the temple of my God, and he shall go no more out."

Rev. iii., 12.

A Preliminary Difficulty.—In our first efforts to understand the nature of enlightenment we encounter a peculiar difficulty. It is embodied in the word " attainment ". There is an air of tenseness about this word, implying as it does a course of action which enables us to accomplish or gain some object. This mood of striving or seeking needs to be examined. Our ordinary moral precepts are based on the assumption that we can acquire virtues by adequate effort and discipline. It is very natural therefore to regard enlightenment as a state of mind which results from diligent application of moral rules and the practice of austerity under guidance.

Those who have studied the nature of the state we call " enlightenment " will detect the subtle danger of " searching " for it.

This will become clear if for purposes of exposition we describe the limited self as the ego. Now the essential meaning of enlightenment is liberation from the illusion of separative functioning. If therefore we set out with our " spiritual brows " knit in a mood of acquiring, we are strengthening those very egoistic tendencies which are the negation of enlightenment. We are seeking the " Kingdom of Heaven " *because* all things will be added unto us.

There is a deeper reason why this egoistic striving must defeat itself. It sets the gaze on a time series, whereas the secret is in the " Now ".

Enlightenment is the revelation of our timelessness. Does this mean merely living in the present and passively waiting for the grace of revelation? If this were so it would be an attitude differing little from the vague drifting state of mind only too prevalent in modern societies. The injunction " consider the lilies of the field how they grow; they toil not, neither do they spin ", was not an appeal to laziness. The mood in which we " seek " enlightenment is exceedingly subtle and difficult to express without misrepresentation. " Living in the present " is not mere quietism. It could more accurately be described as a strenuous exercise practised without concern for success or failure. The mind is held still in order to reflect a truth; to become a dustless mirror. It is not an exercise designed to benefit the egoistic mind but to enable it to register a new order of experience, and this involves a reorientation of the egoic centre within a wider whole.

But as this " wider whole " is our eternal Self, why should it be so difficult to realize this? The answer would seem to be, it is not difficult when in the depths of our nature we really want to realize the truth. Our evolutionary growth can be measured by the strength of our longing. For while the Supreme is not subject to " evolutionary growth ", it includes it. Therefore there is a time for each one of us when we awake from the dream of existence and know that we never left " home ". Must we then wait for the time-cycle to complete itself? Perhaps most will, but many are already stirring in their sleep and they will not be left without aid.

Spiritual Disciplines.—A detailed review of the many disciplines will not be attempted here, but there are certain general observations which are relevant. Each religion has its characteristic methods which are supposed to facilitate a reorientation of the personal consciousness.

Christianity has taken its colouring from the extraverted western races who profess it. It is therefore not rich in the psychological disciplines for interior exploration. This is particularly the case with the Protestant sects. The Catholic church has its tradition of saints, and exercises considerable wisdom in guiding the development of psychic and spiritual manifestations. Many of its techniques of prayer and meditation have their resemblances to those of some Hindu and Buddhist sects. But it remains broadly true that apart from a general injunction to pray, there is little specific technical guidance available to Christian congregations.

Prayer, however, is a term which can represent a wide range of mental attitudes, from simple petitions for personal benefits to adoration of God. Prayer is based on a dualistic concept. We pray to " Our Father who art in Heaven " and for the most part we make our approach to the Heavenly Father with very indifferent faith that we shall achieve a response in terms of our prayers. Some prayers indeed are little more than a wordy haranguing of the Deity, telling Him what He obviously already knew about our needs and spiritual conditions. Yet there is considerable evidence to show that prayer does achieve results not only psychological, but even physical. The results of course need not be attributed to the specific intervention of God conceived in personal form, but rather as being due to the fact that prayer, even in its perfunctory western form, does invoke the operation of psychological laws of some potency. Concentrated thought can produce a centre of energy. The study of psychical phenomena provides evidence of this. Prayer, however, in order to effect specific results, needs to be directed with a knowledge of the laws involved. If I were writing a treatise on prayer it would be necessary to classify the different types of prayer and the devices most propitious for success. It would cover a wide field, including even magical practices, for they involve certain invocatory forms of prayer. But although we would find ample evidence of the power of mind to influence events in a supernormal manner, we would be far distant from the spiritual kingdom which purports to be the supreme object of the highest form of prayer.

Now from what has been said above regarding the nature of enlightenment, it will be realized that if prayer is to be its prelude, it must be pruned of any petitionary elements and become transformed into pure meditation. Moreover it would disclose the inner nature of prayer if it were regarded apart from its Western conceptual frame. Many of the doctrinal associations of prayer are irrelevant. Basically it is a psychological process designed to alter our state of mind. Once we are clear as to the change of mind and heart which is desired we may apply empirical tests as to the effectiveness of the methods practised. Do we, for instance, need the concept God? Or if we do, what idea of God is likely to evoke the best results? Such questions do not imply cynicism regarding the existence or nature of God. Rather may they be considered as a declaration that all our concepts are so far short of Reality that we are at liberty to adopt any or none according to their helpfulness in facilitating illumination.

It is precisely this practical scientific approach which commends to many the Yoga system of Patanjali. Patanjali's aphorisms are admittedly based on a conceptual foundation, but one may disagree with the concepts and yet practise Yoga. Actually the Yoga Sutras of Patanjali are founded on Sankhya, which is one of the six main systems of Indian philosophy. The Sankhya philosophy itself is dualistic, whereas the Vedanta is monistic, but this does not prevent the Vedantist from adopting the principles of Patanjali. There are two forms of Sankhya; one is atheistic and the other accepts God under the name Ishvara. It is the Sankhya with God which is adopted by Patanjali. But the stress is not so much on the existence of God as on the value of the idea of God as a focus to achieve one-pointedness of the mind. In effect Patanjali says, you are more likely to attain non-cognitive contemplation by devotion to God, and thus experience directly what cannot be described. It is therefore the practice of the discipline which is important, for it is a scientific system whereby the mind is tempered to become the instrument of the spirit. Patanjali's dualism consists of Purusha or Spirit and Prakriti or Matter. The Self is conceived as abiding in its own nature, yet It becomes partially entangled with the Not Self (Prakriti). That is, the Seer identifies Itself with the Seen. It is not only the " Seen " in the form of Prakriti with which the Seer becomes identified, but also with the Mind which is the instrument of seeing.

By practising Yoga it is claimed we can detach ourselves even from our minds. This implies that the mind becomes an object. Obviously we must be other than our mind in order to control it. The aphorisms of Patanjali represent a terse epitome, a traditional wisdom and practices of unknown antiquity. It comprises rules for bodily health and the achievement of mental poise and the exercises are designed to free the mind from being at the mercy of external impressions. In the East it is generally regarded as essential to practise under the strict guidance of a master. Unfortunately, the attempts to popularize Yoga in the West have caused it to be exploited by charlatans. The benefits which undoubtedly accrue from " mind-control " have been harnessed to the service of desires instead of to freeing us from desire. Yoga, in common with all spiritual disciplines, is intended as a preparation for perception at a new level, and not to enhance egoistic functioning.

But there is danger of misunderstanding even in this statement. Yoga is not necessarily " other worldly ", as the abnormal practices of some Indian ascetics may lead one to suppose. On the contrary, success in Yoga leads not to an escape from the world but to its reinterpretation. This comes about because we have attained the poise of a spectator who participates in the world but desires nothing from it.

Disciplines need to be adapted to the particular personality types to which each one of us conforms. That there are marked personality types is a fact of daily observation. We distinguish immediately between the jovial Falstaffian type and that of the " lean and hungry Cassius ". The man of thought with his rather slender make-up is a recognizably different type from the large, brawny man whose predominant interests lie in sport and activity. The Jungian description of extravert and introvert are well known, and now we have Dr. Sheldon's more detailed classification of human differences, an excellent summary of which will be found in Chapter 8 of Aldous Huxley's *The Perennial Philosophy*. But whatever classification we adopt it is clear that each of us has inherited to a lesser or greater degree the characteristics of a dominant psycho-physical type. It is interesting to note that a classification of human differences has existed in India for centuries. This is based on the three gunas, or qualities, of Sattva, Rajas and Tamas, words which are variously translated, but may be approximately expressed as Harmony, Activity and Inertia. Every creature is presumed to have a form in which one or other of the gunas predominates, thus causing it to manifest characteristic psychological traits. Corresponding to these three main temperaments are the three Yogas—Raja, Karma and Bhakti. Raja Yoga is the natural path of the intellectual who has a capacity for introspective penetration. The aim of this Yoga is to destroy the illusion of the separate ego and realize identity with the Supreme Self. Union with the Supreme is of course the aim of all the Yogas, but those whose natures are predominantly active and extravert are counselled to practise Karma Yoga, or the path of performance of works without regard for reward. Thus they are supposed to be helped towards the same goal of poised detachment in the midst of action. For the natural devotee Bhakti Yoga is the obvious choice, for these people see life in terms of persons. The wise spiritual advisers of India therefore used this inborn tendency and demanded of the aspirant a dedication of the life to a personal God, and the performance of all deeds for His sake.

What the practice of Yoga teaches us is that we have been seeking the right things in the wrong places. We have been seeking the eternal in the transitory. This is the cause of our suffering. In the world of changing phenomena no experience is absolutely either pleasurable or painful, but contains the possibilities of both. The young in soul contrive for situations which promise perpetual pleasure, mistaken for happiness, but in the nature of things the pleasure stales and discloses its obverse side of pain. All is relative and in eternal flux. We become attached to that which is pleasurable and are repelled by the painful. To seek the pleasurable automatically invites the painful: they are a married couple impossible to divorce. But we need not have either, and the paradox is that by rejecting both we achieve liberation and happiness. This means acquiring an attitude of detachment through discrimination between the ephemeral and the eternal. It is a spiritual " coming of age " and a realization of our true self, sometimes described as living beyond the pairs of opposites. It is not a mood of negative neutrality but one of positive and objective appraisal of all experiences from the standpoint of a wider whole. Freed from the illusion that happiness is dependent on circumstances we can now participate actively in life because we are identified with life itself and not with its changing forms of expression.

This is mere verbiage to those whose time has not yet come. Patanjali assumes the doctrine of rebirth, which is not a process imposed upon us by a deity. The incarnations are to be considered as the result of our own impulses, thus there occurs an " outward moving " of consciousness which seeks expression in limited forms. The infinite nature of our true self is reflected as a cyclic sequence. The practice of a spiritual discipline is the appropriate means for a soul on the " path of return ". We may suppose cycles within cycles—cosmic cycles including infinite expressions of lesser cycles even to the microscopical level. But we must not invest these cycles with some external potency: they are fundamentally expressions of processes in consciousness, and in the particular aspect we describe as rebirth it is our consciousness which is the determining cause. If therefore any of us has arrived at the stage where life has lost its savour it is perhaps a signal from our infinitude to look within. But the search for the Eternal is not to be prompted by aversion to life at the finite level. Aversion is as much an assertion of separative egoism as attraction. Thus again we are faced with the subtle nature of the state of mind which precedes enlightenment. While the Yoga Sutras of Patanjali provide a systematic set of rules for disentangling the mind from its attachments, it is doubtful whether the aphorisms speak a language clear enough for those who do not share the traditional background out of which they arise. But as the western disciplines lack depth and psychological subtlety, the Yoga system is sure to attract increasing attention from those who have lost their moorings in the conventional religious doctrines, yet still see a light which beckons.

An excellent exposition of Yoga for Western readers is that of Ernest E. Wood in his book entitled *Practical Yoga*. Professor Wood has made his own translation of the Yoga Aphorisms, and his commentaries are models of lucidity. That the West is grievously in need of psychological guidance is only too evident from the clinical records of psychiatric practice. In fact there are some who find many principles in Yoga which could be usefully applied in modern psychology. See, for instance, Geraldine Coster's book entitled *Yoga and Western Psychology*.

Actually, the aims of Yoga and Psychoanalysis are similar up to a point. The psycho-analytical technique is designed to force subconscious elements to the surface so that they may be dealt with by the conscious self. This can be described as a process of making whole. As a preliminary to the new synthesis the analyst endeavours to make the patient recognize the subconscious causes of his trouble, and face them objectively. This mood of detachment from our psychological contents is similar to the early Yoga exercises which deal with the five kinds of ideas. This requires the cultivation of Vairagya, or Non-attachment.

The governing principle of all disciplines which purport to assist the neophyte towards enlightenment must of necessity be to destroy the illusions which arise through identification with separative aspects of nature. So closely are we identified with our mento-emotional functions that those who have no skill in introspection are not even sure they are more than their bodies, and are positively bewildered by the statement that they are also other than their separative mentalities. It is not an obliteration of separate functioning which is aimed at, but rather the recognition of its instrumental nature, and the Self as more than its functional aspects.

It may appear from what has been said above that enlightenment can only be achieved by the deliberate practising of some rigid discipline. While it is true that conscious efforts must be made to break down the psychological automatisms which hinder the realization of our true self, yet a discipline cannot be effective until a certain spontaneous reorientation has occurred. I would hazard the opinion that an inner fructification has already begun, and whatever religious practices may be adopted merely hasten the realization. To many, enlightenment has come suddenly without special spiritual exercises. In some cases a great sorrow or joy has acted as a catalyst.

A right attitude to what is happening to us here and now can be the means of liberation. Indeed, the practice of meditation by those who are seeking in the wrong way would suppress egoistic impulses instead of destroying them. Our first task is to understand ourselves. We must consciously become aware of the motives which underlie our daily activities, and allow our inner conflicts to reveal themselves so that we may be in a mood of detached alertness and know precisely the causes which drive us to seek security, power or even immortality.

If these causes are not detected and understood, meditation will almost inevitably concentrate the attention on an egoistic goal, although one dressed up in spiritual garments. Right meditation therefore must be directed to prepare the mind to receive the Eternal by holding it in tranquil expectancy. As we have said previously, no expression in dualistic intellectual terms can make clear the meaning of enlightenment, nor, it seems, can any set system be recommended as a means to attain it. Zen Buddhism lays its main emphasis on this inexpressibility. Dr. Suzuki in his *Introduction to Zen Buddhism* (with a foreword by C. G. Jung) gives a succinct exposition of the main principles.

Zen is neither a religion nor philosophy. It is free from all dogmatic assertions regarding God, the Soul or Immortality. Assertions and denials appertain to logic and Zen is above logic. Nor can it be said, strictly speaking, that Zen teaches anything. Whatever doctrines Zen followers may have are their individual affairs and not part of an official body of doctrine. Zen is elusive and undefinable, yet Zen may be experienced. We must look into our own being to find Zen. It is our non-dual reality. Therefore all definition and logical formulations are barriers to the direct experience. While Zen can be regarded as a form of Mysticism, it employs unique methods for training the mind in preparation for enlightenment or Satori. Its unusualness consists in presenting the commonplace in paradoxical forms so as to evoke an instantaneous response from the deeper layers of the unconscious. It seems to be a method of emptying the conscious mind of its conceptual contents so that Reality may flash directly into the field of awareness. It is hardly conceivable that Zen Buddhism can be profitably transplanted to Western soil, but inasmuch as it is one more statement of the eternal truth of our infinite being it could provide a new viewpoint for us, and make us less dependent on our intellectualisms, which for so many represent reality. The Zen statement that no doctrinal system or belief in deities, even the Buddha, are of the slightest avail in acquiring Satori is a corrective to our over-dogmatized religious outlook.

Those who have listened to Krishnamurti or read his talks will know how he insists on the necessity for complete freedom from beliefs and conventionalized attitudes. Many of his statements have their parallels in Zen literature.

A Re-statement in Psychological Terms.—Perhaps a re-statement in another form may clarify the principles which seem to govern the attainment of enlightenment.

We have for the most part stated the problem in metaphysical terms and regarded enlightenment as a relationship between the Infinite and the Finite. This in a sense is rather an over-intellectualized statement of a state of consciousness which involves our total being. If however for purposes of practical exposition we must regard enlightenment as a relationship between one part of our nature and another, then it might be better to re-cast our remarks in more familiar psychological terms. We could then explain enlightenment as a *rapprochement* between the conscious and the consciousness beyond the waking threshold, variously described as unconscious, subconscious, subliminal, superconsciousness or even cosmic consciousness.

For my present purpose an exact terminology is not important. Specific terms naturally must be invented to classify and describe certain psychological aspects as they reveal themselves, but it is the subliminal as a collective totality which is the relevant concept at the moment. The unconscious thus conceived could be figuratively described as a vast area of simultaneity. It would include the racial memories, and even the collective possibilities for the future. In a sense this almost seems a psychological equivalent of the Infinite, and this indeed is what I intend. But those who are familiar with modern psychology, especially Jung's theory of the Collective Unconscious, may find this approach more practical.

While therefore modern psychiatry aims to make the sick soul whole, that is, to effect a *rapprochement* between the conscious and the unconscious, its scope is limited by its shallow knowledge and lack of subtlety compared with some Eastern systems such as Yoga. Nevertheless its therapeutic value lies in its capacity to unify a consciousness which is severed from elements which have been refused recognition in the waking consciousness. We cannot deny our " wholeness " without penalty, and the first step towards a cure may be described as knowing ourselves. Although it is a commonplace to regard the conscious mind as but a partial expression of a deeper total consciousness, yet most of us set a very high value on our intellectual waking consciousness, and the question arises as to what part our intellectual concepts play in facilitating enlightenment.

What Part do Concepts Play in Facilitating Enlightenment.— We have already seen that no concepts can describe the state of enlightenment. Does this mean that it is a matter of indifference what ideas or beliefs we hold?

This is a difficult question, and we must answer both Yes and No. Enlightenment itself occurs independently of our ideas, beliefs or religion. We may profess belief in any religion or in none, and yet experience illumination. What then are we to say about the vast organizational effort which is being devoted to persuading thousands to say " I believe in Christ " rather than " I believe in Mohammed " or " The Buddha " ? Clearly most of those engaged in these tasks are without the supreme experience, for if they had it they would have passed beyond the conceptual world and realized its relative unimportance.

But apart from the purely religious concepts, how may we regard the ethical ideas? Surely we should endeavour to influence men to think " good thoughts " and practise unselfishness?

We need not go to another for an answer to these questions. A period of introspection with calm detachment can disclose the limits of the influence of our ethical concepts. Many of us will find that the " doing good to others " stems from feeling, rather than being due to an intellectual idea of morality. The moral code arises from a source deeper than the mind. The " hardened heart " must corrupt morality even while practising it. The truth seems to be that all our values of Goodness and Truth emerge from the unconscious realm of our Wholeness. Yet in terms of " practical politics " morality should be preached, because social customs are founded on prevailing concepts and these have the binding power of law which compel the unregenerate to conform at least externally. But those who are attuned from within are compassionate, and while guided by codes, are independent of them. It would be easy to misunderstand statements to the effect that beliefs and doctrines do not assist towards the attainment of enlightenment. Belief looms very important in most religions; to such an extent indeed that the churches are split asunder by their espousal of differing beliefs. Perhaps however what has been said in previous chapters, especially Chapter 12 about the nature of Reality, will serve as a guide to enable us to understand the basis for these statements. Those who are living in the enlightened state know their being as timeless. Now beliefs and doctrines are products of the intellect, which functions in terms of time and duality. From the standpoint therefore of metaphysical infinity these beliefs have no validity. But it will be said, surely our intellectual ideas, beliefs and doctrinal forms are important in moulding our lives, at least on the conscious plane, towards goals generally recognized as good!

It is true we cannot live in the world without ideas and beliefs of some sort, nor practically speaking are we required to do so. But the point is, they have their application on the horizontal level of time-sequence. What value therefore can they have when the direction towards enlightenment is vertical into eternity?

This involves a protest against gradualism as being necessary to attainment. Eternity exists at every moment on the time plane. It is Here-Now just as much as at any future time. When our consciousness is looking backwards and forwards the present moment with its infinite possibilities escapes us, and it is the aim of those who have attained to check this escape from the present.

Consequently even set forms of meditation can orient the mind wrongly. But let it not be supposed that this implies an absence of mental discipline. On the contrary, the discipline is exercised at every moment of time. Our mind is made flexible and alert, and free from preconceptions about reality. What is occurring to us *now* must be deeply understood. In other words, a new viewpoint on the present is to be acquired so that all things are seen as aspects of the eternal. Then we shall become creative because the infinite is like an ever-flowing fountain spilling its contents into time. From this viewpoint what we call evolution, progress or cycles of reincarnation, are within the infinite present. For the infinite and the finite are a duality: one implies the other. Nevertheless those of us who do not breathe at this high altitude require some conceptual aids, and this it has been my aim to give in this volume.

Evolution is an empirical fact, and we each make our ascent from some point on this plane of time. But there is a complementary truth which should be expressed. Diagramatically speaking, there is not only an " ascent " but also a " descent " from "above". This may be called "the Grace of God", but whatever description we adopt it is a fact that illumination often seems to come suddenly as a gift from a higher part of us. Indeed, this is what must be the case, for the ego which symbolizes our separative nature can never command enlightenment. The Self will "decide" when to reveal itself to the ego, and that is why the final object of all discipline is to make the mind alert and expectantly passive. But more than this, we must learn to live without attachment. That is why I feel a scheme of mind-discipline similar to Yoga is in practice essential. But from what has been said above, it will be understood that it must be preceded by a purification of motives; an elimination of craving for specific goals, and a recognition that the daily moments reflect infinity.

It is now generally recognized that our interests, ideas and conscious thinking are determined by emotionally toned biases and more often by complexes below the threshold of conscious awareness. Modern psychological theories have rather destroyed the illusion that our conscious thinking is a dispassionate logical process. We now know this is very rare, even on scientific matters.

For the most part our reasons are only dressed-up versions of underlying and often unsuspected complexes. Current ideas, which most of us accept as originating in our conscious minds, are found on deeper examination to be a sort of outcropping from the subliminal region. The efforts to "change human nature" therefore must be directed elsewhere than merely altering the conscious conceptual patterns. But this does not mean that concepts are unimportant and that we should not consciously endeavour to change certain types of thinking. For instance, narrow sectarianism, racial intolerance and superstitious fears due to ignorance seem amenable to correction on the conscious level of reasoned argument. We have indeed evidence enough of the dynamic power of consciously propagated ideologies as we witness them competing for men's minds. Even so the success on the conscious level is largely illusory and is only an expression of much deeper movements in consciousness. Ideas which gain widespread acceptance do so because they are launched on the heaving tide of human needs which only become articulate in conscious ideas. Clever exponents of the art of propaganda know how small a part reason plays in the success of their campaigns.

Yet, all this being admitted, we must in the first place address ourselves to the conscious minds of those we desire to influence. We however can now do so with less *naïveté* than before the advent of modern exploration of subconscious levels, but it would be a travesty of our view if the intellect were regarded as a mere passive interpreter of subconscious impulses. In some people this may be the case, but in the highest form of abstract thinking we come close to illumined understanding.

Although our concepts have little relevance to illumination, yet paradoxically the state of our conscious mind is of paramount importance. This apparently confusing statement will appear less so if we realize that two different orders of thinking are involved. The ideas which are grouped into what we call concepts are stereotype patterns and arise as convenient mental frames to express our sensory experiences. They are products of life as perceived at the separate egoic level. As such they represent our incompleteness and separative cravings. Our insecurity expresses itself in the concepts of " God " and immortality, and the desire to perpetuate our centres of particularized interests produces every conceivable type of religious and social belief which become refuges for the harassed soul and compensations for its deep-seated sense of insecurity and suffering.

Our first task is to understand the cause of our sense of insecurity and suffering and this requires the application of keen intelligence to our present state of consciousness. We have to become aware of what is actually happening when we experience suffering and frustration. We alertly note the changing stream of consciousness, but our introspection is not in terms of concepts. Rather is it an intense appraisal of our impulses, ideals and goals. The effort at first is diagnostic but the final result is a removal of ignorance regarding our condition. While doing this we must not " desire liberation " or seek to pursue any goals in terms of conceptual beliefs. The assumption behind this exercise is that the separative " I " consciousness is not real, therefore any concepts based on this unreality will prove hindrances.

Perhaps sufficient has been said to indicate the nature of the effort we must consciously make to remove the barriers which block illumination.

CHAPTER XVIII

FINAL REFLECTIONS

"I know I am deathless . . .
And whether I come to my own to-day—or in ten thousand or ten million years,
I can cheerfully take it now, or with equal cheerfulness I can wait.
No doubt I have died myself ten thousand times before."

WALT WHITMAN.

"Why should we be in such desperate haste to succeed, and in such desperate enterprises? If a man does not keep pace with his companions, perhaps it is because he hears a different drummer."

THOREAU, Walden.

"Man's creative energy is caught in the illusion of self-consciousness; and desire, which is energy, encages him in the circle of false values."

"The release of that energy from the prison is man's consummation. When man lives in this pure creative energy then he knows harmony, the blessing of Truth."

KRISHNAMURTI.

WE started this book with the earnest desire to find the meaning of living, and we end it with the realization that any verbally expressed meaning would be a triviality compared with the glorious truth. We could have expounded a doctrine of "spiritual evolution", and to some extent Chapter 11, on Reincarnation, is such a doctrine. We might have developed a theme of eternal progress or alternatively visualized a final perfection achieved by the Grace of God. There is a relative truth in these and similar views, and my sympathy for the need of conceptual aids would lead me to retain them.

They are expressions, in terms of time, of an eternal and timeless Reality. Succession and evolution are, as we have seen, the ways in which aspects of the totality of infinite possibilities become apparent or actual to a limited consciousness.

Although the succession is very real to us, yet it is only an appearance, or partial view of what is in reality the all-embracing Absolute. At any moment of time we may become aware of the eternal, yet this will not abolish the time-series but will enable us to experience the time-series as an aspect of eternity. This is illumination. The degree of significance we perceive in ordinary things and events is determined by the intrinsic quality which marks our stage of growth. While metaphysically speaking all creatures are aspects of the Supreme, yet the empirical fact remains that an evolutionary process does precede our enlightenment, and the most useful and theoretically satisfying expression of this fact is the doctrine of Reincarnation. If it is true that the deepest teachings cannot be given to children, it would seem analogously true that the " young in soul " must await adulthood in other cycles of embodiment. Admittedly this doctrine could act as a soporific and discourage present effort but in practice I doubt whether it ever does because when the bud is ready it must open, and those who feel the inner promptings will be drawn towards the sources of inspiration and the right disciplines will be available to them.

There is no phase of our daily lives which lacks significance in the light of the foregoing principles. Our activities, and indeed all that is perceived through our senses, are correlated with aspects in eternity. A glint of sunshine on the sea or a tender bud in Spring may open the consciousness to Reality.

And finally I think we must return to the mood of our first chapter, which was an expression of a widespread sense of frustration and yearning for happiness. If we were happy we would not need to seek for meaning in living. The vast literature devoted towards " explaining life " is a clinical symptom of psychological dis-ease. Healthy people do not brood over medical books. Happiness and health need no explanation. It is their absence which arouses a crop of question marks.

The cry for light and happiness rises from the void of our darkness and insecurity. Yet would we cry in the abyss if deep within us we did not know there was a way out?

The type of living which makes for happiness has been one of the main themes of this volume. The cause of unhappiness lies in mistaking the transitory for the real, which in our own lives means failure to detect the illusory nature of our separateness.

While the miasma of a false view enshrouds us we traverse a distorted landscape. The hypnotized subject or dreamer must first be awakened before he can understand correctly. Any explanation which fails to detect the falsity of the dream or hypnotized state must obviously be valueless. If our sensory state of separative consciousness is delusive, as the illumined declare, then our concepts, beliefs and theories based on a dream-psychology have no fundamental relevance. Rather should we devote our energies towards awakening, so that our dream-state will automatically be understood and interpreted as an aspect of a wider whole. It is for this reason that I have devoted so much space to a clarification of backgrounds and the nature of sensory perception. We have made a significant intellectual advance even to doubt the validity of the world of appearances as doubt can be the precursor of an awakening.

But there are many false " salvations ". The religions of the world describe their heavens, and we may suppose they are vivid and real states of consciousness, but as they are only enhanced forms of separative functioning they are ephemeral, even though they span aeons of time. They represent survival in time; not immortality. The metaphysical truth incomparably transcends the picturesque prolongation of life in the worlds of form. The final deliverance arises only when ignorance is completely dispelled by knowledge of the Supreme.

" Whoever thus knows ' I am Brahma!' becomes this All; even the gods have not power to prevent his becoming thus, for he becomes their self." *Brihad-Aranyaka Upanishad*, (Hume's translation).

And there are false " salvations " other than those of *post mortem* heavens. The universal yearning for unity and wholeness can find counterfeit expressions in mass movements and forms of Totalitarianism. They are pathological compensations for the sense of separative insecurity in which the mass mind becomes a mystic divinity. In comparison with the prior state of unco-ordinated isolationism the merging into this synthetic unity represents a return to the womb of security. But a forced conformity is not a true unity, and State Absolutism exhibits a failure to advance towards a true organic unity in which individual expressions are enhanced, not obliterated. Of all the false salvations none is more insidious than that of the materialistic Utopia in which freedom of the mind is ruthlessly suppressed in the interests of the things of the body.

All forms of social organization are incarnations of dynamic ideas. Out of the totality of infinite possibilities only certain ideas can manifest in a given situation. Every new idea has to graft itself on, or infiltrate into, the existing patterns of expression. Every civilization has a body of general ideas as its background. Usually these general concepts are unformulated. They provide an enveloping climate characteristic of a period.

But ideas do not incarnate apart from human beings, and if we note periodic recurrence of basic forms of civilization, we are probably witnessing the rebirth of groups of people in whose minds these forms inhere.

The key-patterns are usually established by a minority. The evil of totalitarianism however is not necessarily in the form of organization, but in the methods used to achieve it.

If a social organization is based on the communal realization of compatible aims and on the sharing of common experiences, it will maintain itself with the minimum use of force. Also it will endure in proportion to its capacity for constant changes. It will then function as a living organism which grows and sustains itself in accordance with the laws of life, which are wiser than written constitutions or the logical concepts of the planned State, which usually can only be maintained by a ubiquitous police. Thus compulsion replaces persuasion, and the original ideals of the revolution are inevitably betrayed.

However confused we may be at times, and although tempted by revolutionary short cuts which promise unity, we cannot escape the eternal truth that the spiritual life is only realized by fully conscious individuals. In this task we possess no power of delegation; ours is the realization, and ours must be the effort. That is why engrossment in mass movements or sectarian ready-made beliefs are escapes from the essential task of fearless, independent self-knowledge which enables us to convert " I believe " into " I know ".

If it seems paradoxical that the path to the Universal is through the individual, we must hold steadily to the truth that individuation is the focus for the all-embracing. Vague, diffused states of consciousness are the antithesis of the illumined mind. Also we must suppose that repetition is contrary to the law of manifestation; therefore each focus is potentially unique without being separate, even as are the facets of a single jewel.

Although we ultimately transcend the conscious mind, our efforts must start in the waking self. What we have already written will make clear the direction our intellectual efforts should take. Firstly we must become intellectually aware of a life higher than that of concepts and beliefs. Yet in spite of their relative unimportance as a *description* of Reality, they can prepare the mind for a reception of higher truth.

A volume such as this, for instance, is designed to direct the attention towards certain possibilities, and its value lies not so much in the conceptual forms as in the intellectual mood it engenders, which stimulates an effort of will.

There are some intellectual atmospheres which deaden the mind's receptiveness, and there are others which magnetize the lower nature into responsiveness. The " grace from above " requires preparation below.

The need for some unifying body of truth is painfully apparent to-day. This indeed is little more than a truism, for there is a widespread lament that we are morally bankrupt just at the point where we possess unparalleled powers of destruction, and like apes playing with fire we are likely to find our destructive powers have got beyond control.

Lacking contact with the deeper sources of inspiration, everything we do is corrupted. Noble ideas, such as democracy, are travestied in practice. Conceived as the triumph of the ordinary man, it bids fair to enslave him. His pathetic vote is cast for candidates pre-selected by the party managers, and from then onwards he sinks back into the mass of the ruled, while astute politicians manipulate the levers of power, all the more binding because of the fiction that the common man is ruling when obviously he is not, and never can. Yet democracy must prevail because it is rooted in the truth of man's spiritual identity with the Supreme. Nevertheless it will continue to be distorted because instead of being the inspired expression of a religious truth it tends to become a system for arithmetically ascertaining the economic wants of the multitude. However, democracy forces us to take cognizance of the common man as does no other system of government. This is necessary when the rulers are without spiritual guidance because it checks the abuse of power.

It was believed not so long ago that our salvation would be achieved by the abolition of illiteracy, but sadly we witness the educational forms being twisted into the service of man's competitive instincts. We are educated mostly for a job, and even when our education exceeds our technical needs it is valued largely for the social prestige it brings; consequently passing an examination is valued more than education. Jealousies, competitive bad feeling and all the other symptoms of frustrated human nature are not eliminated by a university training. Indeed it is unreasonable to expect such training to effect a spiritual re-orientation. The curricula themselves would hardly do so, but religion, vital, undogmatic and based on real experience could, accompanied by training in the art of handling our emotions. It is here that we could learn from the Yoga system of Patanjali. But this is impossible under modern conditions of mass education, where the emphasis is on attending lectures with a view to an eventual memory-feat of regurgitation. There is no time for quiet browsing under the guidance of spiritually enlightened teachers. This is not a criticism of our educational leaders, but merely a comment on what inevitably must be when education for a degree masquerades as education.

To-day the blind are leading the blind, although there is a leavening of the wise and spiritually-awakened which may form the nucleus around which a vital re-expression of the ancient wisdom can be given. It is a persistent tradition that sacred beings incarnate in times of crisis to save man from himself. But here again a profound truth becomes travestied when the word " save " is interpreted as relieving man from work upon himself, which means the discovery of his inner kingdom of the spirit.

The religions of the world differ on many points of specific doctrine, but there is a united and continued testimony that our present consciousness is partial and impoverished compared with the transcendent glory of our true nature. The physical world which to many seems the boundary of all possibilities is revealed to us as merely a symbolical expression of realms of infinite dimensions. Our lives are not truncated and meaningless, as they often seem to be, but are charged with the possibility of an infinite expansion of awareness. We may by discipline and right-living become conscious of our eternity even while living in the world. The world in consequence becomes more interesting and significant because it has lost its power over us.

Our power for joyous self-expression is proportionate to the weakening of our cravings. Admittedly it is not easy to maintain a mood of constant self-recollectedness in which inharmonious thoughts and emotions find no scope for expression. Yet it is the path of happiness we are seeking, and provided the warning in previous chapters against egoistic strivings is heeded, it lies in our power to prepare the way for a revelation of our Divine nature, and in knowing our identity with the All we attain to an indescribable Bliss. The Seers of the Upanishads declare that Brahma is Bliss, and our scriptures that God is Love. It is in these teachings that we may find the common ground of inspiration which rightly understood could restore the religious bases of our civilization. The eternal truths require new vehicles of expression, and surely they will be found, for the need is great. A civilization is grounded on a pattern of general ideas which become expressed in innumerable specialized forms. We are at present going through a period when the basic forms are changing and no universal new pattern of general ideas is apparent. But such conditions can be liberating, and often are the prelude to an increased realization of eternal truths. There are indeed even now many witnesses in unexpected places, and their testimony is of a Truth obvious, direct and beyond all possibility of doubt.

And here our search for meaning in living finds its consummation. Our lives have no meaning in isolation, but only as aspects of the wider whole some call God and others the Absolute. No final solution of our personal problems and confusions is possible except by a reference to the wider background against which we live. We have considered the limitations of sense-knowledge and glanced at certain aspects of paranormal phenomena which illustrate awryness of the commonsense world.

This world however is real enough on the plane from which it is perceived, but it does not contain within itself its own explanation, and this forces us to look beyond it.

At the conclusion of Chapter 12 we summarized some general principles which are directly related to meaning in living.

The expression which perhaps might be most helpful to us on the sensory level of experience is to see our lives as ever expanding towards infinite horizons. Each one of us represents a unique viewpoint of the infinite whole. We therefore cannot be spared from the scheme of things. Even though we describe the commonsense world as illusory or of the nature of a dream, this does not imply that it is without value. On the contrary it is of supreme importance, for it is a mode under which the Supreme manifests. What it is desired to emphasize is that the corporeal world is relative and dependent. Its reality is derivative even as a reflection in a mirror. The process of living involves limitation but only as a means of expressing our unlimitedness. In terms of time there appears to be a process of inbreathing and outbreathing; periods of manifestation and of quiescence; an eternal rhythm.

If therefore we view life at this level we can usefully employ all those familiar concepts such as involution and evolution, progress and regress and ever-expanding futures of self-expression both on earth and in non-physical forms. We may contemplate the experience of great happiness and the intense joy of creative living, but also we must accept sorrow and frustration as long as our consciousness is confined to the realms of duality.

Yet, ever abiding at the centre of things is the peace which passes all understanding, which arises from the knowledge of our untrammelled identity with the Supreme.

Our search for security and endurance is really the search for immortality, yet immortality is not to be sought for but realized.

"There is a peace which passeth understanding. It abides in the hearts of those who live in the Eternal. There is a power which maketh all things new. It lives and moves in those who know the Self as One."

LIST OF BOOKS AND JOURNALS

THE following list contains books and journals relating to the subjects dealt with in the various chapters:

PSI PHENOMENA. (GENERAL)

Thirty Years of Psychical Research, Professor Ch. Richet.
The Superphysical, Arthur W. Osborn.
An Adventure, Anne Moberly and Eleanor Jourdain.
The Mysteries of Psychometry and Clairvoyance, Dr. Pagenstecher.
Psychic Research, Sept., 1928, " Some Further Experiments with Jeanne Laplace," Harry Price.
    (Earlier experiments in *Psychic Science* for 1927, vol. xxi, No. 4.)
Evidence for Phantasms of the Dead, S.P.R. *Proceedings*, vol. iii, pp. 146-48.
S.P.R. Journal, vol. xix. (Apparitions at time of Death.)
S.P.R. Journal, vol. xxi, pp. 100 *et seq.* (Apparition at time of Fatal Illness.)
S.P.R. Journal, vol. xxv, pp. 126-28. (Bi-location of the Self.)
S.P.R. Journal, vol. xxiv, p. 402. (Collective Apparitions.)
Census of Phantasms of the Living, S.P.R. *Proceedings*, vol. x.
Phantasms of the Living, Gurney, Myers and Podmore.
Psychic Riddle, Dr. I. K. Funk.
Some Occult Experiences, Johan Van Manen.
Facts of Psychic Science and Philosophy, A. Campbell Holmes.
Modern Psychic Phenomena, Dr. H. Carrington.
Death and Its Mystery, Camille Flammarion.
S.P.R. Journal, vol. viii, p. 180, Dr. Wiltze's experience.
Owen's *Footfalls*. (Cases of Projection of Astral Body cited.)
Owen's *The Debatable Land*. (Cases of Projection of Astral body cited.)
The Night Side of Nature, Mrs. Crowe.
The Projection of the Astral Body, Sylvan Muldoon and H. Carrington.
The Case for Astral Projection, Sylvan Muldoon.
A.S.P.R. Journal, Dec., 1928, vol. xxii, Phantoms of the Dead who Speak (International Notes, p. 713).

Resurrection, Wm. Gerhardi.
  (A novel describing an actual experience of consciousness out of the body.)
Encyclopaedia of Psychic Science, Dr. Nandor Fodor.
Ghosts and Apparitions, W. H. Salter.
The Process of Separation and Return in Experiences Fully " Out of the Body." Dr. J.H.M. Whiteman. S.P.R. Proc. vol. l, Part 185, pp. 240-274.
The Mystical Life, Dr. J.H.M. Whiteman. Faber and Faber. 1961.

TELEPATHY

S.P.R. Proceedings, vol. xlvi, June, 1940.
Experiments in Telepathy, René Warcollier.
Professor Gilbert Murray's Experiments, *S.P.R. Journal*, vols. xxix, xxxiv.
Mental Radio, Upton Sinclair.
Telepathy and Clairvoyance, Dr. Tischner.
Encyclopaedia Britannica, Article on " Psychical Research."
Letter to Manchester Guardian by Dr. Thouless *re* Professor Murray's Experiments, reprinted in *S.P.R. Journal*, vols. xxii, xxiii.
Enigmas of Psychical Research, Professor Hyslop.
Psychic Science, Emil Boirac.
The Widow's Mite and Other Psychic Phenomena, Dr. I. K. Funk.
Hypnotism: Its History, Practice and Theory, Milne Bramwell.
Death and Its Mystery: Before Death, Camille Flammarion. (Chap. v): " Will, acting without the Spoken Word, without a Sign, and at a Distance ", pp. 99-127.
Can Telepathy Explain? Dr. Minot J. Savage.
" *Telepathic Hypnotism* ", F. W. H. Myers, *S.P.R. Proceedings*, vol. iv (1886-87), pp. 127-88.
" *Problems in Hypnotism* ", Dr. Sydney Alrutz, *S.P.R. Proceedings* (1921-22), pp. 151-78.
Supernormal Faculties in Man, Dr. Eugene Osty.
Extra-Sensory Perception, Dr. J. B. Rhine.

PHYSICAL PARANORMAL PHENOMENA
(PSYCHOKINESIS, ETC.)

S.P.R. Proceedings, vol. xlvii, 1945, pp. 277-81.
  Experiments in Psychokinesis, Dr. R. H. Thouless.

S.P.R. Proceedings, vol. xlix, 1951, pp. 107-130.
  Report of an experiment in Psychokinesis with Dice and a discussion on Psychological Factors Favouring Success, Dr. R. H. Thouless.
S.P.R. Proceedings, vol. xliv, pp. 61-78, July, 1950.
  The Experimental Evidence for Psychokinesis and Precognition, C. W. K. Mundle.
The Superphysical, Arthur W. Osborn.
From the Unconscious to the Conscious, Dr. Gustave Geley.
Encyclopaedia of Psychic Science, Dr. Nandor Fodor.
S.P.R. Proceedings, vols. ix and xi, for an account of the phenomena of Stainton Moses, by F. W. H. Myers, published after the death of Stainton Moses.
"*Poltergeist Phenomena*", *A.S.P.R. Journal*, vol. xxiv., p. 122.
"*Poltergeist Phenomena*", *A.S.P.R. Journal*, Aug., Sept., Oct., 1926, and Jan.-Feb., 1927.
Monograph "*Poltergeist*", by Andrew Lang, *Encyclopaedia Britannica*, 11th ed., vol. 22.
Thirty Years of Psychical Research, Professor Chas. Richet.
Clairvoyance and Materialization, Dr. Gustave Geley.
Rudi Schneider: A Scientific Examination of his Mediumship, Harry Price.
Leaves from a Psychist's Case-Book, Harry Price.
Confessions of a Ghost-Hunter, Harry Price.
Modern Psychical Phenomena, Dr. Hereward Carrington.
The Story of Psychic Science, Dr. Hereward Carrington.
The Physical Phenomena of Spiritualism, Dr. Hereward Carrington.
The Projection of the Astral Body, pp. 198-200, Sylvan Muldoon and H. Carrington.
A.S.P.R. Journal, vol. xxii, No. 2, p. 606.
The Reality of Psychic Phenomena, W. T. Crawford.
Phenomena of Materialization, Baron von Schrenck-Notzing.
The Thumb-print and Cross-correspondence Experiments made with the Medium "Margery" during 1927-28, by Mark W. Richardson, M.D., E. E. Dudley, J. Malcolm Bird and Josephine L. Richardson.
Bulletin IV, National Laboratory of Psychic Research.
A.S.P.R. Journal, vol. liii, March 17th, 1933.
A.S.P.R. Journal, vol. xxvi, No. 3, pp. 133 et seq.
A.S.P.R. Proceedings, vols. xx and xxi, 1926-27.
Stella C., Harry Price.
S.P.R. Journal, vol. vi., p. 333, Sir Oliver Lodge on "Telekinetic Phenomena."

Human Personality, vol. ii., pp. 505-54, F. W. H. Myers.
Theoretical and Speculative Aspects of Telekinetic Phenomena. Willi Schneider, " Physical Phenomena ", *S. P. R. Journal*, vol. xx, pp. 363 *et seq.*
Bulletin of the International Institute for Psychical Research on Historic Poltergeists, Dr. Nandor Fodor and Dr. Hereward Carrington.
" Experimental Inquiries into Telekinesis ", Professor Ch. Winther, S.D., *A.S.P.R. Journal*, Jan.-May, 1928.
Haunting and the " Psychic Ether " Hypothesis, Presidential Address, Professor H. H. Price. *S.P.R. Proceedings*, vol. xlv.

PRECOGNITION

Some Cases of Prediction, Dame Edith Lyttleton.
Foreknowledge, H. F. Saltmarsh.
The Superphysical, Arthur W. Osborn.
Supernormal Faculties in Man, Eugene Osty.
Tertium Organum, P. D. Ouspensky.
A New Model of the Universe, P. D. Ouspensky.
Thirty Years of Psychical Research, Professor Ch. Richet.
An Experiment with Time, J. W. Dunne.
The Fourth Dimension, C. H. Hinton.
The Problem of Time, A. J. Gunn.
Death and Its Mystery: Before Death, Camille Flammarion.
S.P.R. Proceedings, vol. xxxiii, " Forecasts in Scripts concerning the War."
Encyclopaedia Britannica, vol. xviii, p. 672.
A Book of True Dreams, Mary E. Monteith.
Enigmas of Psychical Research, Professor Hyslop.
S.P.R. Proceedings, parts 13, 29 and 72. (Articles on " Prevision.")
Clairvoyance and Materialization, pp. 96, 143, 162, 166-72, Dr. Gustave Geley.
Space, Time and Gravitation, A. S. Eddington.
The Mysterious Universe, Professor Jeans.
The Remarkable Premonitory Crystal Vision, S.P.R. *Journal*, vol. xxi. (1923-24, p. 157).
The Facts of Psychic Science, Campbell Holmes.
The Supernormal, G. C. Barnard.
The Future is Now: The Significance of Precognition. Arthur W. Osborn. University Books, New Hyde Park, New York. 1961.

SURVIVAL

Evidence of Identity, Kenneth Richmond.
Evidence of Purpose, Zoe Richmond.
The Superphysical, Arthur W. Osborn.
The Kelway-Bamber Case, *My Life in Two Worlds*, Mrs. Osborne-Leonard.
S.P.R. Proceedings, vol. xiii, pp. 405-6, also p. 396.
Animism and Spiritism chap. ii, Professor Bozzano.
A.S.P.R. Journal, vol. xxv, pp. 246-47, 290-92.
The Arthur Eame Case in *Au Revoir, Not Good-bye*, Appleyard.
The White Case in *The Bridge*, Miss Nea Walker.
The Tony Burman Case, *S.P.R. Proceedings*, vol. xxxix, pp. 1-46.
Death and Its Mystery: After Death, Camille Flammarion.
Revue Metapsychique, Jan.-Feb., 1926, quoted by Bozzano in *Animism and Spiritism*, p. 97.
Psychic Messages from Oscar Wilde, Mrs. Travers-Smith.
Contact with the Other World, Dr. Hyslop.
S.P.R. Proceedings, vol. xx, pp. 213-17.
S.P.R. Proceedings, vols. xx-xxvi.
S.P.R. Proceedings, vol. xxix. (*Ear of Dionysius*.)
The " Walter " Cross-correspondence Tests.
American Psychical Institute, *Bulletin*, I, Reaction Tests.
The Mind and Its Place in Nature, C. D. Broad.
S.P.R. Proceedings, vol. xxxv, pp. 561-89.
The Supernormal, G. C. Barnard.
Spirit-Teachings, by M. A. (Oxon).
Patience Worth: A Psychic Mystery, Casper S. Yost.
S. G. Soal's Paper, *S.P.R. Proceedings*, vol. xxxv.
Human Personality and Its Survival After Bodily Death, F. W. H. Myers.
The Foundations of Spiritualism, Whatley Smith. (A good short discussion of the evidence for survival.)
A.S.P.R. Journal, Dec. 1930, pp. 556-57, also 558-59.
" Les Livres des Revenants ", *A.S.P.R. Journals*.
Some New Evidence for Human Survival, Rev. Chas. Drayton Thomas.
  " Scripts Affording Evidence of Personal Survival ", Gerald W. Balfour, *S.P.R. Proceedings*, part 69.
  " Lethe " Script, *S.P.R. Proceedings*, vol. xxv, pp. 113-217.
  " Observations of Certain Phenomena of Trance ", Richard Hodgson, *S.P.R. Proceedings*, vol. xxxiii.
A.S.P.R. Journal, Jan., 1931, vol. xxv, No. 1. Paper by Miss Gertrude Tuppy (Hyslop Case for Survival).

"*Indications of Continued Terrene Knowledge*" (Finney Case of the Half-Brick), *S.P.R. Proceedings*, vol. viii, 1892, F. W. H. Myers. Investigated by Dr. Hodgson.
Can Telepathy Explain? Dr. Minot J. Savage.
The Story of Psychic Science, Dr. Hereward Carrington.
(See pp. 313 *et seq.* for an excellent summing-up of the evidence for and against survival.)
Dr. Richard Hodgson's summing-up of the Piper Mediumship, *S.P.R. Proceedings*, vol. xiii, p. 370, 376, 378-96.
Oscar Wilde Case, cited in Bozzano's *Animism and Spiritism*.
Disaster to R101. (See *A.S.P.R. Journal*, vol. xxv, No. 7, July, 1931: also *Leaves from a Psychist's Case-Book*, Harry Price.
S.P.R. Proceedings, vol. xxxvi, pp. 517 *et seq.* (Chaffin Will Case.)
Human Personality, vol. ii, pp. 37-40, F. W. H. Myers.
The Widow's Mite and Other Psychic Phenomena, I. K. Funk.
"Finding of a Lost Receipt by Swedenborg", related by Immanuel Kant in a Letter quoted in Borowsky's *Darstellung des Lebens und Charakters Immanuels Kant*, trans. in Frank Sewell's *Dreams of a Spirit Seer:* also quoted by Myers in *Human Personality*.
"Lost Promissory Note Case", report by Dr. Hodgson, *S.P.R. Journal*, vol. viii, pp. 238-42.
Eric Saunders Case, *On the Edge of the Etheric*, J. Ar. Findlay, pp. 105 *et seq*.
The Controls of Geraldine Cummins, E. B. Gibbes.
Polyglot Mediumship, Professor Bozzano.
My Philosophy, Sir Oliver Lodge.
Horizons of Immortality, Erik Palmstierna.
One Hundred Cases for Survival after Death, A. T. Baird.
The Enigma of Survival: The Case For and Against an After Life. Professor Hornell Hart, Rider and Co. 1959.
Challenge of Psychical Research, Dr. Gardner Murphy, Harper and Bros., New York. 1961.
Science and Psychical Phenomena and Apparitions. In one Volume. G. N. M. Tyrrell. University Books, New Hyde Park, New York. 1961.
The Future is Now: The Significance of Precognition. Arthur W Osborn. University Books, New Hyde Park, New York. 1961
Survival and the Idea of " Another World ". Professor H. H. Price. *S.P.R. Proc.* vol. l, Part 182, January 1953.

The "Palm Sunday" Case: New Light on an Old Love Story,
The Countess of Balfour. S.P.R. Proc., vol. lii, Part 189,
February 1960.

REINCARNATION

Gotama the Buddha, Ananda K. Coomaraswamy and I. B. Horner.
The Introductory pages contain a clear exposition of the
Buddhist Doctrine of the Self, pp. 13-38.
A.S.P.R. Journal, vol. xxviii., Nov.
The Soul of a People, H. Fielding Hall.
" *The Idea of Immortality* ", A. Seth Pringle-Pattison, Gifford Lectures, 1922.
" *Some Reincarnationist Automatic Scripts* ", S.P.R. Proceedings, vol.
xxxviii, April, 1928, July 1929.
Reincarnation, E. D. Walker.
The Wheel of Rebirth, H. K. Challoner.
From the Unconscious to the Conscious, chap. i, Dr. Gustave Geley.
Mountain Paths, M. Maeterlinck.
Counter-Attack from the East: The Philosophy of Radhakrishnan,
C. E. M. Joad.
Pre-Existence and Reincarnation, Professor Wincenty Lutoslawski.
The World of Souls, Professor Wincenty Lutoslawski.
The Evidence for Survival from Claimed Memories of Former Incarnations. The Winning Essay of the Contest in Honor of William
James. Dr. Ian Stevenson. This essay now issued in a separate
book was originally printed in two parts of the journal of The
American Society for Psychical Research. (April and July,
1960). This is an outstanding piece of research.
The Tibetan Book of the Dead, W. Y. Evans-Wentz.
The Introduction, pp. 39-61, compares the exoteric and the
esoteric interpretations of the Rebirth Doctrine.

PHILOSOPHICAL AND METAPHYSICAL

Man and His Becoming According to the Vedanta, René Guénon.
The Philosophy of Plotinus, William Ralph Inge.
A scholarly and authoritative work, being the Gifford Lectures,
1917-1918.
The Enneads of Plotinus, translated by McKenna and Page.
Greek Philosophy, John Burnet.

Science and The Modern World, A. N. Whitehead.
Adventures of Ideas, A. N. Whitehead.
The Science of Peace, Bhagavan Das.
The Science of the Emotions, Bhagavan Das.
The Elements of Metaphysics, Paul Deussen.
The Republic of Plato, translated by F. M. Cornford.
    A most readable translation with excellent commentaries.
The Fourth Dimension, C. Howard Hinton.
A New Model of the Universe, P. D. Ouspensky.
Man, the Unknown, Alexis Carrel.
A Primer of Higher Space, Claude Bragdon.
Grades of Significance, G. N. M. Tyrrell.
The Mind and Its Place in Nature, C. D. Broad.
Mind and Body, Dr. Hans Friesch.
    A criticism of psychophysical Parallelism.
The Science and Philosophy of the Organism, Dr. Hans Driesch.
The Problem of Individuality, Dr. Hans Driesch.
The Basis of Memory, Dr. Bousfield.
Matter and Memory, Henri Bergson.
Mind Energy, Henri Bergson.
Materialism, J. S. Haldane.

BOOKS MAINLY INTERPRETATIVE OF THE MYSTICAL EXPERIENCE

The Supreme Identity, Alan W. Watts.
The Timeless Moment, Warner Allen.
The Happy Issue, Warner Allen.
Cosmic Consciousness, Dr. Bucke.
Tertium Organum, P. D. Ouspensky.
The Future is Now, Arthur W. Osborn (Chapters 16 to 19).
Practical Mysticism for Normal People, Evelyn Underhill.
The Varieties of Religious Experience, Wm. James.
The Richest Vein, Gai Eaton.

RELIGIOUS AND PSYCHOLOGICAL, HAVING RELEVANCE TO THE ATTAINMENT OF ENLIGHTENMENT

The Teachings of the Mystics. Selections from the Great Mystics and Mystical Writings of the World. Edited by Walter T. Stace. A Mentor Book, The New American Library. 1960.

LIST OF BOOKS AND JOURNALS

The Future is Now: The Significance of Precognition (particularly chapters 16 to 19), Arthur W. Osborn. University Books, New Hyde Park, New York. 1961.
The Intuitive Philosophy, Rohit Mehta. The Theosophical Publishing House, Adyar, India. 1958.
The Search for Freedom, Rohit Mehta. The Theosophical Publishing House, Adyar, India. 1957.
The Eternal Light, Rohit Mehta. The Theosophical Publishing House, Adyar, India. 1961.
Commentaries on Living: From the Notebooks of J. Krishnamurti. Victor Gollancz Ltd. First Series 1956, Second Series 1959, Third Series 1960.
In Days of Great Peace, Mouni Sadhu. George Allen & Unwin Ltd. 1952.
The Flame and the Light, Hugh I'Anson Fausset. Abelard-Schuman. 1958.
The Book of Mirdad, Mikhail Naimy. N. M. Tripathi Ltd., Bombay. 1948.
Gotama the Buddha, Ananda K. Coomaraswamy and I. B. Horner: contains an excellent introduction to Buddhist doctrine, together with extracts from the teachings.
An Introduction to Zen Buddhism, D. T. Suzuki, with a Foreword by C. G. Jung.
The Secret of the Golden Flower, Wilhelm and Jung.
Modern Man in Search of a Soul, C. G. Jung.
Counter-Attack from the East:
    The Philosophy of Radhakrishnan, C. E. M. Joad.
Sadhana, The Realization of Life, Rabindranath Tagore.
The Code of Christ, Gerald Heard.
The Bugbear of Literacy, Ananda K. Coomaraswamy.
The Thirteen Principal Upanishads, translated by Robert Ernest Hume, with an outline of the Philosophy of the Upanishads.
The Nameless Faith, Lawrence Hyde.
I Who Am, Lawrence Hyde.
The Way of Silence, A. M. Curtis, Burton Bradstock, Bridport, Dorset.
The Buddha's Path of Virtue. A translation of the Dhammapada by F. L. Woodward, Theosophical Publishing House.
Bhagavad-Gita. There are many translations of this Hindu Scripture. For practical devotional purposes the translation by Annie Besant and Bhagavan Das is recommended. Theosophical Publishing House.

The Yoga of the Bhagavad Gita, Sri Krishna Prem.
The Tibetan Book of the Dead, W. Y. Evans-Wentz.
Tibet's Great Yogi, Milarepa, W. Y. Evans-Wentz.
The Legacy of Asia and Western Man, Alan W. Watts.
Meister Eckhart, 2 vols. Translation by C. de B. Evans.
Selected Mystical Writings of William Law, Stephen Hobhouse.
The Divine Life, 3 vols., Shri Aurobindo.
The Cloud of Unknowing. With an introduction by Evelyn Underhill.
" *Dialogues on the Supersensual Life* " in *The Signature of All Things,* Jacob Boehme.   (Everyman's Library.)
Practical Yoga, Ernest E. Wood.
Jnana Yoga. Lectures by Swami Vivekananda.
Raja Yoga. Lectures by Swami Vivekananda.
Yoga and Western Psychology, Geraldine Coster.
Patanjali Yoga Aphorisms. Translated with a commentary by Swami Vivekananda.
Tao Teh King, Lao-Tzu. Isabella Mears' translation.
The Sayings of Tao-Tzu. Lionel Giles' translation.
Spirit Fruit and Voice, Jacob Beilhart.
My Religious Experience, Hugh Walpole.
The Voice of the Silence, H. P. Blavatsky.
Light on the Path, M. C.
   (These two books purport to be translations of ancient manuscripts, and are intended for practical devotional purposes.)
A Search in Secret India, Paul Brunton.
The Wisdom of the Overself, Paul Brunton.
The Imprisoned Splendour, Raynor C. Johnson.
Watcher on the Hills, Raynor C. Johnson.
The Science of Yoga, I. K. Taimni. The Theosophical Publishing House, Adyar, India, 1961.

ANTHOLOGIES OF MYSTICAL AND RELIGIOUS EXPERIENCE

Watcher on the Hills, Raynor C. Johnson.
The Perennial Philosophy, Aldous Huxley.
   With Huxley's commentaries.
The Wisdom of India, Lin Yutang.
The Wisdom of China, Lin Yutang.
The Way of Mysticism, Joseph James.

The Ring of Return, Eva Martin.
The Teachings of the Mystics, Walter T. Stace.

POETICAL AND LITERARY EXPRESSIONS OF THE SUPERSENSUAL EXPERIENCE

Towards Democracy, Edward Carpenter.
Leaves of Grass, etc., Walt Whitman.
The Hound of Heaven, Francis Thompson.
The Candle of Vision, " A. E."
Song and Its Fountain, " A. E."
Time Must Have a Stop, Aldous Huxley.
The Prophet, Kahlil Gibran.

INDEX

A

Absolute, The, 107; and Change, 119, 123; and contingent facts, 124; as Totality, 134, 205; not in Time or Space, 137; beyond Duality, 138,225; and Eternal Now, 143, 175; not a Cosmic Museum, 144; as Brahman, 212; as The One Self and Non-dual, 222, 223
Adler, 89
Adventure, An, 163
Akasa, 162
Allen, Warner, 211
Appearance and Reality, 22-27, 133
à priori judgments, 108, 187
Archetypal Ideas, 144
Astral Counterpart, 66
Atom, The, 107, 110
Avidya, 112, 113, 118

B

Bacon, Francis, 192
Basis of Memory, The, 161
Beilhart, Jacob, 210
Bergson, 117, 120, 171
Berkeley, 105, 106
Besant, Annie, 212
Bhagavan Das, 209, 212, 223
Bhagavad-Gita, 87, 212, 223
Bhakti Yoga, 237
Body, 29, 31, 52, 54, 61-63
Body-Mind, 68, 72
Boehme, Jacob, 208
Bousefield, Dr., 161
Brahma, 87, 250, 254
Brahman, 118, 119, 221
Brain, 29
Brihad-Aranyaka Upanishad, 250
Brunton, Paul, 189
Bucke, Dr. R., 213
Buddhism, 102
Bugbear of Literacy, The, 226
Burnet, Prof., 218

C

Calder, (Case), 155
Carpenter, Edward, 208, 218
Carrel, Dr. Alexis, 62
Carrington, Dr. Hereward, 188
Causality, 133, 134; in relation to Precognition, 149, 151, 153, 157
Chaffin, James L., (Will Case), 70
Chandogya Upanishad, 212
Change, 113, 114; and Changelessness, 117, 118, 120; and Brahman, 119
Changelessness, and God, 113, 114, 118
Chattopadhya, J. C., 221
Christian Science, 111, 112
Clairaudience, 39
Clairvoyance, 39
Clairvoyance and Materialization, 186
Clairvoyant descriptions, 67
Collective Unconscious, 165, 242
Conditioned Reflexes, 14, 169
Contingent Facts, 122
Coomaraswamy, Ananda K., 103, 226
Cosmic Mind, 144
Cosmic Consciousness, 205, 208
Cosmic Consciousness, 213
Cosmic Shorthand, 174
Coster, Geraldine, 239

D

Dante, 210
Death, 57
Death and Its Mystery, Before Death, 172
Descarte, 114
Determinism, 81, 154, 168, 169-172, 176
Dreams, 116, 125-127, 133
Dualism, 109, 115, 216
Duality, 22
Dunne, J. W., 96, 145, 147

E

Eddington, Sir A. S., 64, 107
Egos, 33-35

Enlightenment, 232, 233, 239, 240, 241
Enneads of Plotinus, The, 217
Epiphenomenalism, 30, 159, 199
Eternal Forms, 143, 144, 174
Eternal Now, 123, 127, 138, 143, 144, 145, 157, 175
Eternal Objects, 144, 145, 192
Evil, 21; and God, 111; and Freewill, 111, 112; as illusion, 113; attempts to explain, 121, 122; and good, 128-130
Evolution, and Dissolution, 131; and Involution, 255
Experiment with Time, An, 96, 145, 155
External World, The, 24 f., 104-106, 107, 109

F

Fichte, 215
Firth of Forth Bridge, (Case), 156
Flammarion, Camille, 172
Force, 48, 134, 191
Fourth Dimension, The, 147, 148
Freedom 81, 153; and Precognition, 167, 170, 172-174
Freud, 89
Freewill, 111, 112, 201
Future, The, 146 f.
Future is Now, The, 96

G

Geley, Dr., 186, 187
Gerhardi, William, 60
Gibran, Kahlil, 216
Glandular Secretions, 54
God, 21, 81; and Evil, 111; as Infinite, 113; and Change, 113, 114; Transcendent and imminent, 127; not Good or Evil 130-132; union with, 205, 208
Good and Evil, an aspect of multiplicity, 122, 123; relative terms, 128-134
Gotama the Buddha, 103
Guénon, René, 140
Gurney, 95

H

Hatha Yoga, 188
Hauntings, 39, 163, 166, 178
Hegel, 107, 122, 215
Hinton, C. H., 147, 150
Histogenesis, 64
Histolysis, 64, 187
Hume, David, 80, 106; on Causality, 133
Hume, R. E., 212
Huxley, Aldous, 213, 237

I

Immortality, 51, 79, 225, 250, 256
Ishvara, 235
Idealist Philosophers, 104, 107, 136

J

James, William, 117, 199, 213, 215
Jeans, 107
Jung, 16, 89, 240

K

Kali, 131
Kant, 215
Karma, 81, 82, 84
Karma Yoga, 237
Krishnamurti, 101, 248

L

Law of Causality, 47
Leuba, Prof., 207
Liberation, 101, 246
Locke, 105
Lodge, Sir Oliver, 65
Logical Positivism, 214
Lutoslawski, Prof., 95
Lyttleton, Dame Edith, 96, 155

M

Mace, C. A., 161
Maitri Upanishad, 212
Man and His Becoming, 140
Man the Unknown, 62
Martinique Volcano Disaster, (Case), 155
Materialism, 28-32
Materialization, 178, 186
Matter, 27 f., 62, 108, 109
Matthew, Saint, 212
Maya, 112, 118
Mead, G. R. S., 221
Meaning, 15, 16, 248
Mears, Isabella, 213, 217
Meditation, 235, 240
Memories, past lives, 94, 95
Memory, 87, 91, 92; and Precognition, 159; location, 161
Mescaline, 199
Mind, 29-31, 62
Misplaced Concreteness, 191
Monism, 83, 109, 111, 113-115, 120, 123, 135, 136, 144, 145, 169, 212, 216, 217
Mortal Mind 112
Mula-Prakriti, 225
Muldoon, Sylvan, 60
Muller, Prof. Max., 212

INDEX

Multi-Existences, 77, 80
Multiplicity, 111, 112, 123, 220, 222
Mundako Panishad, 221
Mundle, C. W. K., 180
Myers, 95, 161
Mystical experience, 116, 204-214;
   Implications of, 214-218
Mysticism, 197, 204
Mystics, 35, 120, 140, 204

N

Nature of the Physical World, The, 64
Neutral Monists, 30
Nitrous Oxide, 199
Non-Physical Bodies, 63-67, 82

O

Objective Idealism, 106, 107
Omar Khayyam, 210
Organic Wholes, 54, 55, 188, 221
Osty, Dr., 96, 153, 154, 159, 182
Ouspensky, Prof., 147, 213

P

Pagenstecher, Dr., 181
Paranormal Phenomena, 38 f., 42, 47, 141, 142
Patanjali, 92, 235, 236, 238, 253
Paul, Saint, 211
Perennial Philosophy, The, 213, 214, 237
Personal identity, 52
Personality, 51-60, 62, 64-66, 197, 201, 202
Personality types, 236
Phantasms of the Living, 95
Phenomenal Universe, 118
Philosophical Idealism, 141, 190
Plato, 71, 130, 137, 144, 214
Plotinus, 211, 215, 216
Pluralism, 111, 114, 115, 216
Podmore, 95
Poltergeist Phenomena, 39, 178
Practical Yoga, 239
Prakriti, 236
Pratyag-Atma, 209
Prayer, 86, 234, 235
Precognition, 46, 141, 143, 145, 146, 152, 153, 167, 172, 173, 174, 179, 180
Pre-existence, 79, 95
Prehension, 192
Prevision, 46, 96, 97, 98; in relation to Reincarnation, 97-99
Price, Prof. H. H., 161, 163
Primary qualities, 105
Projection of the Astral Body, The, 60
Proof, 69, 70

Prophet, The, 216
Psi Phenomena, 47, 72, 89, 141
Psychic Ether, 161, 162, 163, 164, 165 184
Psychic Factor of Dr. Broad, 51
Psychical Research, 59, 72
Psycho-analysis, 15, 239
Psychokinesis, 178-180, 182, 185, 186, 188, 190, 191, 193
Psychological Wholes, 55, 58, 59
Psychology, 170
Psychology of Religious Mysticism, The, 207
Psychometry, 39, 181
Psycho-physical Parallelism, 199

R

Raja Yoga, 237
Rajas, 237
Raymond, 65
Realist Philosophers, 104, 107
Reality, 109, 136, 138, 139
Reincarnation, 76-103; 226, 238; and inequality, 74-77; and memory, 87-96; and Prevision, 96-100, 174; and alternative hypotheses, 99, 100
Republic, The, (Plato's), 113
Resurrection, 60
Rhine, Dr., 178

S

Sacred Books of the East, 212
Samadhi Trance, 199
Sankhya Philosophy, The, 235
Satori, 241
Sattva, 237
Science of Peace, The, 209, 223
Science and the Modern World, 134, 139, 184, 192
Search in Secret Egypt, A, 189
Sense-data, 53, 108, 160, 165
Self, 36; and Not-Self, 223; as Universal Self, 123, 220, 222, 223
Senses, 23
Sheldon, Dr., 237
Simple location, 134, 191, 192
Smythies, Dr. J. R., 199
Society for Psychical Research, 43, 96, 141, 163, 186
Socrates, 203; on God, 113
Solipsism, 104, 105, 106
Some Cases of Prediction, 96, 155
Sonrel, M. Léon, (Case), 154
Soul, 56
Spinoza, 215
Spirit Fruit and Voice, 211
Split-personalities, 55, 56, 59
S.P.R. Jour., 181, 199

S.P.R. Proc., 43, 45, 60, 156, 161, 179, 180, 186
Story of Psychic Science, The, 188
Subconscious, 88, 89, 196
Subconscious Latency Theory, 153-155, 158
Subconscious Memory, 89, 91, 200
Subjective Idealists, 104, 106
Substance, 105, 109, 110
Supernormal Faculties in Man, 96, 153, 155, 182
Superphysical, The, 50, 94, 95, 97, 154, 159, 178, 181, 182, 186
Survival, 50-53, 56, 57, 58; and non-physical bodies, 63-68; and proof, 69-73
Suzuki, Dr., 240

T

Tamas, 237
Tao Teh King, 212, 217
Technological Creations, 136, 137, 174, 175, 176
Telekinesis, 46, 178
Teleological Causation, 190
Telepathy, 41, 43, 45, 70, 179
Tennyson, 208
Teresa, Saint, 208
Tertium Organum, 148, 213
Thales, 217
Theosophical, 66
Thought-forms, 165
Thouless, Dr. R. H., 43, 179, 186
Tibetan Book of the Dead, The, 66
Tillyard, Dr., 97
Time, 147, 148, 149
Timeless Moment, The, 211
Timelessness, 150, 233
Time and Space, 116, 124
Towards Democracy, 208, 218
Trance, 197, 202

Transcendental self, 202
Transmigration, Buddhist conception, 102

U

Unity, 110, 113, 114, 117, 118, 126, 216, 221
Universals, 196
Universal Consciousness, 75
Universal Mind, 106, 108, 109, 117, 118, 143
Universal Plenum, 123, 143, 144
Universal Self, 123, 220
Upanishads, 211, 212

V

Vairagya, 239
Varieties of Religious Experience, The, 199, 213, 215
Vedanta, 87, 120, 212, 215, 222, 223, 235
Verne Jules, 175

W

Whitehead, Prof., 134, 139, 144, 184, 191-193
Wholes, 54, 55, 56, 58, 59, 61, 65
Wholeness, 131, 132, 196
Wiesner, B. P., 186
Wiltze, Dr., 60
Wood, Ernest E., 239
World-Mind, 143, 145
World of Souls, The, 95

Y

Yoga, 235, 236, 239, 245, 253
Yoga and Western Psychology, 239

Z

Zen Buddhism, 241
Zen Buddhism, Introduction to, 240
Zener Cards, 45, 46
Zygote, 54